Public Service Broadcasting
in a Multichannel Environment

COMMUNICATIONS

George Gerbner and Marsha Siefert, Editors
The Annenberg School of Communications
University of Pennsylvania, Philadelphia

THE ANNENBERG
WASHINGTON PROGRAM

Communications Policy Studies
Northwestern University

Public Service Broadcasting
in a Multichannel Environment

*The History
and Survival
of an Ideal*

Edited by
Robert K. Avery
University of Utah

Longman
New York & London

**Public Service Broadcasting in a
Multichannel Environment: The History
and Survival of an Ideal**

Longman, 10 Bank Street, White Plains, N.Y. 10606

Associated companies:
Longman Group Ltd., London
Longman Cheshire Pty., Melbourne
Longman Paul Pty., Auckland
Copp Clark Pitman, Toronto

Acquisitions editor: Kathleen M. Schurawich
Production editor: Linda Moser
Cover design: Susan J. Moore
Production supervisor: Richard Bretan

Library of Congress Cataloging-in-Publication Data

Public service broadcasting in a multichannel environment : the
    history and survival of an ideal / [edited by] Robert K. Avery.
        p.   cm.
    Includes index.
    ISBN 0-8013-0479-2
    1. Public broadcasting. 2. Public broadcasting—Europe.
    3. Public broadcasting—United States. I. Avery, Robert K.
    HD8689.4.P83   1993
    384.5'44'094—dc20   91-30930
                                                          CIP

1 2 3 4 5 6 7 8 9 10-MU-9796959493

To the three men who
introduced me to the ideals of
public service broadcasting

E. Arthur Hungerford

James A. Fellows

Fred W. Friendly

Contents

Foreword

Social scientists sometimes contend that "mathematicians and physicists get all the easy problems." They argue that principles of math and physics don't change, but subjects of social science research change constantly. That is precisely the situation in analyzing public service broadcasting today. Technology, environment, politics, and attitudes simply won't wait for us to fit them into well-established, tested principles.

That is why we commissioned this volume for The Annenberg Washington Program. Its purpose is to provide a starting point from which to understand and analyze better the problems and opportunities facing public service broadcasting. These problems and opportunities are not uniquely American, but rather they are global. As the reader will perceive in studying these essays, the problems are difficult, complex, and always challenging. To find the right solutions, we must ask the right questions, not simply answer those questions we find most convenient and comfortable.

Although public service broadcasting developed differently in each country, the difficulties faced in the new multichannel environment are similar for all. The stakes are the same: the survival or extinction of a unique and valuable service. The titles of some of the chapters tell the story: "From Confidence to Uncertainty;" "From Monopoly to Marginalization;" and "The End of Public Broadcasting as We Know It?" Many countries continue broadcast structures that were put in place long before the impact of radio and television was known. These structures will inevitably change, making the next decade a critical one for shaping public service broadcasting in the new media environment.

The reader will notice, as I did, a remarkable similarity among countries in the identification of important public service issues. The struggle in each country is to define the concept of public interest. While there is universal agreement that notions of public interest and common good should drive the future of public service broadcasting, there is widespread disagreement on what these concepts actually mean. Consequently, the standards against which public service broadcasters are held accountable are still ambiguous. Similarly, concepts of diversity and quality remain unclear. Most agree that these should be among the goals of public service broadcasting, but few agree on how they should be measured. The consensus is that public service means information, education, culture, and entertainment, but these concepts are so broad that further refinement is needed.

Another universal problem is the question of funding. Most countries face increasingly competitive commercial markets, with demands placed on public service broadcasters to support themselves and to make a new and better case for public funds. Rising production and programming costs are being met with decreased resources, while national and international competitors proliferate. The pressure to maximize audiences may easily overcome the need to serve minority tastes and may adversely affect the ability of public broadcasters to take risks and experiment. But the new game cannot be played by old rules, and public service and economics must somehow come to new terms.

The globalization of media is also creating serious public service problems in most countries. There are questions of cultural sovereignty, the role of national production, the extent to which local markets will be open to foreign programs, and the degree to which national broadcasting will be subsidized to achieve cultural ends. These questions recur in almost every country, and predictably, public service broadcasting is at the center of this debate.

There is considerable speculation today among communications scholars that potential changes in the availability of media could create a world of "information haves and have-nots." Unfortunately, the scientists and engineers who developed the broadcast spectrum did not produce an accompanying public service manual. It is up to us to create new rules to govern the use of this precious resource and to insure the survival of public broadcasting. We hope this volume will foster public debate about how best to enhance public service programming on our publicly owned airwaves.

Newton N. Minow, Director
The Washington Annenberg Program

Introduction

Public service broadcasting was conceived and fostered within an overarching ideal of cultural and intellectual enlightenment of society. It was believed that broadcasting could uplift its audiences and contribute to their quality of life. The principles of public service broadcasting have long been universality of service, diversity of programming, provision for minorities and the disadvantaged, sustaining an informed electorate, and cultural and educational enrichment. Indeed, since broadcasting established itself as a fledgling industry in the early 1920s, the lofty ideals of public service broadcasting have existed as a persuasive counterstatement to the crass and mercenary tenets of commercial free enterprise. Even within the dominant capitalistic framework of American broadcasting, voices for an alternative system that belonged to the people were raised at every regulatory juncture in broadcasting's evolution. The powerful public service rhetoric of the 1930s and 1940s seemed impervious to attack, at least beyond the boundaries of the United States.

By the 1980s, however, ideals that once stood in bold relief to the callous commercial marketplace had lost their sense of purity. Public service broadcasting throughout the major Western democracies had come under attack, and the importance and legitimacy of the underlying principles had been called into question. The emerging multichannel media environment of that decade changed not only the way the public accessed media products but also the way people thought about the products and services received. Willard Rowland and Michael Tracey argue that from an ideological perspective, "the New Right was questioning the very idea of public culture, and the New Left was calling the national broadcasters elitist, statist, unaccountable, divisive, and exclusive."[1] Programs that once existed exclusively on noncommercial television channels had become successful commercial commodities. The realization of the free market viability of educational and cultural programming led critics of the public service ideal to argue that the model had outlived its usefulness.

These conceptual challenges to public service broadcasting did not develop in a vacuum. They were the product of technological, economic, and political currents that were altering the course of mainstream communications media. Clearly, the introduction of new delivery systems, especially cable television, direct broadcast satellite, and home videocassette players, had greatly increased the availability of program sources and weakened the argument for a public service broadcast system that was itself a response to public interest principles rooted in the reality of limited-spectrum space. Similarly, the move toward a global economy and the deregulation of communication industries as a precursor to the international trade of products and services had awakened a private sector previously blocked from market entry. With the shift away from state-imposed regulatory mechanisms came a change in political posturing that brought into question the utility of such concepts as the "public trust" in favor of more firmly based economic directives derived from consumer preferences and performance. The wisdom of this market-based model was supported by a growing awareness of ever-increasing program production and distribution costs at the precise moment when the public funds available to finance noncommercial broadcasting were at best stagnant and at worst facing continued erosion.

Throughout the 1980s, public service broadcasting advocates mounted a counterattack to the groundswell of political and public discontent with the privileged position afforded state-supported broadcast authorities. Whereas criticism of American public broadcasting had existed from the outset—when the "system" consisted of no more than channel reservations—Britain's British Broadcasting Corporation (BBC) and comparable entities across western Europe had little experience justifying their existence in a competitive market-driven environment where measures of accountability demanded more substance than idealistic rhetoric.

Somewhat ironically, countries that had served as exemplars of strong and healthy public service broadcasting systems began looking to the United States for answers as telecommunications policymakers began to raise troublesome questions concerning new media technologies, economic directives, and public preferences. The American experience argued against the privatization of public broadcasting. Shifting congressional expectations and the associated measures of accountability, along with systemwide survival tactics, such as the Station Program Cooperative and enhanced corporate underwriting, supported the position that new market-driven forces would dramatically change the services provided. Critiques of American public broadcasting bolstered concerns that incentives for experimentation and risk taking would experience a steady decline, and programs designed to appeal to small minority audiences—in both size and demographic characteristics—would simply disappear. Similarly, supporters of public service broadcasting argue that the vision of real diversity in program choices promised by satellite and cable distribution was just an illusion. Increasing the numbers of channels does not necessarily mean a corresponding increase in program choice. Without enormous capital expenditures to develop new program genres and formats, the success record of existing offerings served as the best predictor of what to expect from channel expansion.

Beyond arguments confronting the negative impact of market-driven forces, scholars also stepped forward to debate the issues along more theoretical lines. In 1986, the Aspen Institute Berlin and the American-based Aspen Institute Program on Communication and Society held a joint conference titled "The Challenges to Public Service Broadcasting."[2] In 1987, the Center for the Study of Communication and Culture published a special double issue of *Communication Research Trends* titled "The Crises in Public Service Broadcasting," and in April 1989, the scholarly journal *Media, Culture & Society* devoted an entire issue to "Broadcasting and the Public Sphere."[3]

In this issue's lead essay, Paddy Scannell sets forth one of the most clearly articulated arguments for the preservation of public service broadcasting.[4] Taking on the critical scholarship of Stuart Hall and his associates at the Birmingham School who draw interpretative power from the writings of Marx, Althusser, Foucault, Gramsci, and Habermas, among others, Scannell argues that broadcasting is not the repressive ideological apparatus depicted by Hall that works "to produce a social and political consensus that confirms the dominance of existing economic and political institutions and processes, and of existing structures of class, gender and ethnic relations in capitalist societies."[5] Scannell develops a convincing position statement that views public service broadcasting as a catalyst for greater citizen access to the arenas of public life while facilitating the transformation of political discourse into a more accessible form that is well suited to the norms of everyday life. In a very real sense, he contends, public service broadcasting has done more than any other broadcasting mechanism to demystify the political process and to provide a public forum for political debate. Toward this end, public service broadcasting can be readily characterized in stark contrast to its depiction as a repressive ideological apparatus. Instead, it is seen as a potent positive force for the preservation of democracy through citizen participation. Growing audience fragmentation resulting from the targeted strategies of a commercial-based marketplace could undermine the public sphere so central to democratic freedom, and a universally available public broadcasting system stands as a deterrent to the erosion of public speech within a multichannel environment. Scannell concludes:

> In my view equal access for all to a wide and varied range of
> common informational, entertainment and cultural services, car-
> ried on channels that can be received throughout the country,
> should be thought of as an important citizenship right in mass
> democratic societies. It is a crucial means—perhaps the only one
> present—whereby common knowledge and pleasures in a shared
> public life are maintained as a social good for the whole popula-
> tion.[6]

This book grew out of a mounting concern for the future of public
service broadcasting around the globe. Continuous examination and review by various commissions, agencies, and task forces have made the
purpose, structure, and benefits of public service broadcasting a central
component in the political agendas throughout western Europe, Canada,
and the United States. Even if the structures that would permit a continuation of services were sustained, policy revisions, deregulation, and commercial competition could well undermine confidence in, and commitment to, public service broadcasting. The result could be a demoralized
institution that begins to self-destruct, thus leaving the electronic sources
of culture, education, and political discourse to the prevailing forces of
the marketplace.

Writing in *Communication Research Trends*, James McDonnell set
forth a challenge to scholars concerned with the possible dismantling of
public service broadcasting:

> If we are to continually rediscover the ways of implementing in
> different socio-cultural and political contexts the kinds of ideals
> of public service broadcasting . . . we need a combination of dif-
> ferent research approaches. This research should be based on
> cultural analysis which probes the values held by the public
> service broadcasting, but it should also include political analysis
> exploring the power relations sustaining broadcasting policies
> and historical research into the ideological and cultural
> foundations of present-day broadcasting institutions. In this way,
> researchers can build a potentially more rational basis for public
> policy discussions in the broadcasting arena.[7]

The collection of essays presented here directly addresses the need for
historical treatments that situate contemporary challenges and policy
decision making within the ideological, cultural, and political context of
existing broadcast entities.

The authors who contributed to this book responded to a specific research agenda. Each set out to uncover the most significant issues and
circumstances affecting the evolution of public service broadcasting in

selected European countries, Canada, and the United States. They were guided in their scholarly inquiry by five research questions:

1. How did the concept of public service broadcasting originate and evolve within each country?
2. How was this mandate implemented in the structure, economics, and political relationships of the resulting broadcast entity or entities?
3. Looking at the history of the broadcasting system in question, what have been the most significant structural and institutional crises and conflicts in its evolution?
4. What are the most significant problems facing public service broadcasting in the 1990s?
5. What solutions are being proposed, and what are the projected consequences?

These questions afford an analytical framework for eight case studies. Our investigation begins in Great Britain and moves across the European continent to France, Germany, the Netherlands, Scandinavia, and Italy, before crossing the Atlantic for a look at Canada and the United States. Together, these essays provide a representative profile of the current status of public service broadcasting in Western democracies.

ACKNOWLEDGMENTS

This book was conceived during my tenure as a Scholar in Residence at the Annenberg Washington Program in Communications Policy Studies. Former program Director Robert Pepper was responsible for extending the invitation that took me to Washington, D.C., and his allocation of grant monies made my visit and the commissioning of the essays in this volume possible. Beyond this initiative, I am indebted to Bob for his continued friendship and collegial support that spans nearly two decades. I look forward to the day when we can renew our collaborative ventures as coauthors.

From the inception of this project, Yvonne Zecca, assistant director for the program, has served such multiple roles as financial manager, logistical czar, good shepherd, and patient task master. Her continued encouragement and understanding were central to bringing this collection to fruition, and I thank her for never losing faith in the seemingly strange and often unpredictable practices of overextended academics.

Marsha Siefert, the extraordinary editor of *Journal of Communication*, was an early reader for this manuscript, and her insightful comments and suggestions added markedly to this collection. This is a better book as a result of her involvement.

Each of the authors contributing to this volume deserves recognition for responding to my editorial requests, often at the expense of other assignments. All were exceedingly patient throughout the preparation of this collection, as continuous changes in the European political climate required updates and revisions. I extend my appreciation to each of them.

I am also indebted to the gifted group of professionals at Longman. I will never forget the moment in a San Diego coffee shop when former Executive Editor Gordon "Tren" Anderson caught the vision for this volume. His eyes twinkled and he promised to follow this project through to completion. Although Tren didn't live to see these words taste printer's ink, his gentle spirit, good will, and professional commitment to our discipline are woven throughout the pages of this book. He lives on within the hearts of those he helped along the way. When Tren died, David Fox continued to provide continuity and support until Kathy Schurawich took over the reigns at Longman. All of us connected with this volume owe Kathy our gratitude for her efforts in guiding this book to completion.

Finally, I am indebted to my colleagues at the University of Utah for making the work of scholarship so enjoyable. Edith Welch and Gina Haslam were responsible for typing several drafts of this manuscript with painstaking accuracy. And more than any other single individual who worked on this project, Leonard J. "Leo" Leckie deserves acknowledgement and my expression of respect. Leo is the person who readied countless manuscripts for publication during the first six years of *Critical Studies in Mass Communication*. He brought the same dedication and commitment to excellence to this project that Dave Eason and I came to expect as journal editors. As Thom McCain would say, "This guy is a really outstanding professional journalist!"

To all of you, and to Norma Lee and Catherine Frances who sacrificed in my behalf, I extend my heartfelt thanks.

Robert K. Avery
University of Utah

NOTES

1. Willard D. Rowland, Jr., and Michael Tracey, "Worldwide Challenges to Public Service Broadcasting," *Journal of Communication* 40 (2, 1990), pp. 8–27.
2. A conference report by the same title was prepared by Willard Rowland and published by the Aspen Institute for Humanistic Studies.
3. This was the second time the editors for *Media, Culture & Society* had provided a broadly based intellectual forum for the discussion of public service broadcasting. The first was a double issue (5:3/4) that appeared in autumn 1983, titled "Public Service Broadcasting: The End?"

4. Paddy Scannell, "Public Service Broadcasting and Modern Public Life," *Media, Culture & Society* 11 (2, 1989), pp. 135–166.
5. Ibid., p. 156.
6. Ibid., p. 164.
7. James McDonnell, "Public Broadcasting: Cultural Good or Commercial Commodity?" *Communication Research Trends* 8 (3/4, 1987), p. 13.

Public Service Broadcasting
in a Multichannel Environment

The British Approach to Public Service Broadcasting: From Confidence to Uncertainty

Jay G. Blumler

For nearly half a century, assurance and pride were hallmarks of British broadcasting. The appropriateness of public service principles, as legitimizing creed and policy guide, was unquestioned. Criticisms of performance were more often particular than general. Crises and proposals for change focused more on institutional arrangements than on ideological beliefs. The BBC, especially, served as a model to be emulated (as in the British Empire and later Commonwealth) and envied (as in certain continental European countries, where different arrangements applied).

Today the climate of opinion is markedly different. When the British government declared in a policy paper that "change is coming"[1] and an influential member of a policy review committee declared that "the status quo is not an option,"[2] they had fundamental challenges and restructuring prospects in mind. Of course, much of the shift is due to new communication technologies, the end of spectrum scarcity, the unavoidable growth of commercial competition, and the iconoclastic zeal of a right-wing, market-minded Conservative government. But new standards of evaluation are being applied to radio and television, in which strictly economic and financial criteria are playing a more central part.

Hence principles once taken for granted are now very much on the defensive. Although the long-term fate of the public service idea is unpredictable, several alternative scenarios for its future role can be envisaged. Their outer boundaries are defined by the twofold fact that while nobody is yet recommending the root-and-branch abandonment of public service principles, neither does anyone expect the public service philosophy to reign supreme any longer over all forms of broadcasting service. The future probably lies somewhere at the conjunction of three courses. One would involve a continuing public service vitality in at least some of the commanding heights of broadcasting. On this view, the British system's traditional strengths will somehow prevail: (1) the vigor and creativity of its programming industry, (2) the concern of many producers to make public service–oriented programs, and (3) the fact that the British audience has been "trained" to accept public service programming as something it is prepared to patronize along with all the less demanding fare that it wants to enjoy.[3]

A second outcome could be "ghettoization," giving certain institutions the limited and subsidized task of making the more worthy programs that the market cannot sustain (as in American public television). Explicitly recommended by a government-appointed committee,[4] this is a model that might be entertained for the BBC sometime in the 1990s. Third, there is the prospect of a gradual and irreversible withering on the vine of the public service notion, it increasingly becoming more a point of ideological reference and justification than an influence on practical action.

THE BRITISH CONCEPT OF PUBLIC SERVICE BROADCASTING

The notion of public service encompassed a set of lofty ideals. In presenting the form they have taken in Britain, I do not claim that broadcasting practice has invariably conformed to them. British broadcasting was never exempt from the sociological imperatives that oblige all large organizations to adjust to external political and economic power forces and internal factional rivalries. Nevertheless, throughout its history, a public service commitment has defined the broad purposes of the British broadcasting system, deeply penetrated the motivations of leading executives and producers, and provided the standards by which performance has been assessed. Always central, though ever vulnerable, it is that very commitment that is under challenge today. Its key elements may be outlined under six headings.

A Platonic Streak: "High-mindedness"

British broadcasting was born in the belief that social institutions can be driven by an ethical purpose, avoiding subjection to particular interests, including commercial and political ones. Initially radio and later television were regarded as highly suited to such an approach, not only because they depended on a scarce public resource (the spectrum) but also due to their rich and novel social potential. In an early version of this philosophy, John Reith, the pioneering and towering director general of the BBC from 1926 to 1938, declared that the corporation had a high "moral responsibility" to "carry into the greatest possible number of homes everything that is best in every department of human endeavour and achievement."[5] Although the language seems dated, many British broadcasters are still moved by the assumption that television should positively enhance the quality of life, instead of merely receding "into the background of life . . . a placebo, a resort against boredom, a reference point for information" as (supposedly) in the United States.[6]

From such high-mindedness sprang two other characteristic emphases. One was a certain view of the audience, a readiness to regard it more as a public or set of publics to be served than as a market to be exploited,[7] less as a mass being pulled toward a predominant focal point of gravity and more as a set of overlapping tastes and interests. Programming, then, was supposed to do more for the average audience member than merely entertain and keep him or her abreast of headline news. In addition, viewers and listeners should be presented from time to time with material that would stretch their minds and horizons, awaken them to less familiar values and tastes in culture and art and science, and challenge their uncritically accepted assumptions about life, morality, and society.

Another offshoot of high-mindedness was the assumption that judgments about program quality should play a significant part in commissioning and scheduling decisions.[8] Whereas, according to recent research, many American television executives and producers found it difficult to differentiate quality from hits that attract the largest possible audiences, their British counterparts were at home with the distinction, able to discourse at length on such standards as production values, clarity of objective, innovation, and relevance to audience circumstances and needs.[9]

A Comprehensive Remit

Public service broadcasting in Britain has always been shaped by an ethic of comprehensiveness. This is in direct contrast to American public television, which sees itself as an island of welfare in an ocean of commercialism.[10] Whereas in the United States the commercial networks have provided *Dallas* and public television has provided *Pavarotti*,[11] in Britain public service broadcasters have offered both, embracing such multiple goals as education, information and entertainment, range, quality, and popularity. A source of the ethic of comprehensiveness from the outset was the financing of the BBC by a license fee levied on each household with a radio and later a television set. As Terence O'Brien explained:

> The BBC as a public service form of broadcasting, acquiring its funds
> through equal payments by considerable numbers of the public, has
> a clear obligation to discover and satisfy, so far as it is possible to do
> so, the common denominator of broadcasting demand.[12]

The comprehensive approach was sustained through two subsequent developments. First, when Independent Television (ITV) was set up with advertising finance in competition with the BBC in the 1950s, it was still understood that both parts of the system should dance to the same public service tunes. And although when getting off the ground, ITV companies projected themselves as a system of "people's television,"[13] they were brought firmly back into line in the 1960s following stern criticisms of their "trivial" programming record by the government-appointed Pilkington Committee.[14] Second, although an increase in television channels from two to four meant that majority tastes were more heavily catered to thereafter on BBC1 and ITV, with minority-audience programming on BBC2 (opened in 1964) and Channel 4 (its ITV counterpart, launched in 1982), neither majority channel has treated prime time solely as "fun time," and both minority channels have aimed at including at least some large audience attractions in their schedules.

Program Range and Balance

A core tenet of British broadcasting was that programs should cater to all interests and tastes: "The central aim here is to provide programmes of wide range and diversity, over a reasonable span of time for practically all kinds of taste, for large groups and small."[15] How seriously this principle has been taken can be gauged by the clause in the Independent Broadcasting Act that obliged the Independent Broadcasting Authority to ensure that ITV schedules were balanced, taking account of the day of the week and the time of day when programs appeared. This principle rested on assumptions about viewer choice and audience satisfaction. Meaningful choice depends on a range of programs to select from "rather than the mere multiplication of channels which, if all are focused on the search for mass audiences on every possible occasion, provide more, a multiplicity of the same."[16] Even satisfaction may be increased, as Forman has argued:

> So what does the public want? At any time of the day or night, the majority will want *Dallas* or a game show most. Thus, if you string together an endless belt of soap operas and quizzes, you will get most of the people most of the time but your channel will no longer cater for the minorities, who together are not only just as numerous as the *Dallas* audience but are also the same people watching at a different time, and with much more commitment. . . . So what is the nature of our choice likely to be? Are 16 programmes, none of which you really want to see, better than four programmes, one or two of which make your pulse beat faster?[17]

Universal Provision

This principle is also traceable to the dependence of a major source of programming on a license fee levied on each set-owning household. It follows that every effort should be made to get the full service of all its channels to the viewer, regardless of the expense of such an effort. Where one lives should make no difference to the service one gets. Thus public service broadcasting has differed from many of the new technology-based services, like cable television, which are liable to handpick better-off neighborhoods, in which more people who can afford to subscribe will live, and urban areas, where the cable will serve a larger number of households, as well as all forms of pay television that are sent out in scrambled form only to those who buy or rent a decoder.

Editorial Independence

This is the principle that programming should not be under the thumb of any social or political group but should be distanced from all vested interests, particularly those of the government of the day. The historical record discloses many sources of this idea. Independence was part and parcel of the original "high-minded" concern to ensure that broadcasting served only a public interest, not some particular interest. Universality played a part too: How could broadcasting serve all if it came under the control of some section of the community? The enterprise and imagination needed to develop a new and untried service was also thought to be incompatible with the dead hand of bureaucratic officialdom.

The importance of this principle was reinforced by lessons absorbed during the General Strike of 1926, when threats of a government takeover of the BBC were fended off, on the ground that fatal damage would be inflicted on its credibility. It is difficult to maintain that the BBC's independence was fully preserved during this episode. It assured the government that it was on the government's side (since the General Strike was illegal) and invited no pro-strike speakers to the microphones. Nevertheless, its news of strike developments aimed to be accurate and objective and drew from all available sources—unlike the propaganda sheets issued by the government at the time.

Thus the independence principle cannot be associated with a mythically innocent picture of the historic place of broadcasting in British politics. Concerted attempts were made from time to time by governments, parties in and out of power, and bodies representing other organized interests and causes to influence its news and current affairs output, sometimes being able to elicit the desired response as well, at least up to a point. Nevertheless, the belief that such pressures should be resisted is central to British broadcasting philosophy and very widely accepted in principle, as the Annan Committee on the Future of Broadcasting noted: "The evidence we received reverberated with the plea that the Government, politicians, and indeed quasi-political organizations, should not be permitted to control broadcasting directly."[18]

Independence went hand in hand with two other notions. One was an obligation to preserve impartiality in news and current affairs coverage of controversial issues, which in British eyes required institutions that can be counted on to keep all vested interests at arm's length.

A second association was with the public interest that radio and television were expected to serve, three different versions of which have shaped different national systems of public service broadcasting. One of these equated the public interest with the policies of a democratically elected government, as has traditionally been the case in France, where television has been subordinated to many state-imposed editorial controls.[19] Another regarded the public interest as a pluralistic summation of community sectoral interests. A typical example may be found in Germany, where, according to the *Proporz* principle, councils of the broadcasting authorities have been composed of nominees from a wide range of social and political groups.[20] The British approach, however, regarded the public interest more as an abstraction that was best realized along disinterested lines. Arguably, this presupposed both a broad societal consensus of values and goals from which the public interest for broadcasting could be derived and a corps of public-spirited individuals who, when appointed to the top broadcasting councils (as BBC governors and Independent Broadcasting Authority members), could be trusted to promote the public interest in broadcasting. Such authorities were supposed to combine two functions: on the one hand, to "intervene, chide or even discipline the broadcasters in the public interest" and, on the other hand, to "stand up for the broadcasters' independence and defend them if they consider that in controversy with Government, or with pressure groups of one kind or another, broadcasters are in the right."[21]

Public Accountability

It was considered that, in return for the privileges conferred on them by Royal Charter and License (BBC) or statute and franchises (ITV), broadcasters should be answerable for their fidelity to certain public requirements. These have mainly taken the form of broad expectations, which were spelled out in the original Independent Television Act of 1954 and later accepted in identical form for the BBC (whose charter is mainly an enabling document) in a letter sent by the chairman of the Board of Governors to the government minister responsible for broadcasting affairs (then the postmaster general, subsequently the home secretary) in 1955.

The chief duties were to preserve due impartiality in news and the treatment of controversial issues; not to editorialize; to provide a balanced schedule of good-quality programming; to avoid incitement to crime and offenses to decency; and (for Independent Broadcasting) to control advertising for amount, misleading claims, and separation from program content. There was also an unmentioned but highly influential responsibility internalized by many producers to support the values, institutions, and procedures of parliamentary democracy.

MAIN POINTS OF EVOLUTION AND CHANGE

It would be erroneous to regard the public service idea as a fixed and static creed. In Britain, it has been adapted to social change, to demands for new services, and to organizational reform, of which the most influential was undoubtedly the transformation of the broadcasting system from a monopoly to a duopoly with the creation of ITV in competition with the BBC in 1955.

One major line of development was a move away from explicit paternalism, which was no longer compatible either with competition from a second television service, which rapidly established an image of informality and the popular touch, or with the cultural presuppositions of a more democratic, educated, affluent, and less deferential society. The original notion of public service was avowedly tutelary and contemptuous of any form of populism, from John Reith's view that "he who prides himself on giving what he thinks the public wants is often creating a fictitious demand for lower standards which he will then satisfy"[22] to William Haley's insistence on

> the responsibility which a unified public service has to raise·
> standards. There are many people who believe this task is better
> done if it is not talked about. To a great extent this is true. . . . No
> one wishes to feel perpetually at school. But . . . when one is taking
> stock of British broadcasting as a whole, it should be frankly stated
> that to raise standards is one of the purposes for which the BBC ex-
> ists.[23]

What displaced paternalism might be characterized as *balanced*, *symmetrical*, or *pluralistic*, terms that suggest that, while catering to mass taste, programs in the schedules should stretch beyond it as well. As Sir Brian Young, former director general of the IBA, put it, "The output must consist not only of programmes that pay their way. The same source that puts out cheap and popular programmes must also put out programmes which are expensive and ambitious."[24] Some might discern a lingering hint of paternalism in this position: "Since our natural desires are extremely conservative and lazy . . . it is vital that we should not only have what we like but also learn to like a number of things that we don't yet know."[25] It is as if broadcasting should hold a watching brief for sides of our natures that might stultify and dry up if only our easiest options and preferences were satisfied. Thus the conceptualization of producers knowing best for consumers knowing little was discarded in favor of programming that would cater to the vulnerable best in all of us. A simile for this conception likened broadcasting to a public library, where best-sellers and unfamiliar works can be found side by side on the same shelves.

Another major shift involved a reevaluation of the role of competition. In Reith's day, this was anathema, the thick end of the wedge for the loss and corruption of broadcasting purpose. But little more than five years after the creation of Independent Television, even the BBC was acknowledging in its evidence to the Pilkington Committee that in the field of light entertainment, competition had "done something to sharpen and improve their own pro-grammes."[26] In addition, BBC news presentation was overhauled in reaction to the stimulus of Independent Television News, and after the Granada company successfully challenged certain restrictions on the coverage of elections in 1958 and 1959, both the BBC and the other ITV companies pushed for yet other freedoms in this field. Sometimes competition seemed to set a cycle in motion, with one service pioneering an innovation that was soon adopted by the other.

This new competitive element was thereafter both keen and circumscribed. BBC and ITV producers competed keenly with each other for professional reputation, critical approval, and audience patronage. Both services endeavored to attract approximately half of the total audience over a reasonable span of time. Nevertheless, broadcasting competition in Britain was more circumscribed than the American variety because its consequences for the lifeblood income earned by the rival services was less direct than for the U.S. networks. In other words, a principle of assured finance became part of the British public service philosophy, according to which there should be no competition for revenue between the leading providers. With the BBC funded by the license fee and ITV by advertising, each side could afford to lose out a bit in audience terms and to pursue other goals than audience maximization.

In addition, with the introduction of Independent Television, British broadcasting philosophy became less exclusively metropolitan and more concerned with serving regional and local identities. Whereas the Reithian BBC perceived itself as the "national instrument" of broadcasting, Independent Television was created as a federal group of (eventually) 15 companies, each transmitting programs to a different region of the country. Although much of its service was nationally networked, the IBA strongly encouraged the companies to develop distinctive streams of regional provision (particularly in news and current affairs magazines), to which the BBC responded with similar (though more modest) services. In radio, too, this development was reflected in a buildup, from 1970 onward, of chains of local BBC and Independent stations, which together spread to some 85 percent of the population.

Finally, with the gradual expansion of British broadcasting over the postwar period into a large and elaborate industry, the public service philosophy mingled and had to come to terms with two other strands of normative concern. One was the idea of professionalism, standing for such values as mastery of a body of knowledge and technique (in contrast to amateurishness), commitment and dedication to the assigned task (over and above mere competence), and concern for the quality of performance as assessed by peer professionals inside and outside the broadcasting organization.[27] Another internal development was an increasing respect for the effective and efficient management of financial resources and schedule-building tools.

These impulses were joined to the public service creed in complex patterns of accommodation and tension. Although the inward-looking face of professionalism might appear to dilute broadcasters' motives to serve others (society, democracy, audience enlightenment),[28] its emphasis on commitment, creativity, and standards was in line with public service programming goals of range and quality. Similarly, regard for managerial efficiency and economy was held in check by the tradition of filling senior executive positions in the BBC and the Independent Television companies from the ranks of successful program makers instead of with individuals from the worlds of business, finance, and sales.

IMPLEMENTATION OF THE PUBLIC SERVICE MANDATE

British principles of public service were long supported by mechanisms operative in several spheres—broadcasting organization, economics and finance, politics, and culture. Indeed, much of the past strength of the British system is probably attributable to how these diverse props have complemented and reinforced each other.

The Notion of a Broadcasting Authority

In the British system, ultimate responsibility for ensuring that the national interest was served and broadcasters' obligations were fulfilled has been shouldered by the governors of the BBC and the members of the Independent Broadcasting Authority, who were appointed by the government for five-year terms of office. Of course, their functions differed in one important respect: Whereas the BBC produced programs, the IBA was a regulatory agency, organizationally separate from the ITV production companies.

In the BBC, the distinction between the Board of Governors and Board of Management is crucial. The former appoints the director general and a small number of other senior executives. Otherwise, it receives, deliberates, and approves broad policies, budgets, and schedules proposed by the latter. Traditionally, then, Management has decided and Governors served more as sounding board and ultimate authorizer, commenting after the fact on the particular practices and programs of which they approved or disapproved. In subsequent years, however, the Governors have become increasingly active, occasionally breaching the convention that they should not view individual programs before screening to consider cuts. In early 1987, they even took the unprecedented step of forcing the resignation of a director general in whom they had lost confidence, appointing a successor who was more likely to reshape corporation policies in line with their wishes. This relationship of Governors to Management (and especially of chairman to director general) has been vital, because it forms the meeting point of the principle of public accountability, on the one hand, with safeguards of editorial independence and creative freedom, on the other.

The role of the authority is probably best exemplified by the IBA, the powers of which were considerably greater than those of the FCC in the United States. For example, it was the IBA, not the franchised companies, that was held legally responsible for program content.

The IBA received proposed schedules three months in advance, and its approval was required before they could be implemented. The Authority could ask to see scripts of intended programs, if it thought there was a danger that law or policy might be violated in some way, or to see videocassettes of finished programs for the same reason. It could require cuts or even ban a program from appearing at all, if this was necessary to stay within the legal and policy bounds, as it interpreted them. Above all, it awarded and renewed the companies' franchises at periodic intervals, when rival applications were solicited and seriously considered.

The fact that the franchises were not held in perpetuity and that their renewal was no mere formality was highly significant. When the contracts first awarded in 1955 were reconsidered in 1968, for example, the company then serving the west of England and Wales (TWW) was ousted and replaced by Harlech Television; Granada Television lost a portion of its northern transmission area to a new contractor, Yorkshire Television; a new company was created to serve the London area from Friday to Sunday evening (London Weekend Television); and the London weekday franchise was awarded to a company (Thames Television) formed from a merger of two former contractors (ABC and Rediffusion). Yet again, when the franchises to operate from 1982 were settled in 1980, two companies lost theirs to a competitor, one serving the lucrative southern England area and the other the southwest, and two of the largest companies, Central and Yorkshire, were obliged to make significant changes in their internal financial and administrative structures and also to cater more specifically to subregions of their areas. Thus the companies were under a powerful inducement to work for goals valued by the IBA, since failure to do so could eventually result in the loss of their contracts.

Financial Safeguards

Mention has already been made of the principle of assured access by each branch of the broadcasting duopoly to its own source of funds without competition from the other: BBC license fee, ITV advertising revenue. Each was therefore supposed to be able to fulfill public service requirements without forcing every program to earn its own audience keep.

In addition, the great virtue of the license fee was to protect the BBC's independence from the politics and vagaries of a direct government grant. Despite difficulties of collection (evasion was always a problem), this was a buoyant revenue source for many years, first, after a higher fee was charged for television and, second, when a yet higher fee was fixed for color television. But when, by the late 1970s, most households had acquired color sets and the economy had entered a highly inflationary phase, the license fee fence against political control looked increasingly dilapidated, since the level of the fee had been approved by the government, and to keep pace with rising costs, increases were essential at least triennially.

In the case of ITV, determined attempts were also made to ensure that he who paid the broadcasting piper did not call the programming tune. With a monopoly on the sale of commercial time, the companies could normally earn sufficient income to cover their public service obligations without having to turn cold eyes toward all less popular programs. Moreover, the amount and placement of spot advertising was closely controlled by the IBA, which limited it to a maximum of seven minutes in any clock hour (compared with over ten minutes per prime-time hour on American network television and 16 minutes per hour at certain other times), and ensured its insertion into dramatic programs only during "natural breaks." Thus ITV's nightly half-hour news program, *News at Ten*, was interrupted by only one commercial break (compared with at least four on the nightly news shows of the American networks).

The seriousness of the attempt to erect safeguards against commercialism is well illustrated by the elaborate arrangements for funding Channel 4, which was legally required to provide innovative programming different from what appeared on the other three television channels. The 15 ITV companies were given the right to sell advertising time on the new channel as well as on ITV1, thus preserving the principle of no cross-channel competition for income. The Channel 4 company therefore received its revenue from the IBA on the basis of an annual budget submitted to and agreed with it, which in turn collected the required sums through levies on the ITV companies, proportionate to their varying strengths and resources.

Clearly, the ITV companies were highly favored by these arrangements, enjoying monopoly profits. That is why, to bring the privileges back into reasonable bounds, the government also exacted a special levy, calculated originally as a percentage of company income but subsequently as a percentage of profits earned.

Political Arrangements

The political status of British broadcasting has been complex and subtle, designed as it was with independence and accountability in mind. The principle of broadcaster independence has been safeguarded in several ways. First, though appointed by the government for five-year terms of office, neither the BBC Governors nor the IBA Members were supposed to serve as political agents or representatives. Although certain past choices (including chairmen) had party political experience (in some, provoking suspicions of political motivation behind the appointments), once installed, they were expected to perform their duties according to their own lights, not in response to government direction. Moreover, they were the only politically appointed figures in British broadcasting. Second, all programming decisions were made inside the broadcasting authorities. There was no authoritative line of command impinging on program production and schedules running from some political organ to a broadcasting organ. The home secretary's powers to prescribe or ban individual programs were residual and largely inactive, rather than an operative part of the system. And when Ministers were questioned in Parliament about BBC or ITV programs, they typically replied that program content is not their responsibility but was for the BBC and IBA to determine. Third, although BBC Governors and IBA Members were sometimes recipients of political complaints, a division between their responsibilities and those of BBC Management and IBA staff insulated producers from direct interference. When, during the 1987 election campaign, for example, the chairman of the BBC Board of Governors received an objection from the chairman of the Conservative party to the cancellation of a Conservative spokesman's invitation to appear in a certain program, the former merely informed the director general about it, replying to the complainant that of course he never intervened in Management relations with program makers. Fourth, whenever proposals for an overarching broadcasting commission to coordinate BBC and ITV functions have been made—for example, to collect, pool, and redistribute all sources of broadcast income or to monitor performance and enforce standards—they have invariably been rejected because such a step "would sooner or later lead to one body of people being in a position to impose their views on the whole of broadcasting output" and "would increase the risk of political control over broadcasting."[29]

The British framework of public accountability was distinctive for the remarkably limited role of the courts in its enforcement. Although the IBA and BBC could be and were occasionally taken to court for alleged violations, the judges usually presumed that so long as the broadcasting authorities had taken their obligations seriously and respected principles of natural justice, their decisions should be accepted. The system of broadcasting accountability therefore consisted of the following main elements:

1. The responsibility of the Governors of the BBC and the Members of the Independent Broadcasting Authority to uphold and enforce their specified obligations in their services
2. Occasional broadcasting debates in Parliament in response to BBC and IBA annual reports that were submitted to it or to government proposals for structural change
3. The role of the Minister answerable to Parliament for broadcasting, who had certain sweeping but very rarely exercised powers to ban or require the transmission of certain materials and powers to determine the conditions under which programs are transmitted—for example, fixing broadcasting hours and authorizing new services
4. The Broadcasting Complaints Commission, which receives complaints of misrepresentation and unfair treatment from individuals appearing or dealt with in programs, delivering verdicts that the broadcasting organization concerned must publish
5. Periodic intensive and comprehensive reviews of the organization and activities of the BBC and independent broadcasters, such as the Crawford, Ullswater, Beveridge, Pilkington, Annan, and Peacock committees[30]

Such an account would be seriously incomplete, however, without reference to the informal but potent implications of the fact that British broadcasting is a creature of Parliament. This has favored dispositions to show a degree of respect toward the country's main political institutions and of sensitivity toward expectations for broadcasting that are believed to be widely shared throughout the political establishment.

Examples are numerous and significant. Election campaigns have enjoyed extraordinary treatment, with schedules revamped to include numerous discussion programs and news bulletins lengthened and augmented with many contributions from current affairs specialists. Broadcaster agenda setting has been inhibited by the assumption that the main parties are entitled to set the policy choices before the electorate on their own terms.[31] Between elections, coverage of the House of Commons is so extensive and regular that "for British broadcasting, it can virtually be said that political news *is* Parliamentary news."[32] Moreover, the slant of much of the reporting was measurably less negative than American network news coverage of Congress.[33] Similarly, coverage of the annual conferences of the main parties have been influenced by the assumption that since they were " 'the events of the political parties', . . . the BBC had no business interfering with or reshaping the event's representation on the screen."[34]

Cultural Factors

Finally, the public service approach was historically sustained by its roots in a societal consensus over the purposes of broadcasting. This was most evident in prewar support for the BBC monopoly. The Conservative party regarded the BBC as its own creation, whereas Labour approved it as a prototype of the kind of public corporation it favored for nationalized industry generally.[35] It was especially significant that "the educated classes [were] on the whole . . . well satisfied with the programmes of the British Broadcasting Corporation,"[36] for they dominated articulate opinion in prewar Britain and appreciated the BBC's fidelity to their cultural values.

Across the postwar period, however, the more political underpinnings of consensus gradually eroded. One sign was the increasing number of groups voicing their discontent with television,

> ranging from standard bearers of social causes, such as racial equality and the feminist movement, to inveterate wielders of pressure, such as the major political parties, to even well-entrenched Establishment sectors, such as the police, the trade unions, and the medical profession.[37]

Most significant was a deepening of party divisions. On two occasions, after the Conservatives assumed office in the postwar period (in 1951 and 1970), they effected changes in broadcasting organization over Labour opposition (introducing Independent Television and commercial local radio, respectively). Today, party differences over the future of broadcasting amount to a gulf.

SIGNIFICANT CRISES?

The history of British broadcasting has been punctuated by a series of political crises (serious quarrels in which government or party displeasure over actual or proposed programming was backed by sanctions threatening vital broadcaster interests) and one major structural crisis (proposals for organizational change that appeared to jeopardize the public service framework itself). But in hindsight they pale in comparison with the structural crisis now on the horizon.

Political Conflict

The best single account of many political cases can be found in Asa Briggs's *Governing the BBC*,[38] though this does not cover the General Strike of 1926[39] or political conflicts in the 1980s. The most important of these recent events was the furor over *Real Lives*, a 1985 program about Northern Ireland featuring interviews with Protestant militants and members of Sinn Fein, a political wing of the IRA. The complexity of the political status of British broadcasting is probably reflected in the fact that no single pattern of outcome and resolution has emerged from the sequence of political conflicts. There have been no consistent winners or losers, although observers have increasingly discerned some weakening of broadcasters' resolve and a tightening of their political belts.[40]

In a few cases, the broadcasters won hands down, yielding little or nothing. At the time of the British invasion of the Suez Canal in 1956, for example, the BBC insisted on giving the microphone to Labour opponents and reporting dissent to foreign listeners in its World Service, flouting the wrath of Prime Minister Anthony Eden, who threatened to commandeer the corporation. Similarly, the BBC insisted in 1972 on broadcasting a three-hour program called *The Question of Ulster: An Enquiry into the Future*, taking the form of a tribunal of three judges who listened to representatives of eight different Irish political viewpoints and summed up afterward (without judgment), despite the home secretary's public call to abandon it and his unwillingness to appear in it.

In other instances, the broadcasters more or less capitulated. A case in point was a series of adult education talks on *The Citizen and His Government*, scheduled for delivery in 1935, which included a Communist speaker. In response to government objection, the BBC Governors initially stood their ground, then agreed to cancel so long as public reference could be made to government concern, and finally cancelled without any such reference.

Sometimes broadcasters resisted the immediate point of pressure but behaved more responsively afterward. In 1933, for example, the BBC defended against prime ministerial ire a correspondent who stated that Britain would have acted like Germany in leaving the League of Nations Disarmament Conference had the nation been similarly placed—but later eased the correspondent out of regular employment. The fury of Prime Minister Harold Wilson over *Yesterday's Men*, a documentary about the impact of losing office on the Labour party, prompted similar behavior in 1971. After unprecedentedly viewing the program in advance, the BBC Governors allowed it to be screened with only a few cuts of particularly sensitive material. The internal repercussions were drastic, however, including removal of a current affairs executive from his position, reprimands for others, and tightened oversight of political material generally.

Finally, the *Real Lives* episode veered between several outcomes. After receiving a written request from the home secretary not to show the program, the Board of Governors again breached convention with an advance viewing, after which, in the teeth of strong opposition from Management, the majority voted to cancel it. But after a one-day strike of BBC journalists and much public criticism, Governors and Management compromised, letting the documentary be shown a few months later with quite minor editorial revisions.

Perhaps three conclusions may be drawn from this record. First, British broadcasting organizations have been vulnerable to pressure yet could call on defenses against it. Second, outcomes of conflict episodes were often unpredictable in advance and depended on an array of situationally specific power forces in play at the time. Important factors included a unified (or disunited) reaction in the political establishment (all-party outrage over *Yesterday's Men* weakened the BBC, just as party divisions helped it at the time of Suez), the apparent reasonableness (or irrationality) of the government's position (strong over the General Strike, which was illegal, but weak over *Real Lives*, since its desire to deprive Sinn Fein of airtime conflicted with that organization's eligibility to put up candidates in local elections), and whether the program makers concerned could plausibly claim to have behaved responsibly and with due propriety (strong over Suez but very weak over *Yesterday's Men*, since politicians invited to appear had been misled over the title, purpose, context, and satirical musical background of the program). Third, the BBC was at the eye of political storms far more often than ITV. (They feature hardly at all in Sendall's two-volume history of Independent broadcasting.)[41] This may have reflected the BBC's special image and status as a national institution, the fact that as one body it offered one target (rather than 15 lesser ones), its greater dependence on government decisions over finance, and the lack of a clear distinction between its program making and its regulatory functions.

A Historic Structural Crisis

The most important structural crisis in the past centered on the creation of ITV as a competitor to the BBC in 1955. It had two phases—before and after the passage of the legislation. In advance, the proposal to introduce commercial television appeared calamitous to BBC supporters, but their voiced concerns helped to strengthen the controls imposed on the newcomer. Afterward, many in the BBC were still alarmed—seemingly with good reason at first—but within less than a decade they had learned to live with the situation.

The starting point was the report of the Beveridge Committee,[42] which had acknowledged dangers inherent in BBC monopoly—remoteness, size, secretiveness, complacency, and "Londonization"—and had accordingly recommended the antidote of a stiff dose of regional devolution. These alleged weaknesses were seized on, first, in a minority report by a Conservative member of the committee, proposing commercial television as a vehicle of greater diversity and freedom of expression, and, second, by a coalition of economic and political interest groups who were determined that the advertising potential of television be fully exploited.[43] In response to fears of cultural decline and a collapse of standards, the government had to make significant concessions, rejecting the much criticized American system of program sponsorship and setting up the Independent Television Authority to license broadcasting companies and to supervise their performance in the light of requirements set out in legislation.

The progress of ITV plunged the BBC into tumult in the second half of the 1950s. Staff was being lured away, requiring renegotiation of many contracts to retain the services of individuals the corporation could not afford to lose.[44] Confusion reigned over how to respond to competition, including tendencies to ignore and patronize it. The audience reaction concentrated executive minds mightily, however, with BBC shares versus ITV shares falling from 55 to 46 in 1955 to 38 to 62 in 1956 and to a nadir of 28 to 72 in the summer of 1957. In the following five years, the corporation steadily improved its programming, paying more attention to entertainment, overhauling the news service, learning the art of competitive scheduling, and developing new program forms, including realistic serial dramas, current affairs shows, political coverage, and satire. By 1962, overall parity had been reached with ITV, which had to bear the brunt of the next review committee's criticisms of low programming standards.[45] This paved the way for a stronger regulatory role for the Independent Television Authority and authorization of the BBC to open another television channel (BBC2).

Two main structural outcomes emerged from this crisis. One was the previously mentioned conversion of the BBC monopoly into a duopoly, where public service standards would apply in more or less common terms to both sides of the system within an overall ethic of comprehensiveness. The other was a keen realization inside the BBC that it must not neglect overall audience sizes. As Gerald Beadle put the lesson that was absorbed, it would be "hard to justify the continuing existence of an expensive and comprehensive public service . . . if only a small minority of the people were using it."[46] Thereafter, the BBC felt obliged to keep its overall audience share up as part of its continuing need to sustain its claim to sufficient levels of license fee revenue.

MOUNTING UNCERTAINTIES

By the mid-1980s, British public service broadcasting faced many perplexing problems. Cumulatively, the pressures bearing down on the broadcasters generated much uncertainty and concern.

First, the influence of many factors that had traditionally supported the British broadcasting system was weakening. Societal consensus over broadcasting purposes, standards, and arrangements no longer prevailed. The BBC could never again expect to enjoy a buoyant license fee income, due to a government decision to link it for the rest of the decade to the retail price index, which had never kept pace with rising television production costs. The spectrum scarcity that once justified duopoly privilege legitimized public service controls and ensured that massive viewership of BBC and ITV offerings would soon be a condition of the past. Government intentions were difficult to read. In sum, as they looked to the future, public service broadcasters faced less security: of public regard, income, audience patronage, and government support.

Second, with the introduction of new media, the BBC and ITV faced transformed terms of competition, though at the time nobody could say how many British viewers would really wish to invest in them. Would the range of programming offered across terrestrial broadcasting's four main services lessen the appeal of multichannel abundance and choice?

Cable television was very slow to make headway at first. Even at the time of this writing, only a few scattered urban areas are wired up (though well over 100 franchises have been awarded). Domestic providers of finance were reluctant to invest in cable systems, a gap into which several big American multisystem cable operators eventually stepped. Where systems have been installed, only about one-fifth of the households along the route have actually subscribed. Similarly, the eventual popularity of satellite-to-home broadcasting, particularly for six channels offered by a Murdoch-owned service, is difficult to predict, though over a million households have receiver dishes.

Nevertheless, the BBC and ITV knew that from some time in the 1990s, the terms of competition were bound to change in two senses. First, instead of competing with like-spirited, similarly regulated rivals observing the same rules of the game, they would face what Denis Forman termed an international set of "media mercenaries,"[47] unbridled in their readiness to offer whatever was most likely to win audiences. As Christopher Dunkeley warned, the newcomers seem to have practically no interest in high quality. Whether you look at the increasing number of hours becoming available or at the increasing number of outlets, the overwhelming concern in both cases is the demotic. Television simply cannot get enough darts, game shows, and pop music.[48]

Second, competition for audience members themselves would become tougher, partly because "the greater the number of outlets, the more you have to struggle for attention,"[49] partly because with "access to more entertaining programmes," more viewers may gravitate to "the easy option in any viewing choice at the expense of more serious offerings."[50]

Third, there was an unsettling shift in the normative terrain on which public service broadcasting had rested for many years. The BBC and ITV were operating in a new evaluative climate, in which many of their past achievements, though not necessarily denied, were taken for granted and treated at times as if counting for less than their alleged offenses against economic rationality. In broadcasters' eyes, there seemed to be a frustrating inversion of priorities, with less concern for good programming and more for being lean and fit to wage the good competitive fight in the impending multichannel marketplace. Hence Forman's warning about a recent "change in the mood of our masters who have come to see television as an industry, and an industry in need of reform," plus his call for regeneration of a political will that would "show as much interest in good television as in cheap television."[51] Thus public service broadcasters were often thrown on the defensive, having to justify themselves on issues where they were relatively weak and virtually to keep silent about their traditional strengths.

Fourth, a report of the latest reviewing committee, the Peacock Committee on Financing the BBC,[52] gave the government a rationale for introducing significant structural change into British broadcasting. This is not the place to outline the main themes and recommendations of the Peacock Committee report.[53] Certain features, however, heightened British broadcasters' anxieties and opened paths for government policymakers to explore.

One was the Peacock Committee's advocacy of consumer sovereignty as the ultimate criterion of good broadcasting and its belief that an open and competitive programming market would be the best way to reach that goal. In its words:

It is a good general principle that any service to the public should be designed to promote its satisfaction. If this principle is to govern the provision of a service it can be shown that, provided certain conditions are fulfilled, the public are best served if able to buy the amount of the service required from suppliers who compete for custom through price and quality. In addition, the stimulus of competition provides further benefits to the public through the incentive given to offer new and improved services. . . . The fundamental aim of broadcasting policy should [therefore] be to increase both the freedom of choice of the consumer and the opportunities available to programme-makers to offer alternative wares to the public.[54]

Interestingly, the committee rejected competitive advertising as a suitable vehicle of consumer sovereignty:

An advertising-supported system will lead to programme diversity only to the extent that different advertisers are willing to pay to associate their messages with different programmes. The important point from an efficiency perspective is that there is no reason why the value of programmes to advertisers should correspond to the value attached to the programmes by viewers and listeners. In fact, the value to advertisers and the value to the audience of a particular programme may well differ markedly.[55]

It even conceded that "the BBC and the regulated ITV system have done far better in mimicking the effects of a true consumer market than any purely laissez-faire system financed by advertising could have done under conditions of spectrum shortage."[56] Nevertheless, it also argued that certain features of the present system

make it likely that satisfaction of the consumer is not the driving force behind the activities of the producers. . . . They do not have the same incentive, as exists among competing suppliers who serve the market directly, to be cost conscious.[57]

Thus despite its critique of advertising and judicious (if mixed) praise for BBC and ITV programmers' past records, the Peacock Committee injected an entirely new note into public discourse on broadcasting policy. *Competition*, *commercialism*, and *markets* were no longer perjorative terms for conditions to be rejected or closely controlled but instead were criteria to be embraced and pursued more wholeheartedly.

The Peacock Committee was most radical in its approach to the long-term funding of British broadcasting. It recommended that well before the end of the century, viewers' subscriptions should replace the license fee as the main source of BBC income, after which it looked forward to the installation of a fiber-optic grid of an "indefinitely large" number of channels, into which "electronic publishers" would insert programs at publicized prices, for which the consumer would pay through some metering device. In the short run, these ideas were unlikely to have much impact on government thinking. In fact, a further inquiry it commissioned into the technical and economic feasibility of pay-per-view methods concluded that British viewers would prefer the financial status quo for the present four television channels, supplemented by offerings of "premium" material (outstanding films, special events) on a fifth channel, to be paid for by subscription. Nevertheless, the Peacock Committee's approach suggested that in the long run, the license fee might be phased out.

The Peacock Committee was also thoroughly revisionist, though not entirely dismissive, in its treatment of the public service concept. As channels multiply and market-based competition increases, the role of public service must change. Members recognized that valuable program forms might disappear if their availability depended solely on people's individual willingness to pay for them, including

> news, current affairs, documentaries, programmes about science, nature and other parts of the world, as well as avowedly educational programmes, all of which require active and not passive attention and which may also contribute to responsible citizenship; . . . high-quality programmes on the arts; . . . [and] critical and controversial programmes covering everything from the appraisal of commercial products to politics, ideology, philosophy and religion.[58]

In that event, a subsidy to ensure their continuation would be justified because a market, properly conceived, is not only a device to cater to consumers' known and static wants but also a "discovery mechanism" for finding out by trial and error what the consumer might be enticed to "accept . . . and for trying out new and challenging ideas"[59] and because "viewers and listeners themselves may be willing to provide . . . finance for [such] activities in their capacity as voting taxpayers,"[60] just as many citizens are prepared to contribute to the upkeep of national galleries they never go near.

The definition of public service that emerged from this reasoning was "simply any major modification of purely commercial provision resulting from public policy."[61] The committee accordingly recommended a gradual phasing out of IBA and BBC controls and the establishment of a Public Service Broadcasting Council, which would award grants to channel owners and program makers wishing to make worthwhile programs. In other words, the committee maintained that at some point in the evolution of British broadcasting, the "full-blown" public service model, based on the comprehensiveness ethic, should be replaced by a partial, market-supplementing model, not unlike the one that shapes American public television today.

Probably the most influential part of the Peacock Committee analysis appeared in Chapter 4 of its report, titled "The Comfortable Duopoly." Although this acknowledged the freedom to plan in peace that stemmed from BBC's and ITV's exclusive access to distinct sources of funds, it argued that neither service was under sufficient financial discipline to keep its costs down. Not only was there no mechanism for ensuring that the BBC's periodic bids for license fee increases represented the most economical deal that the government could strike, but the ITV companies, as monopoly sellers of advertising, could charge whatever the market would bear and spend the resulting income with little regard for economy. The levy on ITV profits was unlikely to counter such waste, since this simply encouraged expenditure before it was assessed. There was therefore a tendency for the ITV companies to pad out their costs to the benefit of employees and powerful trade unions, on the one side, and management, on the other side, without regard for the public welfare.

INTO THE 1990s: THE SHAPE OF THINGS TO COME

The last years of the 1980s were dominated by debate over the government's proposals for reconstruction of the British broadcasting system. These were first outlined in a white paper, titled *Broadcasting in the '90s: Competition, Choice and Quality.*[62] After a period for receipt and review of memoranda, evidence, and comments from interested and other parties, these were then incorporated in a bill that was presented to Parliament in autumn 1989. After prolonged discussion, particularly in revising committees of the House of Commons and the House of Lords, the bill was passed as amended into law in autumn 1990, taking effect in January 1991.

As enunciated by Home Office spokesmen, the government has sought to follow a "twin-track" policy, preserving public service capabilities while adjusting the framework to admit new services and forces. In Raymond Snoddy's terms, "the stated aim is to reconcile the traditions of British broadcasting with increased competition and choice."[63] As the white paper put it, "The Government understands and values the rich heritage of British broadcasting; although its proposals are radical they preserve strong elements of continuity."[64] At the level of principle, the innovative track appears to consist of several related objectives: to put new services on a fully commercial footing, with no claim on public resources; to increase the number of significant players in the broadcasting system well beyond the ranks of the duopoly; and to encourage British broadcasters to streamline themselves for participation in the more competitive and financially stringent national and international arenas of the 1990s. Critics of this policy are unsure of the strength and genuineness of the government's allegiance to the first track, however, and many fear that the second may deeply damage or even overwhelm the first.

What exactly are the government's main ideas for transforming British broadcasting without jeopardizing its past achievements? They may be summarized through six measures.

1. The ITV companies' monopoly of the sale of advertising will be broken by allowing Channel 4 to sell its own advertising and by authorizing the creation, sometime in the early 1990s, of a fifth terrestrial channel financed by commercials.

2. Although Channel 4 is expected to become commercially self-financing, its legislative remit to be innovative and different will remain in force. It is to be reorganized as a trust, with trustees appointed by the successor body to the IBA (to be called the Independent Television Commission), unless vetoed by the government. It is also to be given a safety net in the form of a subsidy from the ITC, levied on the ITV companies, should the advertising revenue it earns fall below 14 percent of the total commercial income garnered by the ITV (hereafter to be called Channel 3) and the new fifth channel.

3. When the ITV companies' franchises expire at the end of 1992, new ones will be awarded in a complicated two-stage procedure to the highest bidder in a sealed-envelope auction. At the first stage, all applicants will have to pass a so-called quality threshold set by the ITC, in which they will be assessed for their ability, among other things, to show regional programs including programs produced in the region, to show high-quality news and current affairs dealing with national and international matters, to provide services of religious and children's programming, to provide a diverse program service calculated to appeal to a variety of tastes and interests, to ensure that a minimum of 25 percent of original programming comes from independent producers not employed by the ITV companies or the BBC (a requirement imposed on the BBC as well), and to make a reasonable proportion of programs of high quality. In "exceptional circumstance," the ITC is authorized to decline to award the franchise to the highest bidder, but in such an event it must specify its grounds for doing so.

4. The regulatory role and powers of the supervisory body over commercial television (extended to cover cable franchises) will be reduced, compared with those that had been exercised by the IBA. The government's white paper justified such a lighter regulatory touch on the grounds that "as the UK moves towards a more competitive multi-channel broadcasting market" and "as viewers exercise greater choice there is no longer the same need for quality of service to be prescribed by legislation or regulatory fiat."[65] It is true that the new ITC is expected to look after certain so-called consumer protection requirements: to ensure that the provision of news on the commercial channels is impartial and accurate, that due impartiality is preserved when public affairs programs deal with religion and matters of political or industrial controversy, and that nothing is included in programs that would offend decency, encourage crime or disorder, or be offensive to public feeling.

A key requirement of the old Independent Broadcasting Act, however—that ITV schedules should offer "a proper balance and wide range of subject matter having regard both to the programmes as a whole and also to the day of the week and time of day" they appear—has been dropped. Compared to the IBA, the new ITC is not to concern itself with the approval of schedules and will not be expected to preview scripts or programs so as to order their cancellation or amendment, should some breach of law or policy be anticipated. (Thus legal responsibility for program content passes from the regulators to the program companies.) Instead, the ITC will have a graduated range of sanctions it can apply to companies that infringe on consumer protection requirements or fail to live up to their franchise application commitments, including fines (such as forfeiture of sums deposited in advance with the ITC), warnings, and, ultimately, withdrawal of permission to broadcast.

5. In addition, the new and separate Broadcasting Standards Council has already drawn up a code that deals with the presentation on television and radio of sexual relationships, violence, and bad language that all broadcasting bodies are expected to take into account when drawing up codes of their own on such matters. Individuals who consider that a program or a commercial has violated the terms of the code may complain in writing to the council (which may also initiate complaints on its own); the council may then hold a hearing and deliver a verdict. Should that go against the broadcasting organization concerned, it will be obliged to give appropriate publicity to this.

6. Although in the white paper the BBC is termed the "cornerstone" of public service broadcasting in Britain, in 1991 the government awarded a license fee increase below the going inflation rate. The BBC is also invited to explore the possibility of phasing out the license fee as its principal source of revenue, replacing it with some form of direct viewer subscription. Informed observers consider that the next main object of contention and debate on the British broadcasting scene as the 1990s unfold will be the future of the BBC itself (its current charter will expire in 1996), its role (whether comprehensive or compartmentalized), and its funding.

Underlying all this are two related tensions. The government confidently believes these can be resolved, but its critics are not so sure. One may be termed a tension between culture and commerce—between expecting television to perform a cultural role and expecting it to be run like a business, maximizing custom, income, and profit. In contrast to the government's optimism over this, its critics cite four anxieties:

1. A worry about new players who will enter the system through the auctioning of Channel 3 franchises and the creation of Channel 5. They may fulfill public service requirements only to the degree they are absolutely obliged to, and if they become powerful, they could force others to conform to their patterns of provision as well. External regulation may be no substitute for internal motivation.
2. The worry of unaffordability, arising from the need to win franchises with big bids and the likelihood that surplus revenue from commercial advertising will be squeezed in the new competitive conditions. Spending may then be channeled away from lower-audience public service programs into mass appeal entertainment ones likely to attract more viewers and more advertising income.
3. The worry of unenforceability. With the best will in the world,

regulators are unlikely to be able to force companies facing or fearing real financial difficulty to fall into public service line.

4. Worries about effects on the BBC. Despite its cornerstone status, the BBC might feel that it must aim to keep a near 50 percent overall audience share (at least in comparison with Channels 3, 4, and 5 combined) to sustain a convincing claim to license fee revenue support. In 1990, split signals over this were already evident: Management was openly starting to worry over a slippage of only a few points in BBC1's audience share.

A second tension about the various paths that British broadcasting could take in the 1990s is between different models of the relationship of television to society. Providers, schedulers, and regulators could increasingly become confused over which should apply, by or to whom, and when. They are, respectively, a pluralist and a majoritarian model of such relationships.

In the majoritarian model, pride of paramount place tends to be given to satisfaction of the personal and immediate gratifications of as many individual audience members as possible. Television is just a business, aiming to do this like any other commercial enterprise. A broadcasting market, shaped by consumers' viewing decisions, is like a popular democracy, governed by citizens' voting decisions (on a majority-rule basis). As channels increase, broadcasters should be transformed from public trustees to marketplace competitors, and the public interest should be defined by the public's interest and presumed societal and cultural goals.[66]

In the pluralist model, however, the nature of broadcast communication is conceived of differently. It is not merely a product that may please or displease, a tool for the realization of individual purposes, or a conveyor belt for the transfer of information. It is also a spiritual transaction about meanings and relationships, some of them social; and inherent in public service broadcasting was always an expectation of providing essential services to society. In the British version, this was pluralist at three levels.

It was pluralist, first of all, in the multiplicity of audience types served, audience images catered to, and audience gratifications satisfied. Second, it was pluralist at the level of program making, aiming for a mix that reflected the diversity of the population and prepared to cross-subsidize less popular programs to ensure adequate resources, production values, and effective realization of programmers' intentions. Third, it was pluralist at the level of service to society. Public service implied that all significant sectors of society, divided by interests, values, and commitments, were entitled to have their main concerns reflected in program output—parents bringing up children, political activists, trade union members, industrialists, fans of the arts, sports lovers, gardeners, and so on. This is not to say that British broadcasting always did a good job on all these fronts or that organizations representative of such diverse interests were always satisfied by British television. It is nevertheless to claim that if some group did feel dissatisfied on this count, its grievance was thought to deserve consideration and not be immediately thrown out of court.

Clearly, the majoritarian model is likely to make significant advances in British broadcasting in future years. It would be surprising, however, if public service and pluralist concerns were entirely throttled. Strengths in depth in news and current affairs programming and realistic, socially aware soap opera are most likely to endure, as should arts, science, cultural, and creative children's programming. Nevertheless, the public service framework could come under severe, predominantly commercializing pressures at many points: in managerial policy, to compete in international markets, to satisfy coproduction partners with other programming standards, and to look closely at projects that may not pay their way, however worthy; in scheduling, with yet more prime-time entertainment on the majority channels and less popular fare being pushed further out to the margins; and in producer incentives, with audience maximization playing an ever more central part. The effectiveness of public service controls might also be eroded, as sentiment grows among the authorities themselves that regulation has to work with, not against, the grain of financial and competitive conditions.

In the new era, the BBC, being a single corporation and enjoying sole access to its own source of income, might find it easier to frame a coherent policy for adjustment than the numerous ITV companies, facing growing competition for advertising from satellite channels and cable, if not from a reconstituted Channel 4. Underlying everything, however, is the core question of whether the very rationale for the public service edifice might collapse as spectrum scarcity disappears, regulation becomes more difficult, and the status of the obligatory license fee becomes anomalous, funding only two channels out of a large number of freer alternatives. How the viewing audience distributes its favors could then prove quite crucial. If, even with greatly expanded choices, the public continues to spend a large majority of its viewing time in the company of BBC and ITV programs, the case will be stronger for retaining as much of an all-around public service regime as possible, enabling standards of broadcasting range and quality to be set for the electronic media system as a whole.

NOTES

1. Home Office, *Radio: Choices and Opportunities* (London: Her Majesty's Stationery Office, 1987).
2. Alastair Hetherington, Lecture at the Conference on the Future of Broadcasting after Peacock, York (September 1987).
3. Quentin Thomas, head of the Broadcasting Department, Home Office, personal interview (8 July 1987).
4. Peacock Committee, *Report of the Committee on Financing the BBC* (London: Her Majesty's Stationery Office, 1986).
5. John S. Reith, *Broadcast over Britain* (London: Hodder & Stoughton, 1942).

6. Denis Forman, "Will TV Survive the Politicians and the Media Mercenaries?" *The Listener* (16 July 1987).

7. Asa Briggs, *The Birth of Broadcasting* (London: Oxford University Press, 1961).

8. Jay G. Blumler, "Television in the United States: Funding Sources and Programming Consequences," in Home Office, ed., *Research on the Range and Quality of Broadcasting Services* (London: Her Majesty's Stationery Office, 1986), pp. 73–152.

9. T. J. Nossiter, "British Television: A Mixed Economy," in Home Office, *Research*, pp. 1–71.

10. Blumler, "Television in the United States."

11. Willard D. Rowland, Jr., "Public Service Broadcasting: Challenges and Responses," in Jay G. Blumler and Thomas J. Nossiter, eds., *Broadcasting Finance in Transition: A Comparative Handbook* (New York: Oxford University Press, 1991), pp. 315–334.

12. Terence H. O'Brien, *British Experiments in Public Ownership and Control* (London: Allen & Unwin, 1937).

13. Bernard Sendall, *Independent Television in Britain, Vol. 1: Origin and Foundation, 1946–62* (London: Macmillan, 1982).

14. Pilkington Committee, *Report of the Committee on Broadcasting* (London: Her Majesty's Stationery Office, 1962).

15. Broadcasting Research Unit, *The Public Service Idea in British Broadcasting* (London: Her Majesty's Stationery Office, 1985).

16. Ibid.

17. Forman, "Will TV Survive?"

18. Annan Committee, *The Future of Broadcasting* (London: Her Majesty's Stationery Office, 1977).

19. Roland Cayrol, "Problems of Structure, Finance and Program Quality in the French Audio-Visual System," in Blumler and Nossiter, *Broadcasting Finance in Transition*, pp. 188–213.

20. Winfried Schulz, "Public Service Broadcasting in the Federal Republic of Germany," in Blumler and Nossiter, *Broadcasting Finance in Transition*, pp. 260–276.

21. Annan Committee, *Future of Broadcasting*.

22. Reith, *Broadcasting over Britain*.

23. Sir William Haley, *The Listener* (20 November 1947).

24. Sir Brian Young, *The Paternal Tradition in British Broadcasting, 1922* (Edinburgh: Heriot-Watt University, 1983).

25. Ibid.

26. Pilkington Committee, *Report*.

27. Tom Burns, *The BBC: Institution and Private World* (London: Macmillan, 1977); Lord David Windlesham, *Broadcasting in a Free Society* (Oxford: Blackwell, 1980).

28. Ibid.

29. Annan Committee, *Future of Broadcasting*.

30. Crawford Committee, *Report on Broadcasting* (London: His Majesty's Stationery Office, 1926); Ullswater Committee, *Report of the Broadcasting Committee* (London: His Majesty's Stationery Office, 1936); Beveridge Committee, *Report on Broadcasting* (London: His Majesty's Stationery Office, 1949); Pilkington

Committee, *Report*; Annan Committee, *Future of Broadcasting*; Peacock Committee, *Report*.

31. Jay G. Blumler, Michael Gurevitch, and T. J. Nossiter, "Setting the Television News Agenda: Campaign Observation at the BBC," in Ivor Crewe and Martin Harrop, eds., *Political Communications: The General Election Campaign of 1983* (Cambridge: Cambridge University Press, 1983).

32. Jay G. Blumler, "The Sound of Broadcasting," *Parliamentary Affairs* 37 (1984).

33. Blumler, "Sound of Broadcasting"; M. J. Robinson and K. R. Appel, "Network News Coverage of Congress," *Political Science Quarterly* (Fall 1979).

34. Halli A. Semetko, Jay G. Blumler, Michael Gurevitch, and David H. Weaver, *The Formation of Campaign Agendas: Party and Media Roles in Recent American and British Elections* (London: Erlbaum, 1991).

35. Jay G. Blumler and Denis McQuail, "British Broadcasting: Its Purposes, Structure and Control," *Gazette* 11 (1965).

36. R. H. Coase, *British Broadcasting: Study in Monopoly* (London: Longman, 1950).

37. Jay G. Blumler, *Political Communication: Democratic Theory and Broadcast Practice* (Leeds, England: Leeds University Press, 1981).

38. Asa Briggs, *Governing the BBC* (London: BBC, 1979).

39. See Michael Tracey, *The Production of Political Television* (London: Routledge & Kegan Paul, 1978).

40. Ibid.; Anthony Smith, "Britain: The Mysteries of a Modus Vivendi," in Anthony Smith, ed. *Television and Political Life* (London: Macmillan, 1979), pp. 1–40; Forman, "Will TV Survive?"

41. Bernard Sendall, *Independent Television in Britain, Vol. 1: Origin and Foundation, 1946–62* and *Vol. 2: Expansion and Change, 1958–68* (London: Macmillan, 1982–1983).

42. Beveridge Committee, *Report on Broadcasting*.

43. H. H. Wilson, *Pressure Group: The Campaign for Commercial Television* (London: Secker & Warburg, 1961).

44. Tom Burns, *The BBC*.

45. Pilkington Committee, *Report*.

46. Gerald Beadle, *Television: A Critical Review* (London: Allen & Unwin, 1963).

47. Forman, "Will TV Survive?"

48. Christopher Dunkeley, "The Slide towards the Trivial Gathers Pace," *Financial Times* (25 February 1987).

49. Brian Wenham, Lecture at the Conference on the Future of British Television after Peacock, York (September 1987).

50. Pam Mills, "An International Audience?" *Media Culture and Society* 7 (1985).

51. Forman, "Will TV Survive?"

52. Peacock Committee, *Report*.

53. Samuel Brittan, "Towards a Broadcasting Market: Recommendations of the British Peacock Committee," in Blumler and Nossiter, *Broadcasting Finance in Transition*, pp. 335–358.

54. Peacock Committee, *Report*.

55. Ibid.

56. Ibid.

57. Ibid.

58. Ibid.

59. Ibid.
60. Ibid.
61. Ibid.
62. Home Office, *Broadcasting in the '90s: Competition, Choice and Quality: The Government's Plans for Legislation* (London: Her Majesty's Stationery Office, 1988).
63. Raymond Snoddy, "Turbulent Waters Ahead for ITV Companies," *Financial Times* (24 June 1987).
64. Home Office, *Broadcasting in the '90s.*
65. Ibid.
66. Mark S. Fowler and Daniel L. Brenner, "A Marketplace Approach to Broadcast Regulation," *Texas Law Review* 60 (1982), pp. 207-257.

CHAPTER **2**

French Public Service Broadcasting: From Monopoly to Marginalization

Thierry Vedel and Jérome Bourdon

Over the past two decades, analysts of French broadcasting have generally come to a similar conclusion: Public broadcasting in France has been suffering from two structural problems: continuous government intervention in its operation, particularly in newscasting, and economic and organizational inefficiency. These problems appeared almost as soon as radio and television themselves. From the start, French broadcasting has been a governmental entity intimately linked to political authorities and has repeatedly generated controversy. For this reason, to understand the present situation of public broadcasting, one must review its history; this we shall do in the first section of this chapter.

The past of French broadcasting is both complex and simple—complex because it is made of layer after layer of reforms, reports, and debates, simple because the debates seem to go endlessly over the same topics and because this history can be summarized in one sentence: Long an absolute public service monopoly, French broadcasting has recently moved to a situation of extreme competition among six channels (two public and four private).

The second section will present the current situation of public service in this context of increased competition. One might gather the impression that public service is now suffering the agony of slow death. Both the notion and the institution representing it have finally succeeded in disappointing almost everybody. The debates on public service still mention the same expectations that have been thrust upon it over the years: fair information, quality, variety, and, most recently, defense of the national production of programs.

The third section will go over each of these issues, trying to assess what has changed and what has not, what is bound to last and what is contingent in the present crisis of French public service. We will focus particularly on the question of financing, which has emerged as crucial in recent years. Ultimately, we will try to answer this question: Has public service broadcasting, both the ideal and the institution, been permanently reduced to a marginal part of broadcasting as a whole, or can it still play an important role politically, economically, or culturally?

HISTORICAL BACKGROUND

The Beginning of Radio and Television in France

The prewar period of broadcasting is little known but extremely interesting.[1] France had a private radio sector and some advertising before the war. This period was one of coexistence between "hard" principles (monopoly) and "soft" implementation (numerous exceptions). Following a practice observable with numerous other new media,[2] the government applied the regulatory framework of the medium that seemed most similar. Thus in 1923, the state telecommunications monopoly was extended to what was then known as the wireless telegraph. However, the principle was applied with some flexibility. Exceptions were allowed, and a private sector was created. Some 20 private stations had been set up by 1928. At the same time, the government shored up the public radio network with stations in the form of associations created by the PTT (Postal, Telephone, and Telegraph Office). The establishment of a license fee on receivers allowed the PTT to increase the number of its stations, which, like the private ones, resorted to advertising and sponsorship.

In the mid-1930s, especially under the Popular Front government (1936) politicians' interest in radio grew. They realized not only its social but also its political potential. In July 1939, public radio, until then a PTT department with 3,000 employees, was put under the authority of the head of government (*président du Conseil*); the government also created the Ministry of Information, which would control broadcasting directly until 1964.

Radio played a key role during the war.[3] The Vichy government used it intensively for propaganda. The Allies counterattacked. From London, General de Gaulle broadcast his later famous *appel du 18 juin 1940*, which few people heard at the time.

The first official television broadcast took place in 1935 under the authority of the PTT. The PTT encouraged improvements in transmission technology, but French industry was unable to market receivers, which were, as in early radio, often assembled by users. The war and the vicissitudes of the Liberation period delayed any meaningful development of television until the mid-1950s.

The liberation of France ushered in a new era. Broadcasting was firmly connected with politics. The heads of the new government came from the resistance: They had witnessed the role of radio during the war and sought to prevent any use harmful to democracy. The three dominant parties (Communists, Socialists, and Christian Democrats) saw the state's role as extending far beyond mere regulation. To them, the state was a force for social progress and economic development within society at large. They rejected private interests connected with the collaborationist right-wing parties. They counted on education and the media to raise the political and cultural level of the population and to promote social reconciliation. The powerful means of communication that was broadcasting was naturally imbued with such noble goals.

In 1944 and 1945, all private radio stations—many had collaborated with the Germans during the Occupation—were eliminated and their equipment was requisitioned. Under the authority of the Ministry of Information, broadcasting developed slowly. Sixteen bills were introduced but were not even discussed in Parliament under the first postwar government. Not until 1953 did Parliament vote a budget for setting up a transmission network for television. The number of television sets, then only 24,000, began to grow fast: 500,000 in 1957, 700,000 in 1958, and 1.3 million in 1960.

In 1958, France regained political stability with the new constitution of the Fifth Republic. De Gaulle's presidency (1958–1969) coincided with television's growth. The ownership rate increased from 13 percent of households in 1960 to 70 percent in 1970. At the same time, the government moved from too little management to too much. After public broadcasting was established as a public corporation, with its own administration in 1959, several reforms were passed, but not much changed in its practical operations until 1974.

The Public Service Model of Broadcasting

The 30 years following the war were dominated by what can be termed the public service model of broadcasting. Despite many controversies and accusations (by both broadcasters and the government) of plotting against, destroying, or sabotaging public service, there was an implicit consensus on certain basic principles, most of which would be questioned in the late 1970s and discarded in the 1980s.

The first principle was that radio and television were public services in the sense that they responded to basic needs of the population and had to satisfy the general interests of the nation. Broadcasting had to encourage the education and improvement of the public and carry out some basic missions: "information, education and culture, and entertainment," as stated in the law of June 26, 1964.

Second, broadcasting had to be a public corporation. This stemmed from the traditional philosophical and political belief in France that only the state can look after the general interest of all citizens. Private management was deeply mistrusted and rejected for at least two reasons. For one, private management would not be able to provide universal coverage, since the high costs of installing transmitters in certain areas would far outweigh any additional gains from advertising. Conversely, public service would go by the principle of equality, without consideration of money. For another, relying on advertising, private management would look for the lowest cultural denominator among Frenchmen and develop "demagogic," low-brow programs. It would also be vulnerable to commercial lobbying.

The French model of public service broadcasting was highly prescriptive. It was based on the assumption that radio and television should promote a certain idea of culture and not necessarily try to cater to the immediate tastes of the majority, which audience polls started revealing at the end of the 1960s. This effort to regulate culture fit well with the Gaullist vision of society. General de Gaulle firmly believed he had a mission to restore France to a position of grandeur institutionally, economically, and culturally. This view was reflected in prewar tracts on radio but was brought to a climax with television in the 1960s. When he termed television a "magnificent instrument for supporting public morale" in 1963,[4] de Gaulle unconsciously echoed the 1923 decree on radio, which called it "a magnificent instrument of education."

The Three Monopolies

So far, one of the key words necessary to define French public service broadcasting has not been used: *monopoly*. Monopoly was the essence of public service broadcasting, and nobody seriously questioned it—at least until around 1968. Although monopoly had long been seen as a single principle, the Paye commission in 1969 analyzed it into three different monopolies, one already gone.[5]

The first, the "core of public service broadcasting," was the monopoly of *signal transmission*, which was actually enforced the most strictly and for the longest period until 1986. Even the so-called peripheral radio stations were never allowed to install transmitters on French soil or even to use those of the public service. When local private radio stations were allowed to broadcast in 1982, they had to rely on the transmission networks of public service.

The monopoly of *programming* was also strictly enforced until 1982. It meant the responsibility of putting together and transmitting a complete schedule, as opposed to transmission itself and the making of programs. However, there had been one major exception: the peripheral radio stations, so called because their transmitters were located just outside French territory. They started transmission after the war and had been tolerated since. The French government, through private companies with public capital, held a major share in most of these stations.

The third monopoly defined by the Paye commission, the monopoly of *production*, is the most complex. Production meant the material operations of program making itself. The professionals in public service broadcasting insisted that only they should make the programs. This principle explained why a huge production department was developed within public service broadcasting. It was codified in the law in 1953 and again in 1960 before being discarded in 1964. However, it was never fully respected. A small private sector, fighting with unclear legal rules and the changing directions of public service, was tolerated almost from the outset, like little birds on the back of a rhinoceros, performing tasks the larger entity's bulk made impossible.

Early Criticism of Public Broadcasting

In the late 1960s and the early 1970s, critics of public service broadcasting concentrated on two points. The first was management. According to critics, public management slowed down the production process and was unable to control television professionals, described as prone to strike, unreachable, and unruly. Most politicians and broadcasters still loathed the idea of advertising, but some of them saw private management as a remedy to the numerous ailments of public broadcasting.

Second, acute political controversies started when General de Gaulle became the first leader to use television as a major tool of communication. Convinced that all print media were hostile to him, he relied heavily on television (making 32 official speeches between 1958 and 1962). National television also paid due attention to his travels and covered his masterfully staged press conferences. The Ministry of Information, the only one of its kind in western Europe, watched over television newscasts carefully and directly influenced the coverage of "sensitive" issues (social conflicts, French diplomacy, government actions).[6]

From the government's point of view, political control and cultural ambitions went hand in hand; they both supported the national interest. This is what President Georges Pompidou meant when he said in a 1973 press conference that television was "the Voice of France" (a continuation of the Gaullist doctrine on television). Television had to represent both the political interests of the government and the cultural resources of the nation.

The "Voice of France" doctrine was denounced by the left as crude political cynicism. The left adhered to the cultural objectives for television but claimed that it wanted to reconcile it with higher democratic standards. It rejected commercial interests even more strongly but also criticized the fact that the government used television for political control, especially during electoral campaigns.

"Gaullism is personal power plus the monopoly of television," said Jean-Jacques Servan-Schreiber, in a statement reminiscent of Lenin's quote: "Communism is the monopoly of Soviets plus electricity." Despite the first surveys that showed the limits of television's influence,[7] politicians were convinced (and still are) that television had a decisive influence on public opinion.

The government responded to critiques with a string of reforms of all kinds from the 1960s onward. In 1964, the RTF (Radiodiffusion Télévision Française) was replaced by the ORTF (Office de Radiodiffusion Télévision Française). Supposedly controlled less closely by the state, the ORTF was given a board of directors, but its managing director was still appointed by the Council of Ministers. After the 1968 crisis, new reforms were proposed. In order to make management more flexible, the control of expenses before payments was replaced by a control after payments.[8] In 1969, a modicum of competition was introduced in the area of news with the creation of two independent news units. In January 1973, the government launched a third channel called the "channel of regions," but it remained closely controlled from its Paris headquarters.

Finally, after the death of Georges Pompidou and the election of the more free-market-oriented but still right-wing President Valéry Giscard d'Estaing, the 1974 law introduced more competition within the system by breaking up the ORTF into seven public companies: three broadcasting companies—Télévision Française Un (TF1), Antenne Deux (A2), and France-Régions Trois (FR3); one radio company, Radio-France; Télédiffusion de France (TDF), the public body in charge of transmissions; the Société Française de Production (SFP), in charge of making the most costly and prestigious programs (fiction and variety shows); and the Institut National de l'Audiovisuel (INA), entrusted with archives, training, and research. The major innovation was that, in order to bring "greater variety and quality of programming" together with "political independence," the programming companies had to compete with one another. The government staved off all parliamentary moves to reintroduce any form of coordination or cooperation among broadcasting companies.

The 1974 system, however, did little to change broadcasting's dependence on political powers. Although direct ministerial intervention was reduced, government influence over newscasting continued, especially in the case of FR3 regional newscasts. The heads of news departments were often appointed with the prior knowledge and consent of the government.[9]

The Question of Financing

Radio and television continually increased their hours of programming in the 1960s, but their financial resources did not keep pace. As the percentage of television-equipped households started to level off, so did license fee revenues. The government and the Parliament were wary of increasing these fees. At the same time, a large proportion of the public service broadcasting budget was devoted to the installation and operation of three transmission networks covering the whole country.

To give public broadcasting more resources, advertising came under consideration as a solution. Advertisers were eager to use television. Within the government, advertising was considered a politically safer alternative to increasing the license fee. Radio journalists, who knew the private sector through peripheral radio and often moved between the public and private sectors, did not see advertising as a major threat to their professional ideals. However, the majority of broadcasters, all left-wing parties, and the intellectuals strongly opposed advertising.

After a heated debate in 1967 and 1968 between the government, the opposition, and the press, commercial advertising was introduced on the first channel on October 1, 1968, at the rate of two minutes a day, under the principle that it was not to affect programming in any respect. In January 1971, the second channel followed suit. After the 1974 split-up of the ORTF, TF1 and A2 began to compete openly for advertising revenues and audiences.

Together with advertising and competition, ratings were coming to the forefront of the French broadcasting scene. The task of measuring ratings was entrusted to a public organization under the prime minister's administration. Ratings were confidential and transmitted only to the management of broadcasting companies. However, the popular press—and advertisers—had also developed ways of measuring ratings, and soon broadcasting analysts started using the vocabulary of sport: A2 was "trailing," TF1 was "out in front," and so forth. Nevertheless, unlike the competition of ratings in the United States, this had little effect on the stations' budgets, which were established by Parliament and thus affected only slightly by the size of the audiences.[10]

From 1974 to 1981, conflicting demands started to weigh on public broadcasting. Programming hours increased and competition for audiences developed, but budgets did not grow accordingly. The left-wing parties and many social and political associations born of the 1968 movement were more and more dissatisfied with public service broadcasting, which did not reflect dissenting views and was attacked for being the "Voice of France."

THE NEW ENVIRONMENT: PRIVATE CHANNELS AND OPEN COMPETITION (1982–1990)

Changing Ideologies

Starting in 1982, a major change took place in French politics. At first slowly, then gathering momentum, neoconservatism permeated political thinking. This affected all major policies, but, as usual, broadcasting was used as a flagship for all new governments to assert their intentions. The change was all the more striking as it took place at the time the Socialists came into power, after 25 years in the opposition. In 1981, President Mitterrand and the Socialists (then allied with the Communists) had been elected to implement a program of "breaking away from capitalism." But economic difficulties and the weight of the international and European contexts led them to question the role of the state and to place renewed emphasis on private corporations. The state, lacking flexibility, was no longer seen as the best agent for social change. Private corporations were deemed a source of social and technical innovation, not a profit-making machine thriving on exploitation. In 1984, President Mitterrand stated that French society should move toward a mixed economy, wherein the private and public sectors would complement each other. In fact, France pursued a European-wide movement to redefine the role of the state in light of the problems to which the welfare state and Keynesian policies had led.[11]

"Economic realism" soon became a catchphrase for French Socialists. They started speaking the language of management and money, of financial and industrial constraints. Even cultural and communication activities were affected by the change and began to be considered as industries. Until then, the expression "cultural industries" implied the subordination of culture to capitalism and the transformation of cultural goods into merchandise.[12] Slowly, one moved from criticism to assessment of a situation and from there to a strategy. If culture was an industry, then it had a part to play in an economic recession. This change of outlook was also a change of scale: Broadcasting was increasingly envisioned in an international context.

Local and Private Radio Stations

The first area to be affected by this change was radio. The question of local radio was high on the Socialist agenda during the 1981 electoral campaign. Private local radio stations had begun to mushroom in the late 1970s. Several factors contributed to this: Lightweight transmitters were on the market, specific social groups were not satisfied with public service and wanted their own channels, and advertising resources were available in local markets. In November 1981, the Socialist government authorized private radio stations without advertising. But many stations were soon rife with illegal advertising. In fact, the Socialist dream of thousands of local community stations blooming all over France quickly turned out to be unviable. After 1984, advertising was allowed on private radio stations.

The ideal of an equal distribution of frequencies to all could not resist the trend toward concentration. Networks of local stations organized along various formulas (franchising, national affiliation with interspersed local slots, full affiliation). The peripheral stations benefited from the change and were granted franchises in all major cities. They also bought stock in the new networks.

The 1982 Law on Audiovisual Communication and the Creation of an Independent Regulatory Body

With the law of July 29, 1982, the Socialists introduced a new actor in the French audiovisual system: the High Authority of Audiovisual Communication (Haute Autorité de la Communication Audiovisuelle), whose major task was to regulate broadcasting independently from government. This was agreed on by all political parties, but the implementation was chaotic. In 1986, the right-wing coalition, back in power, changed it into the National Commission of Communication and Liberties. After the 1988 presidential elections, the Socialists changed it again into the Conseil Supérieur de l'Audiovisuel (Higher Audiovisual Council), or CSA.[13]

The reforms of 1982, 1986, and 1989 changed not only the names but also the membership. In 1982 and then again in 1989, the council had nine members: three were appointed by the president of the Senate (usually a moderate right-wing politician), three by the president of the National Assembly, and three by the president of the republic. This system has not won rapid acceptance, and inept appointments have already drawn criticism from all sides—as did the appointment of the heads of broadcasting companies in earlier periods.

Despite changes of membership, the CSA has retained certain major responsibilities to this day. It appoints the managing directors of public television and radio stations. Yet their budgets are still controlled by the government and the Parliament. The directors of public television and radio ended up with two supervisors instead of one: "We were like children complaining to daddy (the government) when mammy (the CSA) was not nice, and vice versa," recalled the first director of Radio France under the new system, Jean-Noël Jeanneney.[14] The CSA must also ensure that public stations fulfill their public service requirements and that the principles of freedom of information and independence of news are respected. The public service requirements themselves, however, are defined by Parliament, and their details are laid down in "specifications" issued by the minister of communications.

The Advent of Pay TV

In 1983, talks about a fourth channel started. The Socialists first thought of a cultural station providing access for social groups and associations. However, following the general evolution of other policies, Canal Plus started as a private, scrambled subscription channel whose programming centered on movies and sports. Although the idea of a subscription channel seemed elitist, the Socialists justified their choice in two ways: The channel does not have to resort to advertising, and French industry must master the technologies of coded broadcasting, which have great economic potential.

Canal Plus, the first private television station in the history of French broadcasting, went on the air in November 1984, under a ten-year public service concession. This was not the only connection with the state. Its majority shareholder was an advertising agency, Havas, which was controlled by the state until June 1987.

Canal Plus is a thriving business. With 910 million francs in profits on turnover of more than 6.13 billion francs in 1990, Canal Plus is the wealthiest station in France. By comparison, TF1 earned 300.3 million on 5.83 billion. (Note that these figures include the companies' subsidiaries.) Canal Plus's stock scores high on the stock market. It has more than 2.5 million subscribers and has exported its formula of encoded movies and sports to Belgium (1989) and Spain (1990), with numerous projects elsewhere in Europe, including Hungary. In addition, the majority of French theatrical movies are now cofinanced by Canal Plus.

La Cinq and M6, Full-fledged Private Stations

For the public at large, however, the real change in French broadcasting did not occur until 1986, when two general interest private stations were launched and for the first time the public could see commercial breaks during the course of a program. It all started in January 1985, with President Mitterrand solemnly announcing that private television stations would be allowed in France. Following a long tradition, the president appointed a noted public figure, Jean-Denis Bredin, to write a report, which was published six months later.[15] The Bredin report stated that private television stations "give viewers more air to breathe and more freedom."[16] After the creation of an independent broadcasting council in 1982, the state backed up even more by letting the market have a real part in the play. In February 1986, two private channels were launched: M6, a (mostly) pop music station, and La Cinq, a general interest channel.[17] The surprise came from the man who controlled La Cinq, Silvio Berlusconi, the private television tycoon of Italy, called the "grave digger of Italian cinema" by the Socialist French minister of communications in 1982. La Cinq and M6 started as public service concessions. Their public service requirements, however, were probably the lightest in Europe.

After winning the 1986 parliamentary elections, the right-wing coalition voted "freedom of communication" into law on September 30, 1986, calling into question the very idea of public service broadcasting. According to the 1986 legislators, communications services were not public services per se. They did fulfill educational and cultural functions, but they also performed numerous other activities, much like the movie industry and sports. Like the Socialists, the right had undergone a major ideological change. The Gaullists, in particular, had forsaken the conception of the audiovisual media as an integral part of the state apparatus. This ideology was obvious in one of the major provisions of the law: France was to privatize its first television channel, a decision unique in Europe. The

decision raised a flood of controversy and prompted demonstrators into
the streets but did not diminish the channel's popularity.

In 1987, Francis Bouygues, owner of the leading building and public
works company in France, was granted the authorization to operate TF1
for ten years by the CSA. Then, with other investors, he bought it from the
state.[18] Until that time, private channels had been marginal and had
drawn only a small audience. Now it was "La Une," the One, as the channel called itself, which surprised viewers with commercial breaks within
programs and with a scramble for resources of all kinds, which the law
did not officially allow but which the whole ideological atmosphere
seemed to encourage.

La SEPT, the Seventh Cultural Channel in Search of Viewers

Besides the six general interest channels, France has a seventh channel
with an overtly cultural aim. It went on the air in 1989. The idea was
launched by François Mitterrand in May 1985, five months after he had
announced the creation of two private channels. French intellectuals and
academics were strong supporters of such an initiative. Pierre Desgraupes,
a senior television figure, wrote a draft, and the idea was quickly put into
practice. As a first step, the new channel was given the responsibility of
producing programs. Money was lavished on it rather generously, compared to the rest of the public service sector. In 1990, La SEPT received 4.5
percent of license fee revenues, although it reaches only a tiny part of the
population.

Although a French initiative, the cultural channel was supposed to
have a European scope, exemplifying, in the area of culture, the renewal
of the European Community and the (would-be) free market of 1992. To
reach an audience outside France, it was decided that it would be broadcast on TDF1, the French direct broadcast satellite (DBS).

Cable and Satellite

Initiated in 1979, the TDF1 project has been continuously criticized for
high costs and uncertain programming. After being postponed several
times, a first satellite was launched in October 1988 and a second one, to
be used as a backup, in July 1990. The major reason, put forward by the
state, is to promote a new television standard, D2MAC, which is to replace the old PAL and SECAM systems and provide a smooth transition to
high-definition television (HDTV)—it can be received on old sets via cable
or dishes. In addition to La SEPT, the two satellites should carry Sport 2/3
(a sport channel set up by the public stations A2 and FR3), Canal Plus, Antenne 2, Canal Enfants (a children's channel), and Euromusique (a pop
music channel). But so far, only La SEPT is available to viewers.
Transponder breakdowns have prompted worry about the technical

quality of this transmission device.[19] Satellite dishes remain costly, as manufacturers are reluctant to start mass production. Most people who receive TDF programs today do it through cable networks, not a personal dish.

Cable television is only slightly better off. The government had long enforced a restrictive policy, limiting the use of cable to retransmitting over-the-air channels. Then, in November 1982, a "Cable Plan" was launched by the PTT, with the objective of wiring 6 million households by 1992. The choice of optical fiber and of a "star" design for cable networks slowed cable development. In 1986, private cable operators were permitted, and more conventional systems were implemented (coaxial copper cables and a "tree" design). By August 1990, around 2.1 million households had been hooked up, of which 387,000 subscribe to cable. French cable systems typically offer a basic package of about 20 channels: the six French channels, major European public stations, and a few thematic channels (sports, movies, children) that, given the cost of development, do not have much to offer in terms of new programs.[20]

To sum up, the new environment in which French public service broadcasting is now evolving consists of three private television stations, two of which have not really broken through. Neither cable nor satellite represents strong competition. Yet the situation is critical, mainly in terms of the interrelated problems of identity and finance.

THE FUTURE OF PUBLIC SERVICE BROADCASTING

Death of a Notion?

Is public service broadcasting a notion now devoid of substantial meaning? Are public stations to see their audience and their political significance fade away? To answer these questions properly, we must review the various meanings of this extremely ambiguous and multifaceted notion. Note that in drawing attention to this ambiguity, we do not mean to criticize it. Other important political notions draw their strength from ambiguity: They are able to reconcile different objectives in a single word or phrase that everybody agrees on. The strength of the notion also depends on its "allies"—the influential groups or individuals who find it useful to their argumentation and are attached to it.

After the war, public service meant universal service. All citizens had to be able to receive the same programs. It also meant, in the eyes of broadcasting engineers (the first influential professional group and the oldest allies of public service), supporting national electronic industries and technologies.[21] In the late 1950s, another meaning emerged, later explicitly expressed in the 1964 and 1974 broadcasting laws: the aim of making accessible to the nation its rich cultural heritage. At the same time, public service television had to produce all or nearly all of its programs itself. Public production had its supporters, but not public broadcasting news, severely criticized for biased news coverage. In the 1960s, another layer of meaning was added by some professionals: Television had to be a new form of art, different from cinema, and the state had to support that aim, which has never been achieved in any respect. During all these years of constructing the notion, broadcasting professionals, backed by powerful unions and associations, were its strongest allies.[22]

All these meanings are tied up together. The cultural-political aim is the essence of public service. It is because public service has such responsibilities that it must be given equally to all citizens (like education or social security) and that it must get enough public money to produce good programs. Problems arose, in the mid-1960s, when public broadcasting, and television in particular, could not meet an increasing number of the expectations placed on it. New expectations, primarily on the part of advertisers, forced the system to change.

After a long tradition of monopoly, the notion of public service was then taken to task by almost everyone. Until the 1974 law, almost all politicians agreed that broadcasting was to remain part of public service. Its cultural goals were supported by everyone. In 1984, the Socialists gave a more restricted sense to the notion of public service. The new private stations were seen as operating under a public service concession, but the demands placed on them were considerably lighter. Private companies could "inform and entertain" as well as public ones. The requirement of equality was forsaken, since the two private channels did not have to provide their programs to all French residents.

The 1986 law on the freedom of communication forsook all references to public service. Public service had no more specific responsibilities. Private broadcasting could do just as well. "What principle gives the State any right to be in charge of broadcasting television and radio programs?" asked François Léotard, the new minister of communications. Ten years earlier, such a question would have seemed out of place, but in 1986, it could be accepted as deserving of an answer and not simply dismissed as irrelevant. Freedom of communication meant the freedom of people to start a broadcasting service and to make money from it. The contents of the broadcasts were less important than the possibility of setting up a station.

The death of the notion of public service broadcasting could also be perceived during the three parliamentary debates of the 1982, 1986, and 1989 laws.[23] There was much talk about the public service, but never as a plain defense or apology. It was mostly in the form of a negotiation, a question, or an attack. Another notion was used extensively, that of the public sector. Broadcasting was seen as an activity divided into two sectors, public and private. The public service channels were mostly referred to as part of the public sector. Only the Communists referred to public service in a positive way and upheld the traditional responsibilities of "information, education, and entertainment" as the essence of public service.

Technologies of Transmissions and Universality of Coverage

That the state and public service companies have to support national technologies is not an opinion widely held anymore, as it used to be in the 1960s. This aim, now completely forsaken by public service broadcasting, was supported by the professional group that is now the weakest, the broadcasting engineers (now superseded by their archrivals, the much more powerful telecommunications engineers). Yet we must be aware of the gap between public proclamations and actual practice. Major technological projects still rely on the state, in particular in the field of telecommunications and space technologies (both connected with the military).

What came into disfavor was the kind of technology supported by broadcasting engineers: the expensive networks of over-the-air transmitters and relays that were built by public service broadcasting itself. In the 1970s and 1980s, the telecommunications engineers started taking the lead. By then, cable networks were preferred to traditional broadcasting transmitters. As for the DBS satellite, supported by TDF (where most broadcasting engineers went to work after 1974), it was to be a public satellite, carrying public channels. Through a small antenna, it would be available to every resident of the country. It was also a tool to support national technologies. As such, it fit old public service ambitions well.

At the same time, the aim of universal coverage was officially renounced by some stations. In 1985, the public service concessions of M6 and La Cinq did not include any requirement for national coverage, not even a schedule for gradually extending coverage to the vast majority of residents. This was a silent revolution—a major traditional ambition of public service was given up. And what had been a major advantage of DBS, in the eyes of public engineers, was gradually losing much of its appeal.

Today, although a lot of money has been poured into TDF, the politics of DBS are very muddled. Economically, nobody is sure about the market for DBS antennas, with increased competition from VCRs, cable, and private networks. Politically, the broadcasters, both public and private, who should go on DBS do not necessarily have long-term plans to use it as a transmission device; they will fall back on other kinds of satellite (plus cable), if those turn out to be less expensive. It is highly significant that nobody points to the universal coverage capacity of DBS as a political argument.

News, Independence, and Pluralism

Until the early 1980s, one area where public service seemed to have failed utterly was news coverage and political information. Peripheral (and private) radio stations were praised for their independence, while the newscasts of the first (and, until 1964, only) television channel never gained recognition and were continuously criticized by opponents—and even by some people among the majority in power. This point is crucial. Despite times of crisis and controversy, major public broadcasters elsewhere in Europe (especially in northern Europe) gained legitimacy in the eyes of the information establishment because the evening news program had become a national institution, independent of governmental intervention. This was not so in France until much too late.

This process of "emancipation," as it is often referred to by newspeople, was slow and difficult.[24] A key event was the setting up of two competing news units (one on each channel) within public service broadcasting between 1969 and 1972. Journalists generally agree that this is when the emancipation started. From this time on, the idea of independence was linked to competition between news services. After the breakup of the ORTF, competition was very strong between A2 and TF1. Despite governmental interventions after 1974 (the director of news for A2 was appointed after the president had given his OK), it is agreed that news got better and more professional at the time. The major anchors of each channel became television stars.

Ironically enough, the process of emancipation was completed in 1982–1984, just before the advent of private channels. Journalists benefited from the setting up of the Higher Broadcasting Council, which acted like a buffer between the government and public channels. After having been derided for so long, broadcast journalists were eager to demonstrate their independence. They increasingly felt free to say no to the minister who "wanted to be on the air tonight." Yet news coverage has remained an extremely sensitive area for politicians, and attempts to influence news can still be noted. This is especially the case in French overseas territories, where state television monopolies continue to reign. The coverage of French "liberation" (or terrorist) movements, such as the National Liberation Front of Corsica, has also caused controversies between newspeople and government authorities. Overall, despite some incidents, French broadcast news has now joined the mainstream of developed countries. Broadcast news is discussed less and less in reference to public service requirements or to politicians' wishes. More and more it is evaluated, criticized, and discussed on the basis of professional criteria.

Many people feared that creating private channels would be tantamount to jumping out of the frying pan of politics and into the fire of commercial interests—journalists would have as much to fear from capitalists as from politicians. So far, there have been few cases of direct intervention by the new private managers into news content. Among the owners of La Cinq is Robert Hersant, a press mogul whose papers have openly supported right-wing parties for years. But he has been shrewd enough to understand that a general interest station could not support specific political opinions. Yet some incidents could still be noted. On TF1 in December 1987, Francis Bouygues put an end to a famous controversial talk show, *Droit de Réponse* (Right to Reply), when the news made fun of him as well as of the Higher Broadcasting Council and questioned its independence. Overall, such crude interventions are very rare, and few French people still worry about private management of the news.[25]

News coverage on private stations is very similar to that on public stations and much more successful. In recent years, the TF1 prime-time newscast has had an audience of around 30 percent, about double that of A2, its main public competitor. With much more money, TF1 can afford original pictures from all over the world. With the exception of M6 and Canal Plus, private stations devote a significant part of their resources to news and current affairs. After starting without the news, La Cinq now emphasizes news in its schedule. Within a few years, thanks to a successful anchorman and aggressive and sometimes flashy coverage, the station established its reputation in terms of news—although this has not been very well rewarded in terms of ratings.

In this new environment, what role can public service broadcasting play? Some professionals claim that there is still a specific niche for public stations. They argue that since public service is less dependent on competition and ratings, it could investigate what private stations do not have the time and the nerve to deal with. There are some examples of this, in particular concerning prime-time programming. The two public stations are broadcasting a current affairs program (A2) and a political talk show (FR3), whereas these are put in late night slots on private stations. To give two recent examples, the coverage of the Romanian revolution and of the Persian Gulf crisis have been very similar on all channels.

Audience and Programming

To date, the problem of greatest concern to public service broadcasting is its audience level. As Table 2.1 illustrates, the private TF1 inherited a dynamic, aggressive programming policy and a 40 percent audience share, which it has maintained. The public service channels have lost 10 percent of their audience share in four years, moving from 43 to 33 percent. The new private channels, La Cinq and M6, get about 20 percent between them. Cable channels and others account for less than 2 percent of the audience.

TABLE 2.1   Audience Shares of French TV Channels, May 1987–May 1990

						Canal		Total Viewing Time	Age
	TF1	A2	FR3	La Cinq	M6	Plus	Others	(min.)	(years)
May 1987	41.0	33.0	11.0	8.0	1.0	5.0	1.0	165	15+
May 1988	43.0	29.0	10.0	10.0	3.0	4.0	1.0	179	15+
May 1989	40.3	24.2	9.5	13.6	6.2	5.0	1.2	154	6+
May 1990	41.3	22.2	11.4	11.5	7.7	4.3	1.6	163	6+

SOURCE: *Eurodience*, the monthly European newsletter of programs and audiences.

The drop in viewership of public channels is also significant because of the dramatic change in the very notion of audience and its relative weight. The way of making the audience speak has varied greatly over time. From influential critics and the press to letters and phone surveys and finally to the present predominance of audience figures, the notion of what the audience is has changed, and the notion of programming has varied accordingly.

Until 1985, the official daily results of ratings were kept secret. In 1985, the department in the prime minister's office that had been in charge of measuring television audiences since 1975 became a private company called Médiamétrie, which perfected the audimeter system it had developed in 1982. Audience figures began to receive more and more publicity, and the press added the controversy over audience measurements to its long list of items for the broadcasting beat. Professionals would like it or loathe it. Ratings became the language to translate the tastes of the public. They had many things in their favor, including apparent scientificity, speed of return (especially with audimeters), and the democratic analogy between ratings and voting in elections.

The drop in audiences can be explained by problems in programming policies. Public service channels suffer from hesitation among strategies. In the 1970s and even more under the extreme competition of the 1980s, the function (and the job) of programming gained in importance in the world of television.[26] Like Janus, public stations realized they had a double face, trying both to compete with private stations on the same lines and to offer a different image and a real alternative to viewers. Thus at some times, FR3 stressed its regional identity, but as soon as ratings started to slip, it decided to program more popular national shows.

As for private broadcasters, they rely heavily on well-established formulas (variety shows, sports), while public service tries to be more innovative. Private channels also do not hesitate to use formats that public stations are reluctant to schedule, such as games offering cash prizes and adult-themed movies or shows.

If private broadcasters learned the rules of programming from their Italian and American counterparts, public broadcasters looked to the BBC for a mode and passed the message to politicians. In August 1989, the chairmanship of the two public channels A2 and FR3 was combined. Foremost among the new chair's responsibilities was the coordination of programming. This moved public service broadcasting back to the 1960s, when public channels were part of a single body. Both public broadcasters now offer a little more diversity in prime time, and their audiences are slightly increasing. However, their strategy is not yet clear. Public service does not emulate the BBC. France does not have a public channel competing head-on with private stations, while another offers alternative programming. A2 and FR3 take turns in the frontal fight against TF1.

Besides, a successful programming strategy does not involve only the ability to make or buy programs but also the competence and the authority to impose programming decisions on all the professionals concerned. In traditional public service broadcasting, programming had traditionally been second to production. On stations such as TF1, production is driven by ratings from the start. Every program is scrutinized and will be dropped if it does not achieve a sufficient market share.

Public service professionals often advance another explanation for the drop in ratings, but it does not carry much weight. They point to the different requirements public channels have to meet. For instance, public service has to carry various community or governmental programs, such as telecasts of religious services, so-called free-expression programs produced by political parties and trade unions, and electoral campaign broadcasts. However, this does not affect prime-time slots. It should also be noted that TF1 is not allowed to carry as many movies as other channels in prime time—170 per year, as opposed to 192 for other channels—and that private stations are allowed a single commercial break inside each fiction program, whereas public service stations cannot interrupt such programs. Overall, however, the requirements that apply to public or private stations do not make a major difference.

Financing Public Service Broadcasting

Public channels are currently experiencing financial difficulties, since their resources have not raised in proportion to their costs. Public service resources come from license fees and advertising, which are both plateauing. License fee revenues increased as households acquired equipment; now penetration has reached the maximum in all categories. Moreover, the French population is getting older, which means an increasing number of senior citizens, who are exempt from the license fee. As for advertising revenues, they tend to decline, reflecting the drop of public channels in ratings.

TABLE 2.2 License Fee Revenues, 1990

	Revenues (millions of francs)	Share of all revenues (%)
INA	130.9	1.8
TDF	27.7	0.4
A2	1,323.6	18.1
FR3	2,694.9	37.0
La SEPT	337.5	4.6
RFO (overseas stations)	711.3	9.8
Radio France	1,851.4	25.4
RFI (world service)	204.6	2.8
Total	7,281.9	

Income from license fees has not kept up with increases in programming costs. It was 3.1 billion francs in 1980, 6.7 billion in 1987 and 1988, and 7.1 billion in 1989. In 1990 (see Table 2.2), it was just under 7.3 billion francs.

In real terms, revenues increased in the 1980s by about 25 percent. At the same time, costs rose dramatically. The main reason is fierce competition among channels to obtain the rights for popular programs, including movies, miniseries, sports events, and variety shows, and their featured performers and producers. In sports, bidding wars are similar to those in the United States. For example, the rights for a soccer game doubled between 1987 and 1989, while the rights for the Tour de France cycling competition went up from 1.5 million to 9 million francs.[27] Faced with increasing costs to feed their schedules, television stations also have to pour money into new equipment, since competition is also a matter of image and sound quality.

The situation is therefore quite uneasy. With declining, or at least constant resources, public channels can hardly fight against a wealthy channel like TF1 to buy appealing programs. TF1's lead in the advertising market is even stronger than in the audience market; it got more than 50 percent of all television advertising revenues in 1989. As a consequence, public stations' audience shares tend to decline, meaning less advertising and fewer resources, and eventually less capacity to fight their competitors. How can such a fatal spiral be stopped?

For the government, a first solution would be a significant increase in the license fee. This would be politically unpopular. Public channels would appear as more and more expensive while private stations seem free. Besides, the license fee is included in the price index, so raising the fee would boost inflation. A second solution for the government would be to reduce the number of television channels—for example, to force La Cinq and M6 to merge (both channels have been continuously in the red since their creation). That would leave more advertising revenues for the remaining channels and soften competition for broadcasting rights. The benefits for public channels would be real but not sufficient.

For public channels themselves, a solution would be to increase advertising revenues. There seems to be some room for this, since commercials amount to 1 hour and 50 minutes per week on A2 and 40 minutes per week on FR3 (versus more than 3 hours a week on TF1). But the strategy of public service in that respect is quite uncertain. The chairman of public channels has said that they may increase the cost of advertising time but not the time itself. The assumption is that even with their present share, public service outlets are necessary for advertisers in order for advertisers to reach a mass audience, an assumption that is not based on audience research and might turn out to be wrong and hence costly.

A fourth solution has recently been proposed by a group of intellectuals, television professionals, and politicians. It consists of suppressing all advertising revenues for public channels. Public channels would make up for this loss through a tax on advertising revenues (from private television and other media). According to its proponents, this system would allow public service broadcasters to be independent from the pressure of ratings and to devote themselves to providing quality programs. This system would also be more dynamic—the more successful the private channels are, the more advertising revenues they would get, and the more resources would go to public service. The question that remains to be answered is, How independent from ratings can a public, national channel be? A decent audience share is necessary to justify financing and to interest the politicians who make reforms.

Production and Competition

Production is an area of public service that has gone from prosperity to crisis. In 1974, when the ORTF was split, France did something that in retrospect seems quite original: It privatized the production department of public service, which had to manage large facilities and an overcrowded staff. In other words, a department of quality, high-cost, and heavy-equipment production was detached from the rest and received the status of a private corporation, the Société Française de Production (SFP). The channels had to commission a certain number of programs from the SFP, fewer each year. But public channels also developed their own production facilities (preferring lightweight film crews). FR3 increasingly resorted to regional production facilities, which had a strong tendency to expand (each one fighting for its own interests). With the advent of private competition, the situation only grew worse. The number of private production companies ballooned in the mid-1980s. Unlike the SFP, they could pass the cost of welfare for their personnel to state unemployment insurance and were much more flexible. Furthermore, private channels, especially TF1 after privatization, tried to build and manage their own big studios.

Since then, the SFP has undergone two reductions (1978 and 1990) and is having more and more problems surviving. A good indicator of its problems is the number of hours of original television fiction produced in France (the majority by the SFP), which has fallen steadily from 471 hours in 1976 to 378 hours in 1985. But it rebounded to 592 hours in 1988. An increasing part of this total is made up of cheap fiction programs, mostly situation comedies. The share of ambitious, costly programs like made-for-TV movies and miniseries is much smaller.

Again, political choices are to be made that cannot be left to the market. First of all, the number of channels still makes profitability doubtful for at least the two minor private channels and definitely delays the possibility for them to invest in production. Second, the competition of channels for audiences and advertising revenues may push up advertising investments, but it will also push up program prices and prompt channels to buy cheap programs from abroad. In that respect, quotas on original or French productions can only hasten bankruptcy and not stimulate production. Third, France has been able to preserve a decent cinematographic sector through a system of public subsidies and stimulation that has been admired and imitated elsewhere. All three public channels have been investing in movies, especially since 1974, and films draw the biggest audiences and advertising revenues on French television. But it remains to be seen whether movies are the best programming ingredient, with so much competition and so many programming hours. Finally, governments calling for both higher-quality programs and more national production must recognize that it is not certain that both aims are financially compatible. At any rate, it means setting the standard very high for private and public broadcasters.

CONCLUSION

The Never-ending Broadcasting Debate

When historians review publications and archives, they are struck by the unlimited energy that the critics of broadcasting have expended repeating the same things over the years and also by the lack of evidence in the arguments.[28] The smallest fact may be picked up to state a charge of "blatant political control" or "disgusting demagogic programming" or "illegal advertising and corruption" or "unlimited greed of commercial announcers."[29] Politicians, members of Parliament, and the press are the most seasoned critics. But sometimes one group of broadcasters would criticize another for the mismanagement of broadcasting (for example, "artists" or "creators" taking "bureaucrats" to task). Taking shots at public broadcasting (and now broadcasting as a whole) is all at once a national pastime, a self-fulfilling prophecy, and practically a self-sustaining activity since, at any given time, one can refer to earlier controversies and comments as proof that "something is wrong" in broadcasting.

What has changed over the years is the emphasis. The earliest controversy arose over the partisan use of broadcasting. Political control remained the major point in the 1950s and the 1960s. Then mismanagement and the lowering of program standards took over. What has also changed is the remedy. State control was vital to broadcasting in the 1950s and the 1960s—and public service was the essence of broadcasting. Competition was developed inside public service in the 1970s, then outside public service in the 1980s.

Both the Gaullists and the Socialists discovered that broadcasting was a matter not only of politics and democracy but also of economics. However, the economic constraints on broadcasting are many and seem hard to understand, and even purported realists have conflicting views on the realities of broadcasting. In any case, it would be naive to rejoice about this new realism, since politicians have tinkered with the system continuously, making it extremely difficult for economic actors (advertisers, advertising departments of the channels, and, above all, producers) to develop a coherent long-term strategy.

NOTES

1. Cécile Méadel, *La radio des années trente* (Paris: Institut d'études politiques, in press).
2. Ithiel de Sola Pool, *Technologies of Freedom: On Free Speech in an Electronic Age* (Cambridge, Mass.: Harvard University Press, 1983), pp. 5-6.
3. Hélène Eyk, ed., *La guerre des ondes* (Paris: Colin, 1985).
4. Charles de Gaulle, *Lettres, notes et carnets, janvier 1961-décembre 1963* (Paris: Plon, 1986), p. 369.
5. Lucien Paye, *Rapport de la commision d'étude du statut de l'ORTF* (Paris: La Documentation française, 1970).
6. Jérome Bourdon, *Histoire de la télévision sous de Gaulle* (Paris: Anthropos, 1990).
7. René Rémond and Claude Neuschwander, "Télévision et comportement politique," *Revue française de science politique* 13 (2, 1963), pp. 325-347.
8. Before that, a reporter could not be sent abroad without forms dutifully stamped and signed by a variety of officials!
9. Raymond Kuhn sees in the political arrangements for television and radio enacted between 1974 and 1982 the very essence of Giscardian politics: increased presidential power, an effort to destroy the Gaullist state apparatus, and a noticeable gap between liberal rhetoric about social relations and continuous governmental control. See Kuhn, "The Presidency and the Media," in Vincent Wright, ed., *Continuity and Change: France* (London: Allen & Unwin, 1984).
10. Advertising revenues were pooled and then distributed among companies.
11. Pierre Rosanvallon, *La crise de l'État-providence* (Paris: Seuil, 1981).
12. Bernard Miège et al., *Capitalisme et industries culturelles* (Grenoble: Presses universitaires de Grenoble, 1978).
13. For simplicity's sake, we will use CSA to refer to this body in all its incarnations.

14. In a seminar on the reforms of broadcasting held at the Institut d'Études Politiques in 1989 and 1990.
15. Jean-Denis Bredin, *Rapport au president de la République sur les nouvelles télévisions hertziennes* (Paris: La Documentation française, 1985).
16. For a thorough commentary on the Bredin report, see Nathalie Coste, Pierre Musso, and Guy Pineau, "Le rapport Bredin: la déréglementation audiovisuelle à la française," *Temps Modernes* (November 1985), pp. 10–34.
17. The creation of private television was hastened in such a way partly to shape a new system before the expected victory of the right-wing coalition in the elections of March 1986.
18. A provision of the law limits the maximum holdings of a given investor to 25 percent.
19. They might also change the allocation of channels on the satellites.
20. On French cable policy, see Thierry Vedel and William H. Dutton, "New Media Politics: Shaping Cable Television Policy in France," *Media, Culture & Society* 12 (1990), pp. 491–524.
21. See John Sysnam, *L'industrie française entre l'État et le marché* (Paris: Bonnel, 1982).
22. Broadcasting in general and French broadcasting in particular is a good field for applying Elliott Freidson's hypotheses on the sociology of professionals. See Elliott Freidson, *Professional Powers* (Chicago: University of Chicago Press, 1986); and Bourdon, *Histoire de la télévision.*
23. Dominique Mehl, "Audiovisuel: le service public, naufrage d'une notion," *MediasPouvoirs* 19 (July 1990), pp. 5–12.
24. Jérome Bourdon, "Petite histoire du pouvoir et de la télévision," *Pouvoirs* 51 (November 1989), pp. 9–16.
25. Nevertheless, the question is complex. In the long run, as has been shown for American television, sponsors do influence programs, not through open censorship but in more subtle ways. See Eric Barnouw, *The Sponsor* (New York: Oxford University Press, 1978). For France, some indications can be found in Jérome Bourdon and Guy Pineau, "Les mutations de l'audiovisuel, des cultures professionnelles aux cultures d'entreprise," *MediasPouvoirs* (October 1990), pp. 16–25.
26. Jérome Bourdon and Régine Chaniac, "La programmation du prime time en Europe," *MediasPouvoirs* (September 1990), pp. 145–152.
27. *L'avenir du secteur audiovisuel public* (Paris: La Documentation française, 1989), p. 91.
28. Jean-Louis Missika and Dominique Wolton, *La folle du logis* (Paris: Gallimard, 1983), p. 45.
29. Jérome Bourdon, "Audiovisuel: les démons du statut," *Le Monde* (supplement, 1 January 1989), pp. 16–17.

CHAPTER 3

Germany: The End of Public Service Broadcasting as We Know It?*

Gertrude J. Robinson and Kai Hildebrandt[1]

Discussions of public service broadcasting in virtually any country today have to deal with the contradiction between "international media markets" and "national broadcasting orders."[2] Perhaps more than in other policy areas, the future paths are likely to be determined by common, intercultural, and technological developments. In this context, however, the future broadcasting scene in Germany will not simply be a linear extension of past national broadcasting practices, rules, and structures. Rather, the past rules should be viewed as channeling devices for new streams of innovation. Yet in Germany as elsewhere, national decision makers find it difficult to alter the technological and commercial pressures resulting from telecommunications developments. To understand these pressures and their effects on public broadcasters, we will first survey the origin and development of German public service broadcasting. This review will illuminate the present state and the specific German conflicts and responses to telecommunications pressures offered by new distribution capabilities. After that, market trends and the influence of conglomerates on broadcast policies in the 1970s will be surveyed. In the end, we will review the options for commercial stations and greater program choice, which are currently being debated in West Germany, as well as the media problems raised by reunification with East Germany.

---

*This article was written prior to German reunification in October 1990. Consequently, it does not take into account changes that have occurred in the German media since October 1990. These changes are discussed in a paper entitled "The Headlong Dash to Freedom: German Media Reunification." The paper will be published in *Promise and Performance: The Media and Change in East Central Europe* (Norwood, NJ: Ablex, in press).

ORIGIN AND DEVELOPMENT OF PUBLIC SERVICE BROADCASTING IN GERMANY

The first German broadcasting transmission took place on October 29, 1923, using a central army radio installation that had been taken over by the Reichspost, the central postal service.[3] Less than a month after the initial broadcast, the broadcasters and the German Post (PTT) signed a contract in which the former received the rights to use the transmission facility and the latter established the right to provide programming guidelines and to collect a license fee of 2 marks per month per receiver. In order to broadcast to all areas of Germany, eight regional stations were established throughout the country by 1925. In 1926, broadcasting was brought even more firmly into public hands when the state-controlled Reichsrundfunkgesellschaft (RRG), the broadcasting corporation of the Reich, took over 51 percent of the private broadcasters' shares, as well as operation of the news division. Programming was to be supervised by Kulturbeiräte (advisory councils for culture), which had veto power over content, and by joint federal or provincial supervisory committees, which were to guard against deviations from strict news impartiality.

Thus barely three years after the first broadcast, all of the basic structural elements of public service broadcasting in Germany were in place and remained unchanged until the mid-1970s. In fact, the level of the license fee remained at 2 marks through three regimes until 1969. And the name of the private broadcasting company, "German Hour, Corporation for Wireless Instruction and Entertainment," provides an interesting preview of the occasionally conflicting dual aims of public service broadcasting and its underlying philosophy.

During the last several years of the Weimar Republic, in the late 1920s and early 1930s, radio increasingly came under direct state control, although Hans Bredow, the "father of German broadcasting," had tried to prevent such a development. The transition to an effective instrument of political propaganda was achieved by the end of 1933, when regional stations lost their independence and control over radio broadcasting became centralized in Goebbel's Ministry for the Enlightenment of the People and Propaganda. Radio played a major part in the Nazi mobilization, and during World War II, it became part of the psychological war effort directed both at the German people and at the Allies.

After the collapse of the Third Reich and Germany's capitulation, the Allies moved quickly to reestablish broadcasting facilities, since the printed press and especially radio were viewed as important tools for German reeducation and the establishment of a new political and social order. The Allies strove, above all, to learn from the past and to eliminate the structures that were thought to have made the Nazi dictatorship possible. Consequently, they set up a weaker decentralized system of government in postwar Germany and patterned the new broadcasting system in the three western (American, British, and French) occupation zones after the public broadcasting model of Britain's BBC. This move implicitly rejected both the American private commercial and the French state-controlled models, which could have been implemented.[4] At the same time, they resurrected many of the features of the Weimar Republic's early radio days.

The broadcasting structure established during the Allied occupation remained essentially unchanged when the Federal Republic of Germany (West Germany) wrote its new constitution in 1949, and it changed only marginally with the rapid introduction of television during the 1950s. Thus the structure of German public service broadcasting contains residues of German history, as well as reflections of new political realities. We can identify several constants in public service broadcasting in Germany from Weimar to the mid-1970s, with the exception of the Nazi era.

First, there is adherence to broadcasting as a public service, which has never been in doubt. Since 1923, the state has always regulated broadcasting, and this has been regarded as legitimate. In present-day Germany, broadcast stations have the status of *Anstalten des öffentlichen Rechts*, a German legal construction similar to American public utility corporations or Canadian crown corporations.

Second, broadcasting fulfills a special function in public life. The West German constitution enshrines freedom of expression and opinion in its Bill of Rights (Article 5). The country's Constitutional Court, the Bundesverfassungsgericht, has consistently interpreted this to include the freedom as well as the responsibilities of the media. In 1987, the Constitutional Court reaffirmed the "traditional functions" of public service broadcasting as "including not only its role in political opinion formation,[5] in entertainment and information, but also its cultural responsibility."[6] Freedom of the press, therefore, has a protective function in Germany, preventing the state from exercising direct control over the media. Offensively, broadcasting's public function legitimizes not only the government's right to mandate certain services but also the role of societal forces (including unions, employers, and churches) in supervising broadcast content.[7]

Third, the limited number of frequencies available demands different rules for broadcasting than for the print media, where the number of "voices" is limited only by the economic power to enter the market, not by technical limitations of the spectrum.[8] In recognition of this difference, the Constitutional Court has developed two contrasting regulatory models for the media: "external pluralism" (*Außenpluralismus*), applicable to the printed press, and "internal pluralism" (*Binnenpluralismus*), for broadcasting. In the former, variety of opinion is guaranteed by the existence of competing publishers. In contrast, variety of opinion in broadcasting has to be achieved *within* each station through administrative councils representing the views of different social groups and political parties.

Fourth, the structure of public broadcasting mirrors the federal nature of the German Republic. Thus the legislative power over cultural matters including education and broadcasting is vested in the authorities of the *Länder* (comparable to American states or Canadian provinces). The federal government has only residual powers in this area, pertaining to uniformity of regulations. Furthermore, the distribution of stations (with the exception of the Second Television Network) generally follows the *Land* divisions. Consequently, changes in the structure of broadcasting have to be legislated and implemented by and in each Land, and the Länder have jealously defended their sovereignty in the domain of communications.

STRUCTURE AND ENVIRONMENT OF GERMAN BROADCASTING

In little more than a decade since the mid-1970s, the German broadcasting scene has changed dramatically and continues to be in flux, at least as far as the addition of private broadcast stations are concerned. New stations and networks appear, and others disappear. We will therefore limit our discussion in this section to the public side of broadcasting. Germany differs from the United States and Canada in that each of the ten Länder have control over their own broadcasting stations. Among them are *Bayerischer Rundfunk* (Bavaria), *Sender Freies Berlin* (Berlin), *Radio Bremen* (Bremen), *Hessischer Rundfunk* (Hesse), *Westdeutscher Rundfunk* (North Rhine–Westphalia), and *Saarländischer Rundfunk* (Saar), each of which serves one Land. The remaining Länder have two stations. Baden-Württemberg has the *Süddeutscher Rundfunk* and the *Südwestfunk*, which it shares with neighboring Rhineland Palatinate, and the *Norddeutscher Rundfunk* services Schleswig-Holstein, Hamburg, and Lower Saxony in the north.[9]

All of the stations cooperate within the Arbeitsgemeinschaft der Rundfunkanstalten Deutschlands (ARD) by coordinating and sharing both programming and financial resources. Programming is shared especially in television, where ARD members joined to create the Deutsches Fernsehen (DFS). DFS programming is usually carried by all stations as the First Program, while each station also produces a more experimental, educational, and regional Third Program. The Second Channel is produced independently by the Zweites Deutsches Fernhesen (ZDF), a station formed jointly by the Länder in 1961. In contrast to the ARD, the ZDF is concerned exclusively with television and produces a single nationwide program. By agreement between the ZDF and the ARD, the two channels usually offer a contrasting program schedule in order to avoid duplication and satisfy the largest number of viewer interests.

While the federal structure of German broadcasting results from the Land responsibility for broadcasting, the internal organization of each of the stations is anchored in ten broadcasting acts. These acts reiterate the social responsibility of broadcasters to create and express the political, social, and cultural diversity of the German Republic.

Though no two institutions are identical, all have a similar organization. A broadcasting council made up of the "relevant social forces," generally elects the station head (*Intendant*). Among the social forces represented are political parties (often in proportion to their strength in the Land's parliament), along with other social groups such as unions, employers, refugees, churches, and women's and youth organizations. In addition, some stations have a program advisory committee to advise the Intendant on program policy issues and to ensure balanced reporting of social issues. The Constitutional Court has repeatedly stressed the crucial nature of this internal pluralism, as long as external pluralism produced by multiple broadcast suppliers was not technically feasible.

The main source of financing for public service broadcasting continues to be the license fee, although most public radio stations and the television channels carry a limited amount of advertising, usually in a block at set times. Income from commercials constitutes between 18 and 38 percent of a station's budget and is the only source of funds over which the stations have direct control. License fees, in contrast, are determined by treaties that have to be unanimously approved by the premiers of all ten Länder. The latter have often tried to use license negotiations to gain influence over a station's programming. Commercials have largely had national or regional reach, so broadcasters compete with the national or regional rather than with the local press.

CRISES AND CONFLICTS: CONSTITUTIONAL COURT DECISIONS

In our discussion of the salient features of public service broadcasting in Germany, we failed to mention two important players: the government and commercial broadcasters. Yet both of these players have in fact been involved in most of the conflicts and crises that have redefined Germany's contemporary broadcasting situation. Attempts by the government to increase its indirect influence over broadcasting have taken various forms. In 1960, the federal government under Chancellor Adenauer attempted—with the aid of industry and Adenauer's party, the Christian Democratic Union (CDU)—to form a second television network. Privately funded, the national network was supposed to carry the government's message. When the Land governments appealed to the Constitutional Court, the latter declared Adenauer's Deutschland-Fernsehen unconstitutional and in a wide-ranging decision set out parameters to insulate public service broadcasting from direct political interference. The decision (the first of the so-called *Fernseb-Urteile* handed down in 1961, 1971, 1981, and several times since the mid-1980s) reaffirmed Land sovereignty over broadcasting and forbade direct government control over programming. The decision did not ban private (commercial) broadcasting in principle, although the Court noted at the time that the press model of external pluralism was inapplicable to broadcasting, due to the limited number of frequencies available.[10] In its 1971 decision, the Court further reduced potential government interference by rejecting the use of the value-added tax to increase license fee income. It noted that through the provision of technical services, license fee setting was within the jurisdiction of Land governments. They too, however, were prohibited from using their financial clout to gain program control.

Yet another way in which political parties and Land governments have attempted to increase their program influence is through appointments to the governing councils of the regional broadcast stations. Formal attempts were made to increase political party representation to these governing councils, as in the amendments to the Bavarian Broadcast Act of 1972. In that case, popular opposition employed a rarely used means of direct democracy to force the Bavarian parliament to pass a constitutional amendment that reaffirmed the public service model and stipulated public accountability for both public and private broadcasters.[11] But even though the influence of the CDU and the SPD (Social Democratic party) is formally restricted, party representatives often attempt to exert their authority informally. They not only elect the Intandant of the broadcast station but also have a hand in hiring and promoting journalistic personnel. This amounts to a form of indirect control over programming through informal pressures on journalists and administrators.

Commercial competition in broadcasting has been another persistent source of controversy with the government. The constitution is silent on this matter, and the Constitutional Court has always left the "mixed system" possibility open since the controversial Adenauer decision of 1960. Only after 1986 did new transmission technologies like satellites and cable force the Constitutional Court to rethink broadcast competition. In the "fourth television decision," the Court acknowledged that a mixed system was constitutional, but how this system would be implemented has yet to be decided. Such crucial questions as supervision over private stations, programming requirements, and funding issues are still unresolved. In a subsequent 1987 decision, the Court reaffirmed the privacy of public service broadcasters in the developing mixed system. In stressing the public broadcasters' important social role in public opinion formation, entertainment, and culture, the Court seems to support the financing of public service broadcasting from both license fees and commercial revenues.

This dual arrangement will surely be challenged by private broadcasters in the future.

FROM NATIONAL PAST TO INTERNATIONAL FUTURE: TRENDS UNDERMINING THE PUBLIC BROADCAST MONOPOLY[12]

The policies implementing public broadcasting in Europe are country-specific. In spite of this, however, all of the continental public broadcast monopolies have faced the same kinds of challenges from commercial interests. These commercial challenges in the 1970s seem to have been fueled by four common sociopolitical trends: technological developments; media concentration (both national and international); political trends toward conservatism, which have focused on the industrial potential of broadcast industries; and changing audience habits. Together these trends have resulted in both producer and viewer demand for "narrowcasting" and a push for new distribution technologies to provide channels for choice.

The introduction of cable and satellite technologies in Europe has intensified pressures and demands for both regulation and coordination of the flow of program content across national borders. Though there always was some spillover from terrestrial broadcast transmitters, the scale of the phenomenon was too small to cause concern. Consequently, until the 1970s, it was assumed that each nation could operate its broadcasting system according to its own cultural mores and political goals. The "gates" of these national electronic systems were formerly controlled by a small number of institutionalized actors who dealt with problems of access, policy formation, and performers' rights. The elimination of channel scarcity through satellite and cable have changed this policy environment and attracted a growing number of actors who were previously not involved with broadcast issues.[13]

Several groups can be distinguished on the transnational and national levels. On the transnational level, they include the electronics industries, both hardware and software, which are in favor of technological development per se. Since the 1970s, they have been joined by political organizations like the Economic Community (EC) and the Council of Europe, which are involved with the development of technical know-how, European integration, and cultural self-sufficiency. Other groups of transnational players are cooperative public broadcast associations like the European Broadcasting Union (EBU) and regulatory associations concerned with aerospace technology and standardization.

Actors on the national political level include state and federal governments as well as parliaments, which have initiated electronic developments for political purposes or are expected to take initiatives as new technologies become available. They are joined by various ministries, such as post and telegraph (PTT), with responsibility for the technical side of network creation and maintenance, and those of culture and industry, which often follow goals contradictory to the PTT's. Though the television receiver in the home opens up opportunities for large-scale personal computer ownership—cinema-at-home opportunities (through VCR), as well as search and database access—European policymakers and the general public continue to view television as a ready source of entertainment and information for mass audiences. All regulatory actors are therefore preoccupied with the political control dimensions of television expansion, while potentially revolutionary changes in relation to telematics are being made by administrative acts without much public discussion.[14]

Media concentration as a global phenomenon is a second trend affecting broadcast regulation since the 1970s because it is most noticeable in Europe, where technological standards are high and demand for advertising is rising. In Germany, five major groups of print and film interests have formed multimedia conglomerates to benefit from the public's demand for greater program choice. In private television production, the two surviving front runners since 1986 are the SAT-1 and RTL-plus consortia, which underwrite and produce the programming for the two new private channels of the same name. Their competition is fierce, though SAT-1 seems to have overtaken its rival and now boasts audiences similar to those of the public stations, ARD and ZDF. Four big cable and print groups hold 85 percent of SAT-1's stock. They are Programmgesellschaft Kabel & Satellitenrundfunk (PKS) (40 percent), Axel Springer Verlag (15 percent), Holtzbrinck Gruppe (15 percent), and Aktuell Presse-Fernsehen (15 percent), which is a group of 165 newspapers.[15] RTL-plus, in contrast, is an international conglomerate in which the majority of stock is held by the Compagnie Luxembourgeoise de Télédiffusion (CLT) (46 percent) and Ufa, a German film producer (39 percent). Leo Kirch, Europe's largest film magnate, is involved both in SAT-1 through the PKS group and in RTL-plus as the majority holder in Ufa. His influence, however, is being challenged by German audiences and the rival Springer concern. Both of these groups are dissatisfied with his programming, which consists of old American films and comedy reruns.[16]

Three other German publishing conglomerates are also deeply involved in both television and radio. Their subsidiaries are bidding for the touristic frequencies that are now being awarded by the 11 Land governments for regional and local programming. They are Bertelsman AG, with huge holdings in book and magazine publishing; the Holtzbrinck group, with press holdings; and Burda, composed of magazine interests. All of these are competing for possible local and regional program projects that will be offered over at least two new private channels in each Land. Cross-ownership issues raised by this development have either remained unresolved or, more frequently, yielded to CDU or SPD political pressures emanating from the Land governments, which hold opposing convictions on commercial competition and development.[17]

Another trend that seems to have undermined the public broadcast monopoly is a political movement to the right in the industrialized world. Though this trend goes far beyond politics, its most visible manifestations have been the conservative governments in the United States, Great Britain, Canada, and Germany. Because conservative governments are more business-oriented, they tend to redefine the social importance of the media in purely economic terms. The conservative Christian Democratic Union's acceptance of market solutions made the federal government of Helmut Kohl generally more open to the demand for privately financed commercial channels than the rival Social Democrats. The CDU has justified this position by emphasizing the commercial media industry's potential contributions to the balance of trade, employment, and the development of data and business communication services. In addition, the political right, more than the left, welcomed the switch to more entertainment programming since this would counterbalance the often critical documentaries and news programs aired on the public networks. Thus for conservatives, there was little or no conflict between support for commercial broadcast alternatives and regulatory issues, because they assumed that what is good for industry is good for the state.

A final trend encouraging the introduction of private broadcasting in Germany can be found in audience demand for more program choice. This demand is anchored partly in the changing media use patterns of the generation that grew up with television. This generation prefers electronic media for its information and entertainment needs both. Though watching television only marginally more than their parents, young people use all the broadcast media as background to other activities. This includes both radio and television, which have become part of an enveloping household ambiance. The perception of television purely as an entertainment medium leads directly to the desire for more choice and thus a push for more channels. The studies accompanying the German cable projects indicate that in Germany, cable only marginally increases total viewing time, but it dramatically changes the type of programming that is attended to. The trend is away from information and documentary series toward films, situation comedies, and other entertainment formats.[18]

The redefinition of television as an entertainment medium has also democratized the concept of culture. German elite cultural concepts, on which public broadcasting was traditionally based, are now challenged. Upper-middle-class tastes for opera, concerts, and theatre, which draw only small audiences, used to constitute the basic programming of public broadcast stations. Today they have been supplemented with popular culture fare, both imported and homegrown, to satisfy the proliferating social subcultures that make up the largely untapped new market for narrowcasting. This is most evident in the 11 new satellite-delivered European programs, both public and private, heavily based on American films and series. Public service programming cannot completely abandon its constitutionally mandated goals to function as serious educational television, which must produce a balanced information and educational program to help citizens understand political and social realities. Its programming is thus at odds with the heavily entertainment-oriented interests of many audience segments, giving commercial channels a competitive edge.

One question still difficult to assess is whether the reunification of formerly communist East Germany (DDR) with West Germany in December 1990 will confound these emerging market trends. In this reunification, Germany's population of 66 million was increased by 16 million new citizens, living in what used to be six additional Länder. These reconstituted Länder will most likely be granted the same kind of media autonomy as that presently enjoyed in the western part of the country. To prepare for the transition, the Media Commission (Mediekontrollrat) was set up in February 1990. Its 24 experts, representing the new parties and other social groups (among them churches, unions, and women), have the mandate to supervise the transformation from a centralized to a democratic media system.

Four issues have preoccupied this commission. The first and most important is the writing of a media law that will implement information freedom based on the 1966 United Nations Declaration of Human Rights. This guarantees all citizens the right to receive information without censorship across national borders and the freedom to assemble and discuss this information with others. Journalistic responsibility in this new system is defined as a "watchdog" function, in which no professional can be forced to proclaim official doctrines running counter to the Human Rights Declaration and in which protection of sources is guaranteed. During the transition period, the Media Commission is furthermore responsible for the appointment of the chief operating officers (*Generalintendanten*) of East German radio, television, and the national news agency ADN. A third set of responsibilities arises out of the necessity to develop rules concerning the operation of private media in East Germany where none existed before and to decide on the role of advertising sponsorship in supporting future mixed public-private broadcasting and a fully private print sector. To develop such a system, the role of foreign participation in the media and the amount of permissable concentration also require clarification, since all European broadcast media presently face competition from Anglo-American producers.[19]

For the East German media, there is particular urgency to confront the issues of West German conglomerates and their potential takeover of existing media outlets. Such an attempt at monopoly concentration in the print sector had already occurred, when four media giants (Grunert &

Jahr, Burda, Springer, and Bauer) tried to corner the emerging print market. They proposed to set up a network to sell 80 papers and magazines of both West and East German origin, parallel to the presently authorized distribution scheme run by the post office. This distribution monopoly by private print interests, if it had been permitted, would have sharply augmented commercialization pressures in the East German broadcast sector, because the conglomerates also own electronic outlets in West Germany.

The Media Commission rejected this incursion and is proceeding extremely cautiously in the face of the general economic crisis engulfing East Germany. Though committed to maintaining information plurality, the commission is nevertheless aware that the economic future of its media industries is clouded. The mix of public and private funding necessary for the maintenance of a possible third television channel has not yet been determined, nor have the needs of the print media been accurately assessed.

Following West German practices, the print media will most likely be largely privatized, and it is already clear that in such a move, many of East Germany's 39 dailies, 30 weeklies, and 508 journals and magazines, let alone the 667 Communist factory organs, will disappear. Only the revamped *Neues Deutschland*, which serves as the new party's political platform, seems to have a relatively assured future. All other publications are experiencing great difficulties, not only in developing new editorial formats but also in securing financial self-sufficiency. Though price increases have already taken place, they alone will not guarantee economic success unless advertising revenues, presently nonexistent, are also introduced. Informed sources claim that papers with a regional and local focus will have the best chances for survival, whereas consumer magazines have already been virtually eliminated from the East German media scene because West German competitors have lowered their publications prices and increased their circulation.[20]

LOOKING AHEAD:
GERMAN SOLUTIONS FOR PUBLIC
BROADCASTING IN THE 1990s

During the 1970s, social and political, as well as media-related, trends led to viewer and producer interest in narrowcasting and support for new delivery modes that provide channels for choice. Sociopolitically, however, these trends have raised issues that are difficult to resolve. Among these are concerns about the effects of commercial competition on public service broadcasting and the redefinition of its mandate. All over Europe, as we shall see, these issues are being conceptualized in a similar manner, though the solutions proposed are influenced by different national and historical realities. In Germany, three types of solutions have been publicly debated: the deregulation solution proposed by the EC's Green Book of 1984, the mixed system (Zwei Säulen system), and the Single Europe 1992 concept. Each solution addresses different issues concerning the balance between public and private broadcasting in the twenty-first century.

THE DEREGULATION SOLUTION
OF THE GREEN BOOK

In 1984, a European Community Green Book titled *Television without Frontiers* proposed the creation of a unified European broadcast market large enough to compete with outsiders. This was to be achieved by deregulating the national broadcast monopolies of the 12 member states while at the same time unifying them into the equivalent of a noncompetitive broadcast union. To make this connection, the document argued that broadcasting is an "information service" that does not differ in kind from other types of services freely exchanged by the EC under the Treaty of Rome. To achieve freedom of movement for television services across national borders, member states were asked to do three things. They were first of all to encourage reception of national channels from *all* member states. They were also asked to reform their national broadcasting systems to accommodate both public and private programmers. In addition, harmonization of technical standards and legal provisions was sought to facilitate the transfer of programs between the 12 countries' broadcasting organizations. According to the Green Book, four types of legal provisions were most in need of harmonization: advertising rules, protection of young people, the right to reply, and copyright legislation.[21]

The German federal and Land governments, as well as the public broadcasters ARD and ZDF, rejected these proposals and thus the deregulation solution on political as well as public service grounds. The federal government questioned the Green Book's constitutionality, Land governments saw it as interfering with their program powers, and public service broadcasters felt it overlooked existing multinational arrangements with the more numerous (21) Council of Europe states. This German debate mirrors the unresolved nature of the struggle between public and private broadcast philosophies in most European countries. It also indicates that the Green Book's assumption of a uniform EC cultural market is mistaken. Germany's federal government argued that the EC's commercial Treaty of Rome provisions were not applicable to broadcasting because they contravened the 1981 Constitutional Court decision that reaffirmed that broadcasting in Germany is both a medium and a factor in public opinion formation. The treaty furthermore explicitly recognized member-state autonomy in the political and cultural realms being breached by the Green Book provisions. Under German broadcast law, as we have seen,

programming must reflect variety of opinion among Germany's major social groups and express balance by presenting different points of view on
public issues. Land governments in turn saw the EC proposal as interfering with their programming powers by requiring harmonization in the
areas of advertising and content quotas. The Land governments noted that
EC states were already supporting a set of similar advertising restrictions
covering tobacco, alcoholic beverages, pornography, violent material,
and false advertising. Yet standards on advertising limits and composition
(block or spot) and program interruption, as well as Sunday advertising,
were incapable of harmonization because they reflected cultural differences and varying religious tolerances in Europe.

Germany's two public broadcasters, ARD and ZDF, voiced yet another
criticism. They objected to the Green Book's call for a 50 percent
European content quota in television and film on the grounds that such
quotas constituted a politically dangerous precedent and were unnecessary as well. They argued that no more European programming than
presently available would be required to fill the 11 new European channels and that by treating member-state programming as though it were
home-produced, the European quota would be automatically achieved.[22]
The public broadcasters also cautioned against the international program
implications of the EC proposal. Here they argued that a "common
market" in broadcasting, regulated by economic criteria alone, was
neither a protection against outside (U.S.) competition nor an adequate
framework for working out the complex public and private regulatory
issues facing contemporary Europe. Instead, variety in cultural broadcast
heritages and extensive voluntary arrangements negotiated within the
larger European Broadcasting Union (EBU) should become the
centerpiece for future planning. Complete commercialization, U.S.-style,
as a solution to Europe's broadcast problems was thus rejected by
Germany on both constitutional and cultural grounds. In spite of this, the
federal and Land governments, who have joint jurisdiction over broadcast
regulation, have not yet made much progress on a common set of minimum standards, which will provide the foundation for new broadcast
laws.

The Mixed-System ("Zwei Säulen") Solution

The massive arguments against the Green Book's purely economic approach to broadcast regulation indicates that Germany, like most other
European countries, is building on its public broadcast heritage and
working toward a mixed-system solution in which public and private
broadcasting will coexist. How this coexistence will be conceptualized
will depend on the kinds of minimum standards that the federal and Land
governments will devise for commercial broadcast competition.[23] While
there is some extension of commercialization in relation to local radio

and cable systems in Germany, both commercial and public broadcasters are at present required to follow the same rules and to provide a balanced program schedule. Commercial broadcasters finance this from advertising, while public broadcasters continue to be supported by a monthly license fee supplemented with some advertising revenues. Land governments set these rates for "unlimited viewing" privileges, depending on the number of receivers a subscriber owns. Such a formula will be increasingly difficult to justify in the light of audience decline due to increased program choice through satellite, cable, and video options. In France, this decline has cost the public broadcaster about half its audience in the first year, and similar declines were recorded in Denmark and Sweden when private channels became available.

Germany's political shift to the right and the concomitant redefinition of the media as "cultural industries" have forced public broadcasters to redefine their goals and justify their existence for the first time in 60 years. Public broadcasters have not found this an easy task, because processes of democratization have undermined the previously accepted paternalistic right of the cultural elites to impose their own values on the tastes of others. Programming for a greater variety of public tastes has had two consequences: It has forced a rethinking of program formats to attract more varied publics, and it has required a reanalysis of the public service goals on which license support is based. Such a reanalysis, it is generally agreed, must be based on more than audience reach. Andreas Wiesand suggests that it include at least four complementary criteria—varied program content, audience needs, cultural objectives, and economic contributions—to encompass the full impact of broadcasting on society.[24] His case study of the Westdeutscher Runkfunk (WDR) station found that in addition to producing a basic service of entertainment, information, and educational offerings for children, adults, ethnic and religious groups, and others, the WDR made additional cultural and economic contributions that are much less widely known. On the cultural plane, its programs reinforce the regional identity of the people of North Rhine-Westphalia and function as a patron of modern music production and performance in the region. Economically, the station is also the largest buyer of cultural productions, such as films and music performances, from independent studios in the state and employs the largest number of artists and creators. The station thus generates substantial state income through taxes on payrolls, products, and services. Public broadcasters, this study demonstrates, not only are culturally productive but also play a substantial economic role in the artistic and technical labor markets of their respective Länder. For providing these extended social contributions, the Land governments argue that public broadcasters are eligible to receive a fee. This fee structure, however, is being threatened by private broadcast competition, whose uniformly entertainment-oriented programming can be bought at a discount. This results in a severe cost-price squeeze and great financial instability for public broadcast stations.

German federal and Land governments have not yet agreed on how the competition is to be handled or how the public cost-price squeeze is to be ameliorated. A variety of proposals have been advanced including tiering, regional fund supplements, direct government subsidies, and increased advertising. Each of these options has its advantages and disadvantages. Increased income from tiering is easiest to justify because it is based on the principle of fees for service. Subscribers are usually willing to pay extra for such new services as all-news and all-sports channels. ARD coffers could be increased by giving the 11 cooperating public broadcasters a supplementary fee based on regional reach and competitive status in relation to private stations.[25] Others have proposed that public broadcasting be supported by a government tax on cable operators' gross revenue, as in Canada, which would be used for indigenous program production.[26] Yet another option suggests that income be increased through more advertising. This option, however, is complicated because the various Land governments disagree about three key issues. Among these are the proportion of public broadcaster income that is to come from advertising (presently between 18 and 38 percent). A lack of unanimity also exists on the maximum amount of advertising to be permitted per hour (12 minutes currently) and the quantity of total daily program time to be devoted to advertising presentations (10 to 20 percent). A secure financial base for the mixed public-private broadcast system in Germany will require a unified nationwide decision on all of these matters and negotiations between the CDU-governed Länder, which favor more advertising support, and the SDP Länder, which want current advertising levels maintained.

The "Single Europe 1992" Solution

The Single Europe 1992 solution addresses a set of problems stemming from the globalization of the entertainment industry. These developments have engendered a glaring contradiction between the capabilities for offering ever more differentiated means of expression and the fact of growing international media concentration, which is capable of undermining and managing public opinion across national borders. Rupert Murdoch, who owns Europe's Sky Channel, argues that globalization of the entertainment industry is inevitable because of business economics. These require companies to expand or go under. Vertical integration and bigness, he argues, are mandated by the industry's three main characteristics: high fixed costs for content production, high risk, and static revenues. Media consultants estimate that 90 percent of a cable programmer's costs are fixed, 80 percent of a radio station's, 70 percent of a newspaper's, and 60 percent of a magazine's—hence the importance of revenue and market share. Because no one knows how to produce a best-seller, a hit record, or a box-office smash, companies cover their risks by making as many books, records, and films as possible and by controlling the distribution system. In this way, the conglomerate's own second-rate programs can be used to fill the schedule. The entertainment conglomerate's fixed costs, high risks, and static revenues put a premium on size and integration. Only the giants can absorb the high costs and wait for the high returns. These giants are still expanding globally. The Murdoch conglomerate increased its size and integration through the purchase of such U.S. entertainment industries as 20th Century–Fox, Harper & Row, and Triangle Publications. Bertelsmann has acquired RCA as well as Doubleday Books, and Time-Warner is poised to make European acquisitions.[27] Such world trends have led to speculation that in the twenty-first century, five or six global entertainment conglomerates, vertically integrated, will control global production. Of these, only two will probably be American: Time-Warner and one other. The European front runners are Murdoch (Great Britain), Bertelsmann (Germany), and Hersant, a French press, publishing (Hachette), and radio conglomerate.[28]

For public broadcasters and European governments, these global monopolies pose three interrelated threats: the evasion of national radio and television rules, the weakening of program production in national languages other than English, and the elimination of an important training ground for cultural workers. The international conglomerate's potential ability to evade German radio and television rules is already being demonstrated in the heated debate about advertising quotas and whether advertising messages should be allowed to interfere with a program's structural integrity. Internationally produced program content, structured by the more lenient U.S. rules, does not adhere to most existing German program practices or advertising rules. Even more problematic are different tolerances and regulations concerning pornography in general programming and violence in children's shows. Not only are conglomerates producing their own or selling others' programs less sensitive to differences in European national and cultural standards, but their marketing strategies, which aim at extending viewership across national borders, tend to soften local rules.

A second threat posed by international conglomerates is the weakening of program production capacities in national languages other than English. Where the ZDF and ARD public broadcasters used to enjoy an uncontested monopoly in the production and supply of broadcast content on the traditional two networks, their capacities today are insufficient to fill the extra numbers of channels now available through satellite and cable technologies. The creation of new European television programming, the EBU demonstrated, is constrained not by national but by linguistic borders. Network television production in Europe's top five languages must therefore be combined with increased regional cooperative agreements in order to achieve savings in scale. These savings, however, will accrue primarily to English-language material because it has a larger world market and is the lingua franca of science, trade, and communications.[29] The fear of Americanization is therefore real, not only on the side of European production needs but also on that of distribution. In the three most populous countries, broadcasters are trying to export their programming to linguistically similar neighbors. Germans are selling or exchanging material with Austria and Switzerland, the French are exporting to Quebec and North Africa, and the Spaniards are involved with booming television markets in Mexico and Brazil. In light of these findings, the EBU argues that program variety and the solution to the public-private dilemma in the European situation require that public service criteria be applied to all programmers equally. Only if every channel has defined and complementary program goals will the inevitable erosion of national public service network viewership through competition be halted. This erosion, however, will be much slower than the private developers of cable- and satellite-delivered programming have expected. The high costs of European network transmission and the low returns from national markets will produce no fundamental change in the publicly dominated broadcast structure until about the year 2000.

The elimination of an important national training ground for cultural workers is the third threat posed by international conglomerates. We have seen that public broadcasters ARD and ZDF create 80 percent of their own programming either through arrangements with independent German producers or through coproductions with other German-speaking broadcasters in Austria and Switzerland. In addition to employing German producers, artists, lighting experts, and other professionals, present broadcast arrangements are offering opportunities for training personnel in educational, entertainment, and news production. Many of these opportunities would be lost if multinationals were able to substitute imported American material for the homegrown product. Such a switch, though cheaper, would further reduce the cultural variety presently represented by national program traditions. Though German regulators at present eschew formal content quotas, the EBU proposal that all European-produced programs count as local productions in effect guarantees the continued viability of European programs against U.S. competition.

The Public Service Ethic Reconsidered

Greater public awareness of globalization's regulatory and program implications has sensitized Germans and others to the fact that the survival of continental broadcast heritages will require a European perspective. The Single Europe 1992 solution acknowledges that Europe does not constitute a uniform cultural market but is instead a cultural mosaic. Each component country in this mosaic speaks a different language and has developed its own broadcast history and unique program formats. The

Single Europe 1992 solution focuses on preserving this variety through at least two strategies: extending the voluntary broadcast arrangements already developed by public broadcasters in the EBU framework and increasing interregional coordination within a European focus.

The EBU's policy framework includes adherence to the spectrum allocation rules of the International Telegraph Union (ITU), the copyright arrangements of the Geneva Convention, and the voluntary exchange of programming between 40 broadcasters in 31 countries. In the early 1980s, the ITU developed cooperative orbiting rules for European direct-broadcast satellites to avoid spillover into adjacent territories. It also endorsed cross-national distribution of programming with prior consent from the receiving country while reconfirming that rule making in cultural production was a national prerogative.[30] Adherence to the Geneva Convention rules of proper compensation for intellectual property have avoided the threat of very high first-show royalties, which would have priced European programming out of its own market. Belgium, Sweden, Norway, and the Netherlands took the lead in devising European-wide flexible copyright solutions, so only the issue of retransmission rights for European programs remains to be negotiated.

Interregional coordination with a European focus was introduced under EBU auspices, which laid the groundwork for bilateral and multilateral cooperative program agreements among public broadcasters. Since the early 1980s, these have led to substantial production savings because they have permitted German, French, and Scandinavian broadcasters to exchange and coproduce much of their programming, in spite of competition from the United States. Interregional coordination has received a substantial boost through the European Community's trade harmonization initiatives. In this sense, the Single Europe 1992 solution constitutes the informational counterpart to these economic goals. As such, it challenges the U.S. interpretation of the free-flow doctrine, which has traditionally been conceptualized in a global trade context. By arguing that television and radio are more than businesses, that they are constituents in public opinion formation, European governments are moving toward an interpretation of free flow as balanced flow. This tempers the free-flow-of-information ideal with the positive concept of cultural sovereignty. It argues that each country has the right to exercise some control over its communicational distribution network, as well as its human-message-creating capabilities.[31] Such control includes the determination of what constitutes important information within a culture and the creation of human and technical networks capable of satisfying local needs by using indigenous resources and frames of reference. Such a notion is similar to that developed in the McBride Commission report of 1980, in response to UNESCO member demand for a more equitable participation of third-world countries in the global communication network.[32]

Germany's continued wrangle over the criteria and financing of the public-private broadcasting system, however, reflects another more fundamental European malaise: the lack of a public discussion of the meaning of public broadcasting in the satellite age. Instead of responding to legitimate public concerns for better access, government bureaucracies everywhere seem to be supporting the transfer of one portion of their centralized control to global conglomerates under the guise of economic necessity. Together, this dual monopoly will make the German broadcasting system less and less responsive to its audiences. Put another way, Germany's public broadcast services are increasingly organized *for* broadcast but not *in response to* the communicative needs of its citizens. The German example has shown that in spite of the rethinking of broadcast issues necessitated by reunification, the bureaucratically organized information and communication sectors continue to work through supervisory boards. These make large-scale public involvement nearly impossible and thus frustrate the communicative competence of individuals and groups in the political communication process. How to remedy this situation and move toward a more democratic system of public communication is at the heart of the public broadcasting debate in Europe. Planning for such an alternative would require the creation of novel conditions for group participation in the social communication process. Canada's 1974 Challenge for Change project was one such attempt. It set up interactive cable networks with and through which individuals and groups could communicate with each other at different social levels.[33] The local radio movement in France, now largely aborted, and Britain's Channel 4, with its programming from independent producers, are other attempts at making access to electronic communication available to different social groups. In spite of these initiatives, European and North American democracies have generally failed to establish new conditions for public involvement in the social communication process.

Such conditions are not created by merely expanding the public's role as consumers of political or economic products or by making media available to a set of limited elites. They grow out of exchanges of experience, language, and culture at all levels of society. To reconceptualize public broadcasting by and for the people, social communication must be viewed as a vital human activity in which distribution technologies play only an instrumental role. Unfortunately, the public debate about the human uses to which technologies are put has been sidestepped in the present European fight over commercialization. The introduction of commercial media alternatives is not detrimental per se. Their social effects depend on the kinds of conditions under which they are allowed to compete with other forms of programming. The German example has shown that these decisions are presently made to protect technological and political goals rather than to democratize access. In the twenty-first century, public service broadcasters will have to rethink their social mission so that they will become more adept at understanding and providing the variety of communicational experiences that European audiences as citizens, not only as consumers, now demand.

NOTES

1. The authors wish to thank Peter Gerlach for his helpful comments on an early draft of this chapter.
2. Our chapter title is borrowed from Wolfgang Hoffmann-Riem's "Internationale Medienmärkte—Nationale Rundfunkordnungen," *Rundfunk und Fernsehen* 34 (1, 1986), pp. 5-22.
3. The historical discussion follows John Sanford, *The Mass Media of the German-speaking Countries* (London: Wolff, 1976).
4. The print media were organized in all three zones on the principle of private ownership, initially under Allied license, later without any restrictions. The press is unregulated, as in the United States, though the Cartel office monitors cross-media ownership.
5. The German *Meinungs- und politische Willensbildung* is difficult to translate but implies public opinion creation.
6. Cited in Hartwig Kelm, "Plädoyer für das 'Unternehmen öffentlich-rechtlicher Rundfunk,' " *Media Perspektiven* 1 (January 1989), p. 1.
7. Jörg Engler, "Rundfunksystem der Bundesrepublik Deutschland," in Hans Bredow Institut, ed., *Internationales Handbuch für Rundfunk und Fernsehen (1988/1989)* (Baden-Baden: Nomos, 1988), p. B74.
8. After World War II, broadcasting frequencies were redistributed in Europe at an International Telecommunications Union meeting at Copenhagen in 1948. Germany, then still under Allied occupation, was not invited. As a result, it received few (AM) frequencies. Consequently, German broadcasters turned to VHF (or FM) broadcasting earlier than North America. See also Sanford, *Mass Media*, pp. 74-75.
9. Until 1953, the Nordwestdeutscher Rundfunk (NDR) served all of what had been the British zone of occupation; first Berlin, then North Rhine–Westphalia split off, leaving the three northern Länder to the NDR in 1955.
10. Arthur Williams, "West Germany: The Search for the Way Forward," in Raymond Kuhn, ed., *The Politics of Broadcasting* (London: Croon Helm, 1976), p. 92.
11. The 1980 NDR treaty adheres to the Bavarian solution and *reduces* party representation to one-third of the administrative council (ibid., p. 95).
12. The heading is borrowed from Colin MacCabe, "Broadcasting: National Pasts and International Futures," in Colin MacCabe and Olivia Stewart, eds., *The BBC and Public Service Broadcasting* (Manchester, England: Manchester University Press, 1986), pp. 106-116.
13. Denis McQuail and Karin Sinue, eds., *New Media Politics: Comparative Perspectives in Western Europe* (London: Sage, 1986), provides a useful framework for the discussion of broadcast regulation "actors."
14. Ibid., p. 125.
15. Bill Peterson, "Out of the Ashes: New from Old," *TV World* 12 (2, 1989), pp. 64-65.
16. Horst Röper, "Formationen deutscher Medienmultis, 1987," *Media Perspektiven* 8 (August 1987), pp. 481-495.

17. Horst Röper, "Der Himmel wird zur Provinz," *Die Zeit* 47 (13 November 1987), p. 38.
18. Rüdiger Schultz, "Auswirkungen des Kabelfernsehens: Passivität und Vereinsamung durch Reizüberflutung," *Aus Politik und Zeitgeschichte* 15 (7, 1989), pp. 25-47.
19. Wolfgang Kleinwächter, "Die Vorbereitungen für ein Mediengesetz der DDR," *Media Perspektiven* 3 (March 1990), pp. 133-139.
20. Jurgen Grubitzch, "Presselandschaft der DDR im Umbruch," *Media Perspektiven* 3 (March 1990), pp. 140-155.
21. European Parliament, Document A2-75/85 (Brussels, 1985), pp. 25-30.
22. Joachim Gerth, "Diskussionsbericht des Round-Table-Gesprächs des Instituts für Rundfunkrechte an der Universität Köln am 7. Oktober 1985," *ZUM* 12 (October 1985), p. 604.
23. Gertrude J. Robinson, "Germany's Satellite Policy Debate: Its Relevance to Europe and Canada," *Canadian Journal of Communication* 13 (3/4, 1988), pp. 28-49.
24. Andreas Wiesand, "Wie gewinnt man Maßtäbe für einen 'produktiven' Rundfunk? Zur Studie 'Der WDR als Kultur- und Wirtschaftsfaktor,' " *Media Perspektiven* 2 (February 1989), p. 64.
25. Udo Michael Krüger, "Ein Programmvergleich SAT-1, RTL-plus, ARD und ZDF," *Media Perspektiven* 4 (April 1985), p. 44.
26. Pierre Juneau, "Television without Frontiers?" paper presented at a meeting of the International Festival of Film and Television in the Celtic Countries (15 March 1989), p. 13.
27. "Meet the New Media Monsters," *The Economist* 310 (3, 1989), p. 65.
28. Fritz Wolf, "The Media in Europe: Communication or Commerce?" *Democratic Journalist* (1, 1989), p. 19.
29. George Wedell, "The Development of Competition between Print and Electronic Media in 17 European Countries, North America, Japan, Australia, and Brazil," paper presented at a meeting of the Intermedia Congress, Hamburg (1985).
30. Rolf Thiele, "Rundfunkversorgung durch Satelliten," *Media Perspektiven* 3 (March 1984), pp. 734-735.
31. Gertrude J. Robinson, "The New World Information Order Debate in Perspective," in Gertrude J. Robinson, ed., *Assessing the New World Information Order Debate: Evidence and Proposals* (1982), p. 3.
32. Sean McBride, *Many Voices, One World: Towards a New More Just and Efficient World* (New York, 1980).
33. Sandra Gwyn, "Citizen Communication in Canada," in Benjamin Singer, ed., *Communication in Canadian Society* (London: Addison-Wesley, 1983), p. 85.

CHAPTER **4**

Dutch Public Service Broadcasting

Denis McQuail

It would be anachronistic to use the term *public service broadcasting* for the system that emerged during the 1920s to exploit the new medium of radio, and even today, the term is only partly appropriate to characterize a system that is not supposed so much to serve the general public as to serve minority interests in Dutch society. This is increasingly becoming an academic quibble, but it is useful to bear in mind how the system started out, since its structure is still strongly influenced by the ideas governing its origin. As elsewhere in Europe, radio did not arrive with any clear blueprint for its functions or any obviously appropriate form of organization, and different societies found the form that suited their immediate needs and circumstances, tending only later to dignify what emerged in terms of principles, traditions, and social theory. The Netherlands was no different, although the form chosen was and remains relatively unique. It is certainly the case that a "settlement" for radio broadcasting was worked out quite early in the 1920s, confirmed in law-making around 1930, survived the war, and still gives shape to the public sector of Dutch radio and television.

The explanation for the original choice of form (insofar as conscious choice was involved) lies in distinctive features of Dutch society and politics. The most relevant feature is the division of society, following vertical lines of cleavage related first of all to religion and secondarily to politics. Traditionally, the country was split more or less equally between Catholics (mainly in the south) and Protestants (mainly in the north), and politics in the nineteenth and early twentieth centuries was characterized by the efforts of the Catholics, in particular, to acquire their fair share of access to the major institutions of society. This was achieved largely by a societywide agreement to share out institutions between the contending confessional minorities. The society became a "pillarized" society, such that each member of each minority could operate within the walls of his or her own confessional pillar, which had its own schools, social facilities, unions, political organizations, and institutions. This solution reduced the chances of conflict, which occur in divided but stratified societies, where one minority tends to dominate others. It led also to a system in which matters of essential national or collective interest had to be handled by leaders of different pillars (in other words, by elites), even if eventually answerable to members. This politicosocial background has left its stamp on Dutch society, which exhibits a distinctive mixture of democratic self-control, elitism, and compromise.

Radio became available at a time when this process of societal pillarization was at its height, and as a sociocultural institution, it became an obvious candidate for development along pillarized lines. Both the educational system and the existing daily press, which was confessionally structured, provided justification and models. The way toward pillarization of radio was facilitated by the fact that no strong central government or industrial interest sought to control the medium, and amateur interest (in cooperation with the electrical industry) was the driving force for adoption of the innovation. The sectionalized structure of Dutch society provided an ideal background for the formation of well-organized bodies of activists who began to use radio for the interests of their parent bodies and for their own satisfaction.

Division by religion was not the only factor at work, since a strong socialist movement had emerged, with no religious attachment, and it was opposed not only to religious parties but also to a liberal, capitalist elite, with secular, even anticlerical traditions. The crosscutting dimensions of right versus left and religion versus secularism gave shape to the original structure of broadcasting in this politicized society. The underlying divisions were deeply felt and sometimes bitter, making it that much harder to achieve the necessary compromises or to change the system, since any proposal for change was open to interpretation as a sectional move. The relatively small size of anything like a neutral, uncommitted center is one reason why the idea of public service in general is a somewhat inappropriate notion. The system was guided by a public service notion, at least in the sense that it was never private in the commercial sense and it was established to serve the needs of several different publics within the society and thereby to serve the state. Although this expresses the primary sense in which the broadcasting system was a public body, it will also be evident from the description of how the system was implemented that it had other features of a public service institution, since it was from an early date regulated and guaranteed by the state and was subject to some fairly universal kinds of rules against the disturbance of public order and good morals.

IMPLEMENTATION OF A PILLARIZED BROADCASTING SYSTEM

By 1926, four of the eight broadcasting organizations that still provide the most television and radio had been instituted, and a fifth was established in 1928. The first four were KRO (Catholic Radio Broadcasting Foundation), VARA (Association of Workers' Radio Amateurs), NCRV (Netherlands Christian Radio Association), and VPRO (Association of Protestant Radio Broadcasters). The fifth was AVRO (General Association of Radio Broadcasters), which was distinctive for not having a religious or political basis and specifically setting out to provide general information, culture, and entertainment.

Each of these organizations was self-governing and self-financing, managed according to a set of statutes, which in each case states goals that relate to the political or religious ideals implied in its constitution. The statutes of the neutral organization, AVRO, state that it aims to offer a full range of programs with a reasonable balance of entertainment, culture, information, and education and to be representative of all streams in society. Although the statutes have been adapted in the ensuing six decades and the reality of their expression in programs has changed a great deal, they are nevertheless important to public policy, for broadcasting still takes them seriously.

The broadcasting organization, now as in prewar days, is the key unit in the broadcasting system. It produces radio and television programs, employs staffs, formulates policy, publishes a program magazine, and cooperates with other organizations and the central broadcasting body (now the NOS, Netherlands Broadcasting Foundation) on matters essential to offering a coordinated and complete broadcasting service. The formal position of the broadcasting organizations was first regulated by acts of government in and around 1930 by an extension of the 1904 Wireless and Telegraphy Law and the issue of Radio Regulation, which stated the criteria whereby an organization could qualify for a share of radio time and the proportion of available time it could have. This regulation was, to a large extent, a confirmation of the status quo, which is true also of most subsequent regulations. The regulations offered a description, more or less, of the existing bodies and confirmed that allocation of airtime would be determined pragmatically according to the relative number of members in each organization. Within limits, this establishes the principle of representational access for society as a whole.

The nature and functions of the broadcasting organization are stated in succeeding legal documents in much the same way as in the original regulations, and the following statement, taken from the draft of the new Media Law (1988), gives an idea of the original intention, as well as the current formal position. Article 14 of the law states (in summary) that a broadcasting association is one that fulfills the following requirements:

1. It is set up legally.
2. It has, according to its statutes, the exclusive or primary objective of providing a national radio and television program service.
3. It is representative of a particular social, cultural, religious, or spiritual stream in the population and is concerned with satisfying needs related to these ends.
4. It must be able to show that it has at least 150,000 members.
5. It must have had broadcasting time in the previous years or have been a candidate organization. In order to advance from candidate status, it must be able to demonstrate that its programming differs enough from that of the other organizations to increase the overall diversity of broadcasting.

This statement points up three key features for understanding what lies at the core of public service broadcasting in the Netherlands. First, the organizations should represent different interests and, among them, advance diversity—thereby embodying the ideal of representative pluralism. Second, the organizations should not have ulterior purposes. Their aims should be shaped by the character of the sector of the public that they represent, but they are no more supposed to be a purely propagandist instrument for a church or a political party than a commercial undertaking with a goal of profit. Their primary aim is to provide appropriate broadcasting of good quality. This underlines both the independence and the noncommercialism of the typical broadcasting association. Third, although not fully expressed in the clauses quoted, there is a strong requirement of democratic self-management, which reinforces independence and noncommercialism.

The core of the Dutch broadcasting system remains a set of eight organizations of the type set out, but certain other essential elements of structure and control have grown up gradually with the system. First, there is the element of central control and coordination, currently represented by the NOS. This was established by the first Broadcasting Law of 1967/1969, but its origins date from the early days of radio, in three factors: the wish to provide some general, nonconfessional programming, if only to cater to minorities without airtime or who objected to the political and religious coloring of everything; the practical need to coordinate the activities of several independent broadcasters sharing the same technical broadcasting facilities (which were, since 1935, mainly in the hands of the PTT); and the facilitation of control by the responsible government minister for observance of the law. The NOS had several predecessors, which grew in significance over time, but it is sufficient to describe its form and function as established in the law of 1967/1969 and confirmed, with modifications, in the 1988 Media Law. The NOS is managed, according to the law, by a board consisting of representatives of the other broadcasting organizations, of interests in the society, and certain nominees of the crown (relevant minister in practice). Its functions are (1) to produce and transmit its own programs, for which it has had a share of up to one-quarter of the total time and during which it provides nearly all news bulletins, much documentary and cultural material, and programs for minorities and special purposes not covered by the other broadcasters; (2) to look after all matters to do with broadcasting in general, including representation of the system in international contacts; (3) to coordinate the programming of other broadcasting organizations; (4) to set up and manage studios and all other necessary facilities and services; and (5) to collect and make available information necessary for the evaluation of the performance of the other organizations according to the terms of the law.

It should be stressed that the NOS is a broadcasting and a coordinating body, first of all, and not an instrument of control. Even so, it does represent something that deviates from the original concept of the system, and it does make control easier. It is different in being specifically national and unifying and connecting rather than dividing Dutch society. It is also different in its imposed neutrality and balance, as opposed to the other organizations, which are allowed, even expected, to express editorial views in favor of the sector of opinion and belief with which they are associated.

It is mainly as a source of information and a channel of communication from the government that the NOS can be viewed as an instrument of centralized control. It collects data about audiences on a systematic basis, which enter into public debate, although the allocation of time is not based on audience share. More important, it has the task of monitoring the output of all television and radio according to a system of program categories. The Broadcasting Law says nothing about what should or should not be broadcast, but it does require each broadcasting organization to offer a full and balanced program within its share of broadcasting time (which, for the large bodies, is currently about eight hours a week). The intention is twofold: to ensure a certain kind of public service goal in terms of the quality of what is offered, especially in terms of culture and information, and to prevent unfair competition between the broadcasting organizations for audience attention, which might ultimately be translated into membership and upset the balance of time allocation. This certainly happens, but the control, by way of NOS research, holds it within limits.

This brief account of the system designed to put the original principles into effect would be incomplete without a reference to the mechanisms of control available to any administration wishing to enforce the law in a complicated area. There are two main structural devices: First, there is the existence of a media commissioner, whose main task is to supervise the allocation and disposition of the revenue that pays for broadcasting, which comes from the license fee paid by the public and collected by the post office, and also of income from controlled amounts of advertising at certain times. The commissioner has no power over content but is a key figure. Second, there is a Media Council. This is an advisory and consultative body, appointed by the crown but intended to represent sectors of opinion in society and also to provide impartial expert advice. Its function is to reply to requests from a government minister for advice over any matter of broadcasting that is not clearly regulated by law or needs interpretation. A minister is unlikely to use the sanctions available for transgression of the law without reference to the council. The body can and does comment on matters of public policy within its remit. The powers of control of the minister over any of the broadcasting organizations take three forms: public reprimand, imposition of financial penalties, and suspension of access to broadcasting time.

ISSUES, CRISES, AND CONFLICTS IN THE HISTORY OF DUTCH BROADCASTING

Built into the original settlement in the 1920s were sources of strain that have come to the surface since and have sometimes emerged as serious conflicts. The most relevant aspects of this settlement concern the choice of a system divided among competing (or coexisting) interests in the society; the limited scope for central, nationwide control; the basis in voluntary, noncommercial finance; and the politicoreligious coloring of the system. Between them, these features have led to a number of recurrent problems. One is the question of access to the system, a valuable social and political right that has acquired potential economic value over time. The qualifications for access have to be specified in a clear and acceptable way, and the key whereby airtime is allocated to qualified broadcasters must also be set, both theoretically and in practice. The choice of a system with a pluralistic structure, employing politicoreligious criteria, was not wholly acceptable at first. From the beginning, there were demands for a more secular, central, national, state-controlled system from various parties. The question of finance has two aspects: whether to be commercial or not and how to raise enough money to provide broadcasting services that meet accepted professional standards and public demands.

Each of the issues can be dealt with briefly in turn.

A Pillarized or National System?

The original choice for "pillarization" was made without very much appreciation of the significance that broadcasting would acquire for society as a whole. The claim on behalf of a national system is not made only in the interests of the state, which naturally likes to have control. There were arguments against the extreme degree of pillarization on the grounds of efficiency and coordination, the interests of groups or individuals who did not feel included in the groups that had access, providing a full and balanced service to a general public, and meeting certain national interests for common broadcasting services. A general problem with the system as instituted is that it was strongly resistant to change and adaptation to new circumstances, since change requires a consensus or a large majority among parties with vital interests of their own, which they are not likely to surrender to the general interest.

Debate over the pillarized system was suspended by one major event in the history of broadcasting, the German occupation from 1940 to 1945. To advocates of unity, the Germans' implementation of a national radio system was counterproductive, and the former system was reinstated with little change after the war. The issue was again prominent in the debates leading up to the Broadcasting Law of 1967/1969, but, as after the war, the political interests in favor of the status quo were strong enough to resist fundamental change. Much the same could be said of the new Media Law of 1988. Even so, we can observe a steady increase, over the history of the system, in the number and degree of unifying, centralizing, or nationalizing features. The law of 1930 already gave central power of control to the relevant minister. In 1935, broadcast transmission facilities became essentially a state-run company. After the war, financing through a nationally collected license fee on all households came effectively to replace voluntary funding. With this came powers of supervision of expenditure. Central coordinating bodies were instituted after the war, leading to the relatively powerful Netherlands Broadcasting Foundation in 1969. There has been much more streamlining and coordination of services to make the program, on the whole, very similar to those of other public broadcasting services in Europe. One can interpret the developments as a de facto development of unity in framework that is still, de jure, a federal system.

Terms and Conditions of Access

The original settlement, as described earlier, was a reasonable enough reflection of divisions of society and of the balance of forces in the prewar Netherlands. It really only came seriously into question when society appeared to change around it, from the 1950s onward, quite apart from the long-term dissatisfaction of secular elements in the society. The less people were attached to a religious or political movement, the less they wanted a system based on these principles. It was not only a matter of religious believers versus nonbelievers. Even believers wanted from radio and the television quite a lot of things that had not a lot to do with religion or politics—entertainment, music, films, culture from abroad, sports, and so on. The broadcasting organizations themselves were actually run by professionals who wanted to be broadcasters above all else (as, in fact, required by the law). The pressure for changing the rules of access was increased during the 1950s and 1960s by the availability (across national borders) of increasing amounts of foreign television and the activities of radio and television pirates.

The law of 1967/1969 responded to pressures for change by formally opening the system, which had been monopolized by the same five organizations for 40 years, to newcomers. Essentially, they had only to find a sufficient number of supporters to get a foothold in the system, which could then be used as a base for further expansion, since the new law laid down precise rules and stages for gaining entry. During the 1970s, three new organizations became established, delivering on the legal promise of open access. Two of these, significantly, were associations that unequivocally set out to offer what the public was thought to want—more entertainment, music, lively and neutral information, and the like. One of them, TROS (the Television and Radio Broadcasting Foundation), gave a new word to the Dutch language, *trossification*, meaning something like cultural trivialization. The second and more recent, Veronica, appeals especially to youth. The third, the fundamental Protestant EBO (Evangelical Broadcasting Organization), is an entrant wholly in line with the original principles of the system. It should be said that the rules for access (more or less confirmed in the new law of 1988) are strict enough to prevent extensive splintering of the system, and on the whole, the rules worked quite well. They have not worked without what seems excessive argument over details, but details that have considerable practical consequences over the way in which access is allocated. It is still the case that membership is largely determined according to the criterion of subscription to one or another of the program guides, which all eight broadcasting bodies publish and in which a membership component is included. A major change in the 1970s was to allow all individuals (rather than households) to be counted, and at one time during the same period, there were strong demands for broadcasting elections to determine the relative allocation of time. It is likely that, if implemented, this would have further weakened the position of the original "confessional" broadcasting bodies. One tricky aspect of the access question is the implication that a limited amount of airtime has to be divided up between a theoretically quite large number of separate broadcasters (each of which is national rather than regional or local) and that some bodies can lose the right to broadcast by falling below a given number of members. In reality, steady increases in the permitted airtime (another power of government) have accommodated the newcomers without loss of time for the others, and none of the broadcasting organizations has ever been "demoted," thanks to demonstrated powers of survival and adaptation, which must be considered a merit of a very complicated and unusual system. The question of access in the new media age will be examined shortly.

The Financing of the System

The original choice not to finance through advertising was very much in line with the general prewar European model. In the Dutch case, this was not only out of principle but also because of the interests of other advertising media, especially the press. Until very recently, the Dutch press, itself with certain ties to the pillarized system, has opposed "commercialization" of broadcasting on grounds of self-interest, despite the inconsistency with the market freedom that it claims for itself. In the 1960s, there was renewed pressure to admit a commercial element to the system, following either the British or West German models. The main arguments were advanced on practical grounds of paying for the system, but areas of the country were being subject to advertising from West German television and pirate broadcasters, and the lack of opportunities for Dutch advertisers was seen as holding back national commercial and economic development. Ultimately, a typical compromise was reached by the law of 1969, allowing a limited amount of advertising time on television and radio, at certain times and under conditions that strictly separated this service from programming. Proceeds from the sale of such airtime were devoted exclusively, by way of a separate public body (STER, the Television Advertising Foundation), to general program costs of the system. They were simply added to the license revenue, which the government then divided up on a pro rata basis among the different broadcasting organizations and the NOS (which, by the 1980s, was taking 60 percent of total revenue, itself a measure of the degree of unity and centralization achieved). But the financial issue, in both its aspects (total revenue and type of revenue), did not go away.

Control of the System

The question of control does not seem to have been addressed very centrally or have been a matter of controversy in the Dutch system, but a few words of clarification are in order. One of the advantages of the pillarized and federated form is that it does limit the power of central authority. The theory of the Dutch case is that the role of the state is to guarantee and to make practicable a system in which there is a large measure of self-control, not only by professional broadcasters and managers but also by members of the public as audience and as members of the organizations. The management of each broadcasting organization is in some degree answerable, according to the Media Law, on a regular basis to members in a formal way. The government, in practice the minister with the relevant portfolio (formerly the Minister of Waterways, now the Minister of Health, Culture, and Welfare), is supposed to enforce democratically reached rules and regulations. Enforcement takes place under the scrutiny of parliament and with advice from the Media Council. There are specific rules against interference in content matters, aside from a general legal requirement that all broadcasters offer a balanced program service within their share of time. Constitutionally, broadcasting has acquired, aside from the special provisions of the broadcasting law, the same rights of freedom of expression as the printed press.

Nevertheless, the state, in the form of the administration of the day, inevitably has considerable power. It can, and does, make major policy proposals for broadcasting; it holds the purse strings, especially on such matters as determining the absolute level of the license fee, which is not regulated by the law; it looks after anything to do with the security of the state and overriding national interests; it takes care of key matters of international negotiation, which become increasingly salient in a satellite age and as a member of the European Community. It could be argued that the question of governmental power is raised much less by its competence within the established broadcasting system, which is strictly limited by law and convention, than by what it can do in the environment of the system with consequences for the broadcasters. We can at least conclude that government interference in editorial matters or conflict with the system has never been a burning issue, despite occasional incidents and friction. Broadcasters have as much trouble, if not more, with their audiences, active members of broadcasting organizations, and people who feel that they should be doing more to implement the founding statutes.

THE MAIN PROBLEMS FACING PUBLIC BROADCASTING

Most of the relevant topics of current concern have already been introduced, since few are really new, but they need a more specific and up-to-date restatement before describing the policy responses that have been adopted. Current problems do, in the main, stem from changes in the operating environment of society, communication technologies, and the international context. Before dealing with these, it will help to say a few extra words about problems internal to the system. These have mostly to do with potential conflicts between broadcast professionalism, the confessionalism of the system, and a tension between the serving of more intellectual or cultural goals and satisfying baser or more material demands. There have been signs that professionals find it difficult to accommodate to a system run, in theory, for and by amateurs (their "members"). They also find it difficult, even impossible, not to compete actively for audiences directly, as well as for "supporters," by way of programming and publicity, which often have a commercial look to them. There is some tension between the formal goals of the system and the most vocal of audience demands in an increasingly competitive national and international context. These tensions are complicated by limited public finance and poor prospects for gaining more. The more ambitious bodies within the system, without strong confessional commitments, see a limited future in general for public broadcasting, and some want more freedom to operate commercially.

The financial question can be taken further, although its elements are not at all unique to the Netherlands. Broadcasting costs, especially those of production and purchasing, have tended to exceed the general level of inflation. For several years, governments have been unwilling to concede significantly higher income from public sources. At the same time, there have been demands for more airtime (until the early 1980s, the system offered only about 100 hours of television a week; it now provides around 150 hours), and there is increasing competition from foreign television channels as well as rising audience expectations. Imports can be much cheaper than home production, but popular items are becoming more expensive in an increasingly international market. There are strong and growing pressures to have a larger domestic program supply and also to expand the sphere of regional and local broadcasting, which is extremely undeveloped, for lack of finance.

There are increasing reasons of an economic kind, not to be left behind in the development of new communications technology, especially advanced cable networks and information systems. The country also has aspirations in the software field, with a large international publishing industry. The obvious alternative to direct public funding is funding by advertising. This has traditionally been resisted both on culturalist grounds and in the interests of the press, but there are signs that resistance is weakening under the pressures just described.

The environmental pressures, some of which have special force in the Dutch case, can be summarized briefly. First is one peculiar to the Netherlands but not unique in its potential impact on public service broadcasting. Dutch society had been characterized as undergoing a long and active period of "depillarization," or secularization, since the early 1960s. Essentially, this means a considerable weakening of the foundations of the whole confessional system described earlier. The result is a challenge to the legitimacy of the main features of the system, as well as the practical consequence that people have voted with their subscription money (and some with viewing time) for the secular-neutral broadcasters, without completely deserting the traditional bodies. This social trend has been especially damaging to the public service system in the Netherlands, which is based on confessional differences, but it has its parallels, under different names, in other countries, where it may be called "consumerism," "hedonism," "privatization," or "decline of ideology." It is a trend that encourages market solutions to program provision, since the reasons for public intervention in the interests of political or cultural welfare are weaker or command less support.

For a decade, between the early 1970s and the early 1980s, debate about the broadcasting system seems to have centered on internal conflicts and tensions. On the one hand, there were the supporters of the traditional, confessional system, sometimes in alliance with secular defenders of public (noncommercial) broadcasters, who deplored the abandonment of the original ideals and the increasingly open, if indirect, commercialization of the system. This showed itself often in aggressive self-publicity and competition for audiences, but also in practices very close to real commercialism, such as merchandising, plugging of music, and showing products or advertisements on the screen as a form of sponsorship. It also showed itself in styles and forms of programming of the kind thought to go with commercial broadcasting. On the other hand, there were many who saw these as necessary changes, in line with the principles of an open and pluralistic system. The advocates of open commercialism were sometimes joined by others who simply wanted more television supply and more choice.

Two other aspects of the context and time reinforce the pressures already mentioned. One, cited earlier, is the desire of the government and a good many interests in the society not to be left behind in the commercial exploitation of new technologies of communication, which are seen as essential to the economic future of the country. The Netherlands is, culturally and ideologically, a curious mixture of the practical and materialist, on the one hand, and the moralistic and the principled, on the other. In the end, the need to survive economically in a competitive world may transcend principle, or it may be transformed into a principle.

The second reinforcing factor has to do with the international agreements and arrangements in which the country is now involved, especially as a member of the European Community. The policy developed for broadcasting in Europe that is now being implemented envisages a broader scope for commercial operation and a harmonization of national regulations concerning advertising.

Another major environmental change that has already been referred to carries special weight in the Netherlands because of local conditions. This is the challenge from abroad by way of cable and satellite. Increasingly, all European countries are receiving the attention of cross-border broadcasters, sometimes fueled by domestic demand as much as by the motives of the senders. The Dutch case is characterized by both. The Netherlands is an attractive target for commercial broadcasters from abroad, a relatively homogeneous, developed, and prosperous market that happens to be extremely accessible by way of the numerous local cable networks. In the future, it could equally offer an ideal target for direct satellite broadcasting. The domestic forces encouraging this invasion include the relative scarcity of home-produced television of a widely popular kind and the interests of some national advertisers in having opportunities not provided by the existing system. Although the

Dutch government was more liberal than seemed strictly necessary in allowing access to foreign cable and satellite services, it is also a fact of geography and an accident of technical infrastructure that it is hard to hold back these trends. The most recent development in the story of the "foreign media invasion" was the addition to the Dutch cable system of a purely commercial television channel, RTL Véronique, transmitting from Luxembourg, under the guise of being a foreign channel. In fact, Véronique is partly Dutch-owned, and its main aim is to serve audiences and advertisers in the Netherlands. It has been rather successful in this aim during the early years of its existence.

It may seem from this account that some of the central questions facing public broadcasting in the rest of Europe, especially those to do with cultural and informational quality, the independence of broadcasters, and the fear of "deregulation," do not seem as prominent as might be expected. In fact, they are present in the Netherlands but are obscured somewhat by other issues. For instance, the question of independence is still resolved largely by the relative autonomy of the main broadcasting associations and guaranteed by law. Cultural and informational quality, as a goal of public service broadcasting, have tended to be defined in terms of pluralistic access and diversity of program types offered (with a premium on informational and cultural offerings). The issue of confessionalism thus stands in part for the issue of cultural quality, and it is central in the debate. However, the Dutch have never seemed overly preoccupied with the dangers of "cultural invasion" and have tended more to appreciate the benefits of other cultures, both European and North American. Though the protection offered by language seems, over time, to be less effective as a defense of the national culture, there is little sense of a crisis of culture.

PROPOSED SOLUTIONS AND CURRENT PLANNING

Debate, proposal, and counterproposal seem to have been a permanent feature of Dutch broadcasting for decades. In general, each succeeding settlement tends to be an elaborate compromise that is under attack as soon as it is implemented, in part because it is the solution to yesterday's problems and because no radical change has ever been implemented. The new Media Law, which replaced the previous broadcasting law, cannot escape being branded an elaborate compromise. The earlier legal change, at the end of the 1960s, carried with it the implicit promise of a new review of its working after a trial period, and that has taken place. Toward the end of the 1970s, the government of the day commissioned a national think tank, the Scientific Council for Government Policy (WRR), to prepare an advisory for changes in the law. The task was made a good deal easier, as well as necessary, by technological changes in communication, especially the means of distribution, since this served to depoliticize the issue somewhat and shift attention to more technical issues. The WRR commissioned much research and produced a weighty recommendation in 1982. Succeeding governments eventually produced and implemented the new Media Law, which formally took effect on January 1, 1988. It is convenient to regard the provisions of the law and the underlying policy it expresses as still representing the solutions envisaged for the problems facing public broadcasting in the Netherlands that have been mentioned. It is also clear that the new law has already been overtaken by events.

As indicated, the provisions of the Media Law are a compromise, made necessary by coalition politics between the reaffirmation of the existing and long-established system and adaptation to the challenges of the 1980s. The following points summarize the main elements of the set of changes. Some elements have more symbolic than real value, and as with many such packages, it is hard to assess which elements will have the most future influence.

An Integrated Policy Response

One aim, which may count among the more symbolic features, is to have a single media policy, covering the press, broadcast television, cable, and satellite. The title of the new Media Law reflects this aim, and it does, for the first time, put economic support for the press on a firm basis and provide a framework of regulation for cable and satellite and, for the first time, for regional and local broadcasting.

The Traditional Pillarized System

The new law reiterates basically the same terms and conditions for access as before. However, there is a subtle difference of wording, and it looks as though an effort has been made to convert the long-established tradition of pillarization into a more general and also more secular principle of pluralism or diversity. The specifically religious, political, or philosophical basis of pluralism is diluted, allowing a wider interpretation. In the new law, however, there are even firmer rules requiring balanced content and noncommercialism. There are also clearer financial penalties for deviation. The law also provided for the innovation of a new (third) television channel, cultural and informative in content, run primarily by the NOS.

Adaptation to Social Change

At the same time, the new law recognizes that much has changed. First, it draws a line around the existing broadcasting system and recognizes and legitimizes an alternative system based on cable and satellite operating under different rules. Second, in the setting up of the new system, a duality is acknowledged between confessional broadcasters and those offering more entertainment and neutral information. The same legal requirement to offer balanced programming will apply equally, but the requirements are likely to be interpreted differently. Each group now has its own channel, offering viewers a much clearer choice. Though not in the law itself, the new deal goes a good way further, since it opens the possibility for any three (or even two) of the organizations eventually to opt out of the public system and "go commercial," if they can agree together and are prepared, after a short transition period, to do without any money from public sources. Although such a move has been held up, the possibility is a legitimization of a mixed system and a further step toward reducing the relative size of the public sector.

The New Media

The main feature of the new legal settlement concerns the cable networks. These have, for years, operated on a local and highly variable basis, without clear regulation. Under the new proposals, they acquire certain rights and obligations (including a must-carry rule for the national channels). They are allowed to carry foreign public service channels and satellite channels, subject to rules about advertising. There remain restrictions on the linking up of networks, and the cable system (with about 80 percent of the country hooked up) is not envisaged as an alternative national system. Cable networks are now allowed to carry subscription television services. They are encouraged to look to program sources outside the existing public system (the broadcasting organizations are specifically excluded), and the press and other business interests are encouraged to provide information services by way of cable. Advertising finance is not yet allowed, although advertising of certain kinds is inevitably carried on several of the channels that cable carries, and advertising to support local television is expected soon. The restrictions imposed on cable networks are relatively slight with respect to carrying foreign-originated or subscription services. But if they provide local (community) television, there are rules for diversity and access similar to those for national television. There are also new rules for the proportion of cable content that has to have a Dutch cultural character.

Financial Provisions

The arrangements described are supposed to contain the solutions to the financial problems that have been mentioned. First of all, the publicly subsidized system is being limited in the range of its activities, although a third national channel has been introduced. Second, there is significantly more advertising carried by way of the officially controlled system and at more flexible times. In this way, more revenue can be raised without altering the basic nature of the system. As noted already, if some broadcasting organizations have ambitions for commercial independence, they will have to leave the system and fend for themselves. One of the problems of finance, however, is that it has always been doubtful if the domestic economy can itself generate enough revenue from advertising to support significant expansion. Other financial measures include the encouragement given to subscription television on cable. The new settlement has leaned toward giving more chances to private enterprise in audiovisual media and—a policy reflected in the semiprivatization of the NOS Service Department—allowing them to work outside the public broadcasting system and changing accounting methods. The public service broadcasting organizations are also now allowed to assign a proportion of their work to companies outside the system.

OVERALL ASSESSMENT: THE FUTURE PROSPECTS FOR PUBLIC SERVICE BROADCASTING

It is very handy to have a new legal settlement with which to describe the current policy response in a fairly objective way. However, it gives a misleading impression of certainty and predictability about the future. Such interventions rarely work exactly as intended, and the national and international context is changing. There is no doubt about what recent governments, with a fair degree of consensus support, have been trying to do, and this new settlement is not likely to be radically undone for a few years, given the struggle to put it together. The aim has been to reaffirm the old order, but within newly drawn boundaries and with a modernized version of the principle of pluralism; admit significantly more commercial elements of various kinds; encourage the development and exploitation of cable systems and other telematic media (not mentioned earlier); respond to popular demands for more television and the more popular varieties of it; adopt an open and cooperative stance in the international, especially European, context; and open a number of options for the future, in which outside business interests can take more of a part.

It is hard not to interpret the whole complex of measures as, on balance, a move away from public broadcasting as it has been known in the Netherlands. However, the response among the broadcasting organizations has not been unanimously negative. Some like the challenge of more commercial-style competition; some hope for some protection from commercial pressures and more limited and realistic cultural tasks. Whatever it may be, the policy response described can hardly be designated as deregulation, and only in a limited way is it privatization. It does at least seem true to the principle that the society should have the chance to choose for itself what sort of broadcasting system (and options within it) it should have, and this, after all, from one point of view, was what the original radio settlement in the 1920s was also about. Despite changes, which are still occurring (more under the pressure of circumstance than by choice), the Netherlands retains the core elements of a system that to a reasonable degree gives reality to the principles of broad access and cultural, social, and political diversity. The scope and ambitions of the public service system have been reduced, but there remains guaranteed space for cultural quality and authenticity, for uncommercial sources of programming, and for minority points of view. The policy commitment to these things remains, although the system as a whole is more fragmented, less coherent, and subject to increased commercial and transnational influences and trends.

CHAPTER 5

Scandinavian Public Service Broadcasting: The Case of Denmark

Preben Sepstrup

THE PUBLIC SERVICE CONCEPT IN SCANDINAVIA

In the Scandinavian countries, radio and television have so far been totally dominated by the national broadcasting institutions, which all rely on the same basic concepts and principles of public service broadcasting: radio and television must not be a commercial business, radio and television must not be a state business proper, and radio and television are obliged to serve the public interest. These basic principles of public service broadcasting imply that the broadcasters must not have any profit goals, that they must not be instruments of any government, and that they must be versatile about program content and target groups served by the programs.

In summary, the Scandinavian broadcasting acts state four basic *obligations* of the public service broadcasters: The public service broadcaster is obliged (1) to supply the public with a versatile program mix, which is relevant to all groups of the population, including minorities and including prime time; (2) to produce a substantial part of the programs and, in doing so, maintain its integrity toward both economic and political interests in the society; (3) to distribute the radio and television signals so that they can be received at the same price by all households in the country; and (4) to support the national production of cultural products (for example, by buying manuscripts, maintaining orchestras, and supporting national artists and entertainers).

Except for the final paragraph on future challenges to public service broadcasting, the text of this chapter uses Denmark as an example of the development and state of public service broadcasting in the Scandinavian countries, which are all characterized by having a population of 5 to 8 million people, independent languages, an old and independent cultural tradition, a long democratic tradition, and the structure of a welfare state with one of the highest per capita incomes in the world.

PUBLIC SERVICE BROADCASTING IN DENMARK, 1926–1980: CONFLICTS AND DEVELOPMENTS

The obligations I have outlined reflect the prevailing philosophy on the role of national radio and television from 1926 to this day.[1] The scarcity of frequencies was used as a main argument for regulating broadcasting by law for the first time in 1926. This first broadcasting act created a monopoly headed by a nine-member board (the Radio Council). Three members represented organizations formed by listeners, one member represented the hardware producers, two the daily press, and three the various ministries.

The 1926 act stated that broadcasting should be financed entirely through a license fee to be collected by the broadcaster, totally separate from any state taxes. The Radio Council was to make sure that the programs were versatile, cultural, and informative. It became the responsibility of the P&T (Postal and Telegraph Service) to ensure that the radio signals reached all parts of the country.

There is no doubt that the first broadcasting act was inspired by the principles governing Britain's BBC and influenced by the "vested interests" of the newspaper industry, which for a long time ran the news service for Denmark's Radio and ensured that there would be no advertising. Radio became a mass medium very fast in Denmark, and the politicians soon realized that broadcasting might exert a cultural and political influence beyond the control of parliament. In 1930, the broadcasting act was changed to increase the number of members in the Radio Council from 9 to 15, and 4 of the members were to be appointed by the four dominant political parties.

In 1959 the broadcasting act was changed again. The name of the monopoly was changed to Denmark's Radio (DR) and television was formally integrated into the organization. (See Box 5.1.) The most important change, however, was that the composition of the Radio Council was altered to reflect the powers of parliament very closely. This change mirrored a long political debate on the meaning of the concept of democratic public service broadcasting. One point of view advocated "neutrality" in programming; the other advocated "versatility."

The concept of neutrality has never found its way into any Danish broadcasting act, whereas all have stated that programs must be versatile in their political, topical, factual, and artistic dimensions. Therefore, the political discussion—which led to a higher ratio of parliament members on the Radio Council—was on the interpretation of versatility.

BOX 5.1   Danish Broadcast Corporation (DR)

The Danish Broadcast Corporation (Denmark's Radio, or DR) is an independent public corporation financed by license fees paid by households having radio and/or television.

DR provides one national television channel, three national radio channels, and nine regional radio channels.

DR is directed by a board of governors responsible for all operations of the corporation. The Financial Committee of parliament sets the license fee for three-year periods. The chairman of the board is appointed by the minister of communications, nine members are appointed by parliament, and one member by the staff of DR.

In addition, the Program Advisory Committee, representing a number of organizations, discusses DR's programs and may submit its opinions to the board and the management.

According to the broadcasting act, the radio and television programs of DR must cover the dissemination of news, information, entertainment, and the arts. In the planning of programs, decisive importance must be attached to considerations of freedom of information and speech, and DR must endeavor to provide quality, diversity, and variety. In the dissemination of news, importance must be attached to objectivity and impartiality.

DR transmits around 3,000 hours of television a year. Two-thirds of that is produced by DR itself. About 50 percent of the foreign programs come from other western European countries (mostly Great Britain), about 30 percent from the United States, about 10 percent from other Nordic countries, and about 10 percent from other countries.

In round figures, the distribution of DR's television program categories in 1990 was as follows: news and current affairs, 15 percent; children and youth, 15 percent; drama, 15 percent; entertainment, 15 percent; regional programs, 10 percent; culture, 10 percent; sports, 10 percent; music, 5 percent; and educational programs, 5 percent.

To the right of the political center, versatility was basically seen as a possibility for banning certain topics and viewpoints in individual programs on the grounds of "one-sidedness." The advocates of this point of view wanted the programs to be neutral and to avoid controversial issues. The opposing point of view stated that the purpose of democratic public broadcasting is not only to reflect prevailing ideas but also to open the eyes and ears of the audience. So versatility is interpreted to include an obligation constantly to expand the scope of the programs and to find room also for challenging and different views and to produce certain programs irrespective of the popular demand for such material.

An important change of the broadcasting act took place in 1973, when an amendment stated that versatility was not to be met by an individual program but by the overall composition of total program output. This has not prevented politicians from most parties, from time to time, from criticizing individual radio and television programs for a lack of balance, and the political parties to the right of the political center tried during the 1970s to substitute for *versatility* the term *fairness* and to apply that concept to individual programs. In some periods, this strategy had some success in the Radio Council's evaluation of individual programs. But the broadcast act was never changed to reflect this point of view, and since the end of the 1970s, the fairness doctrine has not had any practical influence.

But discussions of the interpretation of versatility continued until 1986, when the board of Denmark's Radio was changed radically. The practical consequences of this discussion for Danish broadcasting reflected the political majority of the Radio Council, which again depended on the political composition of parliament. One might therefore say that the ultimate freedom of Denmark's Radio for a period of more than ten years depended on the political tolerance or political culture of the parliament members of the Radio Council. As a grand total, it appears that the political process created the necessary tolerance and, to a large degree, allowed program policies to reflect the progressive interpretation of versatility. But the process certainly had its ups and downs.

In 1964, the Radio Council gave up its attempt to control program planning and for all practical purposes delegated its program decisions to the directors of Denmark's Radio. The Radio Council continued to approve the general program plans and tried continuously to influence programming by "subsequent censorship"—which, of course also influenced future activities. It also happened again and again, as long as the Radio Council existed, that the politicians, the press, or the audience found the progressive interpretation of the public service obligations to be exaggerated in specific programs and made complaints via the Radio Council. As long as the Radio Council existed, the issue of control of programs was a constant source of conflict between the Radio Council and the employees of Denmark's Radio.

Summary of the Basic Historical Conflict Areas

When the 1980s started, the historical development of public service broadcasting in Denmark had produced a system that financed three radio channels and one television channel by license fees only, had a board with heavy political representation that was responsible for appointing a large number of executive positions in DR and for discussing the program output, and was obliged to serve the public with a versatile program output.

From 1926 to 1980—and in essence to this very day—the most significant conflict areas produced by this system have been the interpretation of the call for versatility as discussed earlier and the financing of broadcast activities. From the organized birth of radio in 1926 and since the introduction of television in 1954, there has been constant demand from advertisers for access to both radio and television.

Starting with the British ITV in 1955, almost all of western Europe's public broadcasters had gone commercial at the beginning of the 1980s in the sense that they carried advertising.[2] The best explanation for the Scandinavian countries' staying out of this mainstream is probably the welfare state ideology of these countries, which placed a relatively high priority on consumer interests and cultural viewpoints.

The most heated discussions developed around the issue of the extent of political influence on the economy and on radio and television programs. Denmark's Radio was never a state business. But as long as the Radio Council existed, the organization and its products reflected a complicated, political influence. Though democratic in nature and reflecting the composition of parliament, this influence was considered dubious by many, including the employees of Denmark's Radio.

A paternalistic, elitist, we-know-better attitude can easily become typical of a public monopoly with a dominant position in the cultural sphere, sworn to versatility, the protection of minority interests, and the production of certain programs irrespective of popular demand. Until 1988, the audience had no alternative but to stay with the "schoolteachers" of Denmark's Radio. A widespread criticism was that the audience could not get what it wanted; instead, it had to learn to love what it got.

At the beginning of the 1980s, Denmark's Radio had a 54-year history of crises and conflicts, only briefly touched on here. It is fair to say, however, that during most of its history, Denmark's Radio has continuously moved toward an increasing realization of its public service obligations. Except in the very early years, the principles and consequences of public service broadcasting have really never been questioned but rather taken for granted in Denmark and the other Scandinavian countries. Only the implementation and exact form of the basic elements of public service broadcasting have been discussed and developed.

PUBLIC SERVICE BROADCASTING IN DENMARK, 1980–1990: PROBLEMS AND SOLUTIONS

The conflicts I have outlined continued into the 1980s, when some of the most significant problems of public service broadcasting in Scandinavia also started to develop.

As is well known, the development in information technology during the 1980s influenced media patterns heavily, due to the increased speed of transmission, increased capacity in communication distribution systems, and reduction of physical distances. Cultural influences from major broadcasting countries became more pervasive, media products were to an increasing degree internationalized, and the electronic media, especially television, became more and more commercialized. None of these were new phenomena. But during the 1980s, they moved with startling speed and power due to developments in information technology. Some of the basic problems of public service broadcasting in Denmark during that period were caused by these technological developments. Others— especially those related to programming—were made more visible by the technological development.

A Small Country with Big Problems

The transnationalization and commercialization of television, which appear to follow the developments in information technology and the parallel search for new sources of profit, are felt most in countries, like the Scandinavian countries, that kept to a noncommercial, one- or two-channel public service system.

Denmark is a small country with a population of 5 million people in a relatively small area that is very easy to cable. Until the second half of the 1980s, the electronic world to most Danes consisted of a public service system comprising three radio channels and one television channel.

At the beginning of the 1980s, this situation was disintegrating. Starting in the 1970s, there had been much talk in Denmark about a gap of confidence between the politicians and the electorate and a growing understanding that a country with a very homogeneous and highly educated population might nevertheless have information gaps and cultural gaps. Research demonstrated a high amount of viewing of Swedish and West German television among two-thirds of the households,[3] which was closely related to the fact that more than half of all Danish households were passed by cable in 1982. Though obviously not new, the extent of this viewing surprised most observers. The first pan-European satellite channels started transmissions of new transnational, commercial channels. The telephone companies in Denmark started to build a giant, national fiber-optic cable network that by the end of the decade had bridged so many local cable networks that 34 percent of all households received between 15 and 18 channels of foreign origin.

From 1975 to 1985, the average person spent about nine hours per week in front of the screen. In 1984, the two-thirds of viewers who received either the two Swedish or the three West German channels watched 30 percent more television than the national average for Denmark's Radio.[4] Attention was focused on the fact that many Danes were exposed to West German television advertising. Also, it was pointed out in the public debate on the television situation that in West Germany with three channels and Great Britain with four channels, the consumption of television was much higher than in Denmark—and on the horizon was the frightening figure of 28 hours per week in the United States. By 1990, the average viewing time from age 6 in cable-equipped multichannel households in Denmark was actually 19 hours, the majority spent on foreign, mostly commercial channels.[5]

Foreign television was not unknown to the viewers left with Denmark's Radio single channel: Between 1984 and 1987, some 34 percent of the hours supplied and 38 percent of the hours watched were of foreign origin (mainly from the United Kingdom and the United States).[6] There was some concern over the expansion of the percentage of nondomestic hours available to viewers and much concern over the increase as such in viewing time due to the expanding supply of foreign national and transnational television. The worries in the public debate ranged from the economic effects of foreign transnational advertising to speculation on the effects of the editorial content and concerns over the sheer amount of time spent on television. On top of that, penetration of VCRs accelerated in the first half of the 1980s from zero to 20 percent. (In 1990, it was close to 40 percent.)

Some of the questions asked in the public debate were, What would the effect of this be on values and norms? On the "Danish way of thinking and living"? On the national culture and language? What would happen to Danish manufacturers of consumer brands competing with transnationally advertised brands? From what activities would more time for television consumption be taken? Why is this small country, without any raw materials, so well off? What do the Danes do while the Germans, the British, or the Americans watch television? What would the implications of more television be for social and educational policies, knowing that the less educated would take the lion's share of the inflated consumption?

So, probably for good reason, the Danes—or at least their politicians, public debaters, teachers, and representatives from the cultural sphere— felt a bit uncomfortable about the media, especially television, since the national radio stations were not really challenged yet. An old and well-known world was breaking down. The monopoly-based public service broadcasting company realized that it had competitors, both commercial and noncommercial, and that more were on the way.

All this does not mean that foreign influence was new or especially threatening to the Danish society. Traditionally, Denmark has always been very open toward the rest of Europe and the United States. But in the electronic field, this new transnational influence seemed more and more a threat to national, cultural, and political integrity and perhaps even the language. The potential influence from a commercial, transnational television culture was new. Many domestic advertisers felt that the admittance of foreign advertisers to Danish television screens was unfair competition since they were not allowed to advertise on Danish television and costs prohibited them from advertising on the nondomestic channels to which the Danes were exposed.

Most people probably considered the whole development a step forward. They wanted more than they got from Denmark's Radio. The decision makers fully understood this and probably shared this wish. And they fully accepted the consumption of foreign television. But they did not want it to be out of a lack of national alternatives, and they knew that the viewers in general preferred national productions. They were probably also a little worried about Danish culture and the Danish way of life (whatever these concepts may be), as well as the language.

Changes in Danish Public Service Broadcasting

As a consequence of the developments of the 1980s, a large political majority and the majority of the population and the advertising industry felt an urgent need to introduce a second national television channel. Many politicians hoped that two competing channels would give them more exposure and that the new channel would be less critical than Denmark's Radio. The idea of breaking the monopoly of Denmark's Radio was very popular with the population, which hoped for more choice and more attractive (that is, entertaining) programs. And the advertising industry saw a new chance for turning television into an advertising vehicle.

After a long and heated debate, the broadcasting act was changed in 1986 to make room for a new national public service channel, partly financed by advertising, to start in June 1988, together with eight regional channels. (See Box 5.2.) The board was to be businesslike, with no political representation, though appointed by the minister of culture. What really heated the debate on the second television channel (TV 2) was the proposal from the conservative government that the channel should be 75 percent advertising-financed, copying the rigid West German system, with advertising restricted to five minutes before and five minutes after the news.

Advertisers and advertising agencies—led by the big U.S. agencies—mobilized all their lobbying and opinion-building resources. For both economic and ideological reasons, the issue was crucial to the parties behind the government. And a noncommerical solution was for ideological reasons very important for the parties to the left of the political center. In the end, the government's proposal was accepted by a two-vote majority for the commercial model.

The broadcasting act of 1986 also replaced the Radio Council with a small, professional, traditional board. But the politicians were not ready to give away all their influence, so it was decided that the professional board should be appointed by parliament. Behind these changes was an

---

BOX 5.2   TV 2 (Denmark)

TV 2 started its transmissions in late 1988 and provides both a national and regional service. The latter is produced by a network of eight regional stations in different parts of the country.

TV 2 is an independent public corporation financed mainly by advertising, with a maximum of 27 minutes per day in 1991. All advertising must so far be placed between programs in a maximum of five blocks. Rules corresponding to those of the EC television directive regulate the content of advertising, including products that cannot be advertised, such as cigarettes, alcoholic beverages, and medicine.

Advertising sales are handled by an independent state-owned corporation (TV 2 advertising). An advertising committee appointed by the minister of communications ensures that advertising rules are observed.

TV 2 is governed by a board of five members appointed by the minister of communications, one member appointed by the staff, and one by the regional stations.

TV 2 is so new that few statistics are available. The station produces about 30 percent of the programs itself, mainly news and current affairs programs, including sports. The broadcasting act states that at least 50 percent of the station's total output must be produced in Denmark or one of the other Nordic countries.

---

understanding that Denmark's Radio needed more freedom from political influence with the introduction of competition. The same motive was behind a decision to introduce three-year budgets, so that from 1990 on, parliament has to approve the budget and license fee only every third year. Another element of the act was seen also as a tool to counteract the influence of foreign television. After a trial period, local radio and local television were introduced—with no public service obligation and dominated by the labor movement, religious organizations, and, to a lesser extent, grassroots organizations.

In discussions of the introduction of television advertising, opponents argued that advertising and competition would influence program quality in a downward direction and that advertising would soon appear to be a cuckoo in the nest that would need more room all the time. It is open to discussion what has happened to the quality of the programs of DR and TV 2. There are both positive and negative effects, and there is no doubt that a certain commercial style of presentation and self-promotion has come to stay, together with, for example, more entertaining news, less time for children's programs, and a proliferation of Brazilian and American series.

And there is no doubt that television advertising has acted like a cuckoo in the nest. Between 1988 and 1990, there were several revisions of the advertising part of the broadcasting act for the purpose of increasing advertising income through a more flexible advertising system. From 1991, TV 2 will be almost totally advertising-financed, and there will be advertising between all programs. From the beginning of 1992 there will be more advertising time, and advertising is expected to be allowed in "natural breaks" in programs. In 1990, the broadcasting act was also changed to allow sponsorship in all electronic media, including Denmark's Radio. Advertising has also been introduced as a source for financing local television and radio.

Commercial radio stations have succeeded to such an extent that they have become serious competitors to the national public service radio channels. DR is losing the young listeners and will lose even more if a fourth, commercial, national channel is introduced, as suggested in 1990. Public service radio is close to a crisis because it is losing its grip on the young audience. It is uncertain how DR will react and what the consequences for public service radio will be. For one thing, it depends on whether national networking of commercial local radio will be allowed and what will happen to the fourth national radio channel. If commercial operation gets the go-ahead, which is likely in a not-too-distant future, many of the problems outlined next for television will be pertinent to radio also.

CHALLENGES TO SCANDINAVIAN PUBLIC SERVICE BROADCASTING IN THE 1990s

As outlined earlier, the media scene has changed radically during the 1980s and so have the conditions for the old, monopoly-based public service broadcasters.

What, then, is the situation today and the problems and possibilities for tomorrow for public service broadcasting in the Scandinavian countries? The competitive situation of television changed during the 1980s and will probably change even more in the future. The monopoly situation will never come back in Denmark and commercial, national channels will start in 1992 in Norway and Sweden. (See Box 5.3 for a description of the Norwegian Broadcasting Company.)

Funding

The first challenge for public service broadcasters will be to keep the present level of funding. The national license fee has been almost the only

---

BOX 5.3   Norwegian Broadcasting Corporation (NRK)

The Norwegian Broadcasting Corporation (Norsk Rikskringkasting, or NRK) is a public service broadcaster financed by license fees. NRK provides one television channel, two radio channels, and 17 regional stations.

NRK was a state-owned company until 1988 but is today independent of the government and parliament.

NRK is governed by a board of seven members. Five are appointed by the government and two by the staff of NRK. The board submits budget proposals to parliament, which decides on the license fee. NRK has a broadcasting council that meets every month to discuss program matters. All members are appointed by either parliament or the government.

According to the rules of NRK, the corporation must provide a variety of programs that cover all forms, themes, and opinions, including those of minority groups. NRK must stimulate interest in social issues as well as provide cultural experiences and entertainment. The programs must be characterized by impartiality and objectivity. This pertains to the total output and not necessarily to individual programs. And this rule must not prevent artistic freedom or freedom of expression.

NRK is required to reject attempts from outsiders—including governmental authorities—to influence its programming. The total output of programs must strengthen Norwegian culture in a wide sense. The corporation must also ensure that its programs reach all areas of the very large but sparsely populated country.

NRK transmits around 3,400 television hours a year. Around 60 percent is produced by NRK. The remaining 40 percent is mainly imported from Great Britain and the United States.

In round figures, the distribution of NRK's television program categories in 1990 was as follows: news, current affairs, and documentaries, 34 percent; sports, 14 percent; drama, 14 percent; miscellaneous, 14 percent; children and youth, 9 percent; educational programs, 5 percent; music, 5 percent; light entertainment, 4 percent; and religious programs, 1 percent.

---

entrance ticket to the electronic media for the Scandinavians. In the future, however, the license fee will become one of several "electronic expenses" in most households. Many families already pay to be connected to a cable network or subscribe to a pay TV channel, they rent videocassettes, and sometimes they also support their local station.

The permanent, almost traditional discussion of the size of the license fee will therefore become more critical, and the arguments for substituting advertising income for the license fee will fall on even more receptive ears in the many households that believe commercial television is "free." The best legitimization during the time of monopoly for the license fee was the very high percentage of viewers watching the national broadcaster's programs and the popularity of these programs.

Swedish television has experienced a serious cutback in ratings in cable-equipped areas. (See Box 5.4 for a description of the Swedish Television Company.) And shortly after TV 2 was introduced in Denmark as a partly advertising-financed public service competitor, the average ratings of Denmark's Radio were cut almost in half, the new channel taking the other half. It also immediately became very important for the two competing public service broadcasters not to lose the ratings race (winning was actually less important). For TV 2, ratings are important because of the advertisers, and for DR, they are important as a legitimization of the license fee.

The politicians anticipated the immediate decline in DR's ratings. But what will happen to either of the two stations if they lose further ratings points to the national competitor or to foreign channels? If either license fees or advertising income does not keep up with costs (skyrocketing due to the entrance of private, commercial channels on the European television market), attractive programs cannot be produced, resulting in lower ratings, which will lead to less advertiser support or less political will to support the license fee.

Programming

The second challenge to public service broadcasters will therefore be programming policy. It is obvious that the national public service broadcaster cannot maintain the high ratings of the past. When all the new competitors are established (or have failed), ratings for most programs must fall relative to the situation in the 1980s.

Then the crucial and critical question will be whether the public service broadcasters, financed by license fees or advertising, dare to uphold their public service obligations (to serve all interests, including minority interests, even in prime time, and to maintain versatility in entertainment, news, cultural events, and information). Will the public service broadcasters be able to do so when most competitors, driven by a commercial motive, turn the news into entertainment and concentrate on popular movies and series to attract as many viewers as possible?

Around 15 percent of the hours broadcast by DR, Sweden's television, and Norway's television are directed toward children and teenagers. These programs are known for their high quality and have for years been very popular within their target groups. There is no doubt, however, that

BOX 5.4 Swedish Television Company (SVT)

The Swedish Television Company (Sveriges Television AB, or STV) is a subsidiary of the Swedish Broadcasting Corporation (SR), which also includes the Swedish National Radio Company and the Swedish Educational Broadcasting Company. SR has exclusive rights to nationwide terrestrial broadcasting in Sweden. It is a joint-stock company owned by big labor organizations, consumer cooperatives, churches, industry, commerce, and the press.

The board of SVT has 11 members appointed by the board of the parent company, which is in turn appointed by the government and the shareholders. The staff of SVT appoints two members, and the managing director is also a member of the board.

SVT operates two national television channels. SVT 1 broadcasts programs produced mainly in the capital, Stockholm, whereas most of the programs broadcast from SVT 2 are produced outside the capital by the ten SVT regional offices. Both channels also broadcast programs produced by SVT's sports department and by the Educational Broadcasting Company.

SVT is financed by a license fee, which every Swede who owns a television set must pay. The license fee is determined annually by parliament.

The radio act and a so-called agreement between SVT and the state provide the guidelines for SVT activities. The radio act states that SVT must exercise its broadcasting rights impartially and objectively and allow total freedom of expression and information. The act also prohibits censorship and the examination of programs before transmission by any authority or other public body. After transmission, the Broadcasting Commission can raise objections to specific programs and consider complaints from viewers.

Each of the two channels air around 3,000 hours, including 500 hours produced by the Educational Broadcasting Company. Two-thirds of the output is produced by SVT itself. Around 25 percent is imported from Great Britain and the United States and around 10 percent from the Nordic countries.

In round figures, the distribution of SVT's television program categories, excluding educational programs, in 1990 was as follows: nonfiction, 26 percent; drama, 21 percent; light entertainment, 11 percent; sports, 11 percent; children's programs, 10 percent; news, 10 percent; music, 6 percent; and minority programs, 5 percent.

the young Scandinavians are very attracted by, for example, the European MTV (Music Television)[7] and the private, commercial TV 3, which broadcasts to all the Scandinavian countries. How will the Scandinavian broadcasters react if and when young people turn to MTV and TV 3? Will they fight fire with fire? If not, what will the politicians do if a big proportion of the target group not only tunes in MTV and TV 3 but also abandons the national programs?

Will the political system—which eventually determines the income of the public service broadcasters (and also those financed by advertising)— be able to withstand the pressure and maintain the license fee while the public service ratings are declining? It may be serious enough from a national and cultural point of view if many viewers turn away from the programming of the public broadcaster. Another thing—and perhaps the real danger—is if these programs cease to exist as an alternative to commercial broadcasting (that is, if the public broadcasters start competing on commercial terms by being less versatile, by increasing popular common-denominator shows, by scheduling minority-interest programs at odd hours, or by dropping costly in-house productions).

The basic principles of public service broadcasting will be under attack in the Scandinavian countries in the years to come. Europe—and hence Scandinavia—will, in the 1990s, experience the "American rules" of competing commercial stations. It is an open question whether the public service broadcasting tradition will be able to survive that.

The reason the question is open is that most commercial channels have no obligation to be versatile in the public service sense of the concept. As a consequence, their costs are lower, and they may be very attractive for prime-time consumption. They will follow the well-known pattern of commercial television in the United States (based on movies, sports, music videos, series, and serials). There is no reason to complain about that, except when measured by the public service yardstick. Competing commercial channels keep to the political and cultural center; they keep to what is acceptable to most viewers, which is unfortunately not what is most attractive to individual persons or any single group.

The commercial (private) channels in Europe produce very few programs themselves. They rely heavily on buying, especially from the United States.[8] They must aim for high ratings. They cannot use all their income on new programming, since they have to earn a profit. They do not have to support national, cultural productions. They are searching for the transnational common denominator in their program policy. They must not rely on specific, individual, or national characteristics but on the (little) common background, knowledge, and interests of all the peoples of Europe.

All this said, one must still ask why viewers in Scandinavia would let down their public service broadcasters. This is a burning question if one believes in the superiority of the principles of public service broadcasting.

Why is it a fact today in Scandinavia that the audience in general—and the low-income and less educated groups, and perhaps the younger part of the population, in particular—appears to abandon the informative, educational, and entertaining programs of the public service broadcaster for commercial competitors, now that technological developments gives them that chance?

One hypothesis offered here, as part of the answer, is that a large share of the programming is not seen as relevant by a majority of the audience; these programs do not deal with subjects *they* find interesting and do not relate to *their* point of view, *their* experiences, *their* way of understanding, or *their* language. These programs are not really propagating *their* culture or expressing true diversity and versatility. Seen from this point of view, the social groups that are most readily attracted to transnational, commercial television are the same groups that have been let down the most by the old public service broadcasters, due to what might be called the paternalistic and elitist tendencies of these public service institutions.

If public service broadcasting in the Scandinavian countries wants to maintain its audience, it will, in all likelihood, be forced to adopt a new general programming approach and to learn a new television language. The problem is to stay competitive and fulfill the public service obligations at the same time. It is an advantage for the Scandinavian public service broadcasters that they have a national platform and a unique language to start from, but it will probably not be enough to counterweigh continued paternalistic or elitist attitudes and practices, and technology will soon wipe out the comparative advantage of language.

Perhaps the most serious threat to public service broadcasting would be the public service broadcasters' choosing, in the sacred name of ratings, to fight fire with fire. The second greatest threat is to continue the paternalistic approach. The only alternative is to develop a public service tradition that would seriously contradict the majority of viewers' beliefs about the relevance of most national public service productions.

Advertising

The third challenge concerns public service broadcasters who are or will be financed by advertising in one way or another. A general problem for these public service broadcasters is the effect of advertising financing on programming. The decision in Denmark, in 1986, to allow advertising on the second channel was based on the assumption that it would be possible to regulate tightly the use of advertising on television in the same way as other restricted systems in Europe. The hypothesis offered here is that the rather rigid rules regulating advertising on many European public service channels cannot be maintained in a situation of competing commercial stations.

Because of the transnationalization of television, the existing advertising-supported public service broadcasters are or will be involved in competition for advertising revenues. The guidelines for television advertising, as decided by the European Community,[9] are less rigid than most national rules for advertising on public service channels. This may eventually devastate the values and purposes of the public service broadcasters.

On top of this—and perhaps in the long run the most serious threat to the quality of commercial public service channels—comes the "electronic dilemma of television advertising"[10] (that is, the declining effects of traditional television advertising). Here it suffices to note that due to remote controls, VCRs, the large number of channels, the many narrowcasting channels, and pay television, exposure to traditional television advertising is on the decline. And the most regulated advertising systems are of course also the most vulnerable in this process.

To counteract the electronic dilemma of advertising, which is an economically devastating process for both advertisers and stations, the commercial channels allow advertisers and their agencies to develop new "traditional advertising methods," like 10- and 15-second commercials and the "minimovie commercials." Most important, advertisers are allowed to develop a new breed of "integrated advertising" (programlike advertising, advertiser-initiated product-related shows, advertiser-initiated non-product-related shows, and other kinds of sponsorship).

By offering advertisers better conditions to parry off the electronic dilemma of television advertising, the commercial channels make it more difficult to attract advertising to highly regulated systems limiting commercials to scheduled blocks of airtime. If a public service broadcaster for some fraction of the income is dependent on advertising and to some degree competes with commercial channels, the public service broadcaster must offer the advertisers the same attractive conditions as the commercial competitor, as is the case of TV 3 in Scandinavia, which in both 1990 and 1991 was the main argument for new, more flexible rules for advertising on TV 2 in Denmark and also during 1990 became a main argument for introducing commercial television in Norway and Sweden (as happened in 1992). The consequences for programming and advertising are not in line with the principles and obligations of public service broadcasting.

The public service broadcaster's dilemma, with regard to advertising, can be summarized in two questions that reflect a very pertinent problem for the Scandinavian broadcasters: Should public service broadcasting organizations be allowed to accept advertising on the assumption that this will enable them to compete more vigorously and effectively with their proliferating rivals for maximum viewership? Or should public service broadcasting be expected to fulfill a different function from that pursued by single-minded market entrepreneurs, depending on noncommercial sources of funding compatible with it?[11]

NOTES

1. Details on the historical background are from Roar Skovmand et al., *DR 50* (Copenhagen: Denmark's Radio, 1975).
2. See Preben Sepstrup, *Transnationalization of Television in Western Europe* (London: Libbey, 1990), for a discussion of the concept of commercial related to broadcasting and for a categorization of western European broadcasters and their program output according to the degree of commercialization.
3. Erik Nordahl Svensen, *'Danskere med flere tv-kanaler'* (*Danes with several TV-channels*) (Copenhagen: Denmark's Radio, 1984).
4. Ibid.
5. Niels J. Jensen and Lars Qvortrup, *Program valg og seervaner i Grenaa Byantenne* (*Program choice and viewer behavior in a local cable net*) (Grenaa: Grenaa Kommune, 1990). Further details in English can be found in Sepstrup, *Transnationalization of Television*.
6. Sepstrup, *Transnationalization of Television*.
7. Westrell (1989); Jensen and Qvortrup (1990), in Sepstrup, *Transnationalization of Television*.
8. See Sepstrup, *Transnationalization of Television*.
9. Commission of the European Communities, *Television without Frontiers* (Brussels: COM [84] 300 final, 1984). Compare the final version of the EC television directive, adopted in October 1989.
10. The determinants of this dilemma in Europe and the United States, the countermeasures taken by advertisers and broadcasters, and the consequences of these countermeasures are described in Preben Sepstrup, "The Electronic Dilemma of Television Advertising," in Jay G. Blumler and T. J. Nossiter, eds., *Broadcasting Finance in Transition* (New York: Oxford University Press, 1991), pp. 359–381.
11. David Poltrack, "What Happens When Competition Comes: The American Experience," *EBU Review* 36 (6, 1985), pp. 14–18.

CHAPTER 6

Italian Entrepreneurial Initiatives: Public Service Broadcasting in Transition

John F. Kramer

THE UNIQUE SITUATION OF PUBLIC BROADCASTING IN ITALY

Public broadcasting in Italy is in a situation unlike that anywhere else in the world. It is unique in two respects, both immensely important for its future and the definition of its role in Italian society. First, the public broadcasting system in Italy, a strong, well-developed, multichannel radio and television system known as RAI, is almost completely lacking in autonomy from the government. From almost its very beginning in 1924 until the reforms of 1975, the public system has been directed and controlled by the government or by a particular faction of the political party that controls the government. Since the reforms of 1975, control has been more widely shared among the major political parties and their representatives in parliament. Despite this, as will be described, RAI has gained little in autonomy and has exchanged one set of governors for another.

The second unique fact of Italian broadcasting is that in Italy, a developed public broadcasting system is for the first time strongly confronted by a virtually unregulated and increasingly powerful private radio and television system, which is not only challenging it for audiences and revenues but is also beginning to raise questions about the role of public broadcasting in a mixed public-private system.

Contrast the state of public broadcasting in Italy with that in the United States. In the United States, the private commercial broadcasting system was the first to develop; it laid claim to the best radio and television channels and to rich sources of funding and through its power won from the government protection from competition and even from much regulation. Thus in the United States, the public broadcasting system is the decidedly weaker system. It operates on inferior channels with only a fraction of the funding of the private system (and is threatened with the loss of the portion of the funding that comes from the public purse). Finally and ironically, despite its second-class status, it is more often a victim of political interference.

In Italy, as in most of the western European democracies, of course, these positions were largely reversed. The public system was the established, strong, well-funded system that was allotted the best frequencies and interconnections and was held in the highest regard. Until the mid-1980s, it was the private commercial system that was struggling for a place in the broadcast system and for legitimacy. But now the two systems are virtually equal.

PUBLIC SERVICE BROADCASTING

Given the two systems, one public and one private, what is "public service broadcasting"? For most Italians, it is still the broadcasting of the state radio and television networks, RAI (Radiotelevisione Italiana) or "Mamma RAI," as it is sometimes called.

For most of the history of broadcasting in Italy, from the beginning in 1924 until the mid-1970s, RAI was the monopoly Italian broadcaster for programming ranging from the weekend soccer games to opera from La Scala, from instructional programming for the schools to news and public affairs. Today, at the start of the 1990s, RAI operates one of the world's most developed systems, broadcasting over three national television networks and three national radio networks as well as over regional television and radio networks, plus a foreign radio broadcast network. RAI is one of the largest broadcasters in Europe (after the Soviet Union and the BBC), with an operating budget of about $2 million and more than 13,000 employees.

But in the mid-1970s, the RAI monopoly on broadcasting was broken. Private commercial and noncommercial broadcasters began to challenge RAI very successfully both for audiences and for advertising revenues. As RAI began to meet this challenge by programming ever more commercial entertainment programming, including American commercial programming (such as *Dallas* and *Little House on the Prairie*), critics in the press and academia began to raise concerns about the proper role of RAI in a mixed public-private broadcast system. Moreover, the failure of the reforms of 1975, which only briefly brought forth a flowering of broadcast journalism on RAI only to be crushed by the political parties, have added to these concerns.

Yet for all its problems and uncertainty about its ultimate role, "Mamma RAI" is at present *the* public service broadcaster in Italy. It is the major or sole source of broadcast journalism, educational and instructional programming, and cultural and religious programming; for the most part, it provides the highest-quality entertainment programming; and even today it attracts by far the largest audience. For these reasons, we will focus largely on RAI, its historical role and evolution, its recent history and the attempt at reform, and its struggle to adapt to the new environment of mixed public-private broadcasting.

RAI has four problems. First, the control of the public broadcasting system by the government and the political parties has resulted in a generally acknowledged inefficiency or ineptness in management and production. Second, the professionalism and creativity of those engaged in news and public affairs programming have been stifled by the power of the parties, leaving these programs at best boring and at worst irrelevant. Third, stemming from the rise of the private networks and the competition for audiences and thus for programming, costs are rising much more rapidly than (politically controlled) revenues. Finally, the ideological or theoretical underpinnings are weak for a definition of public service that would justify an entity of the scale of RAI funded both by the public and by revenue from advertising.

POSTWAR RAI: AN INSTRUMENT
OF POLITICAL PATRONAGE

At the end of World War II, RAI had been operated as a part of the patronage system of the ruling Christian Democratic party. With the loss of their absolute parliamentary majority in 1953, the Christian Democrats began to broaden the base of the party by creating and filling patronage positions not only in the government agencies but also in the "subgovernment" or "*sottogoverno*," the vast array of quasi-public corporations dependent on government funding.[1] This "colonization" of the public sector replaced the heretofore professional managers with party members who would owe their first loyalty to the Christian Democrats. Possession of the party card, the *Tessera*, and an important powerful political sponsor became, by all agreement, a more important criterion than competence for appointment to positions in the *sottogoverno*.[2]

RAI, as the government-controlled institution of the mass media, was most thoroughly subjected to political colonization. Beginning in the mid-1950s, RAI became a "citadel of . . . patronage" of the Fanfani faction of the Christian Democrats.[3] From this time to the present, the issue has not been whether RAI should be an organ of political patronage, but rather which political parties would be allowed to share in the patronage.

Prior to 1963, the Christian Democrats had been able to satisfy their coalition partners with a few low-level positions in the *sottogoverno*. But with the formation of the center-left government in 1963, the Socialists demanded a more representative portion of the patronage, especially within RAI. Still, these positions were fewer than and subordinate to the Christian Democrat positions. Thus in 1964 as a result of the center-left coalition, Socialist, Social Democrat, and Republican party members were added to the Administrative Council and top management of RAI. A Socialist and a Social Democrat were named as vice-presidents.[4] This was the beginning of the "*lottizzazione*" of RAI.[5]

Commenting on this *lottizzazione* of RAI, one observer described RAI as "one of the eldorados of the patronage system, employing thousands of unnecessary people including over 20,000 special contributors."[6] An early 1970s article in *La Stampa* described RAI Director General Barnabei "as an eastern potentate, surrounded whenever he goes to the Houses of Parliament by a hoard of supplicant MPs asking him to employ their protoges."[7]

Along with the rigorous division with respect to patronage came great caution with respect to political reporting. All political reporting had to be cleared with party officials. When, for example, an important political meeting was reported, the footage would show the party secretaries speaking to the reporters, but the sound was eliminated and a carefully constructed and innocuous report was read over the visual footage. One former RAI personality, and later editor of *La Stampa*, described RAI's political coverage as resembling fish in an aquarium, "their mouths move, but no sound emerges."[8] Moreover, most of the strikes and demonstrations, of which there were many during the 1980s and early 1970s, were not covered by RAI because of their political character.

> The Milanese who was delayed at getting home at the end of the day by an uproar in the Piazza San Babila would never learn about it on that evening's news broadcast; the Roman who saw pitched battles between radical students of the right and left wielding chains and monkey wrenches could be certain that his favorite medium would not carry a word of it. . . . For more than a decade the major evening news broadcast typically began with the fish in the aquarium, moved from that to a series of what television journalists call talking heads—RAI correspondents reporting [from foreign capitals]—and concluded with a feature or two about the monuments of the past and the beautiful countryside. . . . Add to this extreme caution in covering politics a general practice of not covering crime or highway accidents, and the country was left with what was for years the world's dullest news broadcasts.[9]

THE MOVEMENT OF REFORM OF RAI

At the beginning of 1965, upon the death of the director of television programming, RAI's Director General Bernabei attempted to restructure the management. This precipitated a nine-month-long crisis with the resignation of the Socialist vice-president and a Republican councilor (board member). For the first time, a wide cross section of the Italian public became aware of the internal problems of RAI.[10]

From this time and into the 1970s, support for the reform of RAI grew. Demonstrations, sit-ins, and wildcat strikes by RAI workers in Rome, Naples, Turin, and Milan called for reform, access, and the democratization of RAI. These became especially intense during the "hot autumn" of 1969.

The 1970 convention of the Catholic Press Union had as its theme "Television Journalism: Reform for RAI-TV." The Socialist party convention theme was "The Conditions of Democratic Information."[11] The regions, the unions, and the Republican, Socialist, and Communist parties were all calling for the "democratization" of RAI. These groups were asking that control of RAI be exercised by parliament rather than by the government. RAI should be transformed into a public organization that would allow a right of access and decentralization of program conception and production, and there should be administrative positions for the representatives of the regions in the direction of RAI.[12]

There was, moreover, a second theme in the growing chorus of criticism of RAI: the breaking of the state monopoly of broadcasting. Indeed, private radio stations had sprung up occasionally throughout the country, beginning in the mid-1950s, but RAI would have the Ministry of Post and Telecommunications shut them down as a violation of the RAI monopoly.

This part of the chorus sometimes included the unions and political parties of the left, who had a vision of alternative, community-based broadcasting. But it also included Socialists and factions of the Christian Democrats, as well as Republicans, other parties of the center-right, and their allies in the press and industry who saw this as a way to break the lock on broadcasting of Bernabei and the Fanfani faction of the Christian Democrats. For these groups, there were commercial as well as political gains to be had. In addition, the regional governments wanted to break the monopoly of RAI for the political and social value of regional broadcasting and for possible tax revenues from local broadcasters. This debate was also energized by the fact that the RAI concession was due to expire in 1972. In January 1972, *L'Espresso* carried an article by Eugenio Scalfari titled "And Now, Liberty of the Antenna,"[13] and the phrase "liberty of the antenna" came into common use throughout the press.

The pressures on the political parties markedly increased in 1973 when an ex-RAI television director, Beppo Sacchi, built a small cable system for a few hundred households in the town of Biella, in northern Italy. The minister of Post and Telecommunications, Giovanni Gioia, a Fanfani Christian Democrat, moved to shut down the cable system, and Sacchi took the case to the Constitutional Court. Because of the closure of the system, the leader of the Republican party in the coalition government, Ugo la Malfa, called for Gioia's resignation. When Gioia refused, la Malfa and his party left the government, and the government collapsed.[14]

With its decision of July 10, 1974, the Constitutional Court began dismantling the RAI monopoly. While the ruling confirmed the concession to RAI of national radio and television broadcasting, it also affirmed, for the regions, the power to regulate and to program broadcasting of a local character that is part of a decentralized radio and television system. Thus the local cable system was constitutional.

The justification of the state monopoly over national programming was based on the limited availability of channels and the duty of the state to guarantee to everyone the possibility of free expression in a pluralistic society. It required, however, that these channels be used in an affirmative manner to provide access to all the relevant information that is required in a pluralistic society: "The public monopoly by definition must be understood and configured as a necessary instrument for the enlargement of the area of an effective presentation of a plurality of voices."[15] At the same time, in a second decree, the Court authorized foreign broadcasting into Italy. Télé-Monte-Carlo and then the Swiss and Capodistria television networks began setting up relays on Italian soil, spurred by the lure of potential advertising fortunes.[16]

Within a few months, a young entrepreneur, Silvio Berlusconi, who had built a new town on the outskirts of Milan, set up a cable system for the 10,000 residents in his community. Within ten years, Berlusconi would dominate Italian commercial television as owner of the three major private networks and with advertising revenues far surpassing those of RAI. And on August 10, 1974, a station calling itself Firenze Libera began broadcasting in Florence, breaking RAI's monopoly on television broadcasting.[17]

THE REFORMS OF 1975

Finally, responding to the public outcry and the Court decrees, parliament passed a reform law in May 1975, which still largely governs RAI. The law seemed to respond to many of the public concerns. A parliamentary oversight commission, known simply as the Parliamentary Commission, was set up to oversee RAI. The commission appoints 10 of the 16 members of the Administrative Council (the RAI board of directors), 4 of whom must be nominees of the regions. The Institute for Industrial Reconstruction (IRI) has 6 appointments to the council. The Parliamentary Commission is responsible for enforcing the principles of impartiality and professional autonomy laid down by the Constitutional Court. Major social groups were to have regional and national access to radio and television.[18]

The reform also required autonomy for each of RAI's radio and television networks and ordered that they organize separate autonomous journalistic units, each with its own director. These became Tg1 and Tg2 for television and Rg1, Rg2, and Rg3 for the radio networks.[19] A third television network, Tg3, was to be developed with an emphasis on regional programming. The cap on RAI's advertising revenues was to be set as a proportion of total press advertising revenues after an annual consultation between RAI and the Federation of Italian Publishers.

LOTTIZZAZIONE OF RAI AND THE SMOTHERING OF BROADCAST JOURNALISM

One of the first effects of the new reform was an even more complete *lottizzazione* of RAI (distribution of patronage among the political parties roughly on the basis of their relative strength). Shortly after its passage, the commission named a new council, allotting its ten council appointments to the parties of the coalition government on the basis of their proportion in the government. The council named a new director general, a Christian Democrat from the Fanfani wing of the party. RAI's journalists were invited to choose which of the news organizations they wished to join: RAI-1 (TV network 1) and Tg1 were controlled by the Christian Democrats, RAI-2 and Tg2 by the Socialists and "lay" parties, and later, RAI-3 and Tg3 by the Communists.

A similar system was set up for radio, the first network being a Socialist network, the second a Christian Democratic network, and the third a Communist network.

From early 1975, even before final passage of the reforms, the press headlines told the story of the *lottizzazione*. Here are some examples: In April, "Reform of RAI-TV: A Good Law That Awaits the Deeds," "Already They Are Outlining the *Lottizzazione* of RAI-TV, Born of the Reform," "The *Lottizzazione* for the Seats at RAI Has Begun"; in September, "RAI-TV, but It Doesn't Change"; in November, "Savage *Lottizzazione*," "Assault on RAI"; and in December, "The Battle of via Teulada [RAI headquarters]: Party Cards, Talent and Liberty," "RAI-TV, the *Lottizzazione*: Reform Is Necessary Again," "The Tragic Comedy of the Reform of RAI-TV."[20]

For a brief period, however, during a window of opportunity before the parties tightened the political controls, RAI's journalism and public affairs programming flourished. The autonomous news services were very quickly in competition with one another, and for the first time, the Italian public was treated to an open and even exciting presentation of public affairs broadcasting.

Tg2 began asking embarrassing questions of party leaders, and Tg1 soon followed suit.[21] The chief editor of Tg2 recalls finally being able to interview a political leader, a minister being investigated by parliament during the Lockheed scandal, who agreed to a live interview on the evening news:

> His press aide had prepared a series of questions . . . but we asked the minister our own questions. The interviewee couldn't hide his surprise. He began to beat the table and became so red in the face that we feared for his health.[22]

The smaller third radio service began interviewing spokespersons for unconventional causes: militant feminists, organizers of protests in prisons and mental hospitals, homosexuals, and leaders of a movement to democratize the military.[23]

A writer of television documentaries for RAI recalled the period:

> The reform gave rise to a happy and brief season, lasting perhaps less than two years, of a springtime of television information, which saw more than a flowering of weekly reports of documentaries of news programming, which saw in particular the second opening of a professionalism and a richness and completeness of information that until that time had not been known.[24]

This freedom of broadcast journalism was short-lived, however. In mid-September 1976, the Parliamentary Commission had organized oversight subcommissions for RAI's two important political news and election programs, *Tribuna Politica* and *Tribuna Electorale*, the subcommission members chosen for political balance.[25] By the 1979 elections, the parties had secured from the Parliamentary Commission "the right to produce *all* RAI campaign programming . . . [as well as] protection from attractive competitive programming on the other of [RAI's] two channels." Analysis of audience data indicated that the resulting *Tribuna Electorale* drove away listeners by the millions.[26]

The domination of RAI by the parties continued through the 1980s and up to the present time. In 1984, on the thirtieth anniversary of the introduction of television in Italy, *Corrière della Sera* ran an article titled "RAI in the Mortal Embrace of the Parties: Information Dead from the Pressure, Demands, and Underhanded Poison of the Pallazzo." The radio network news directors were quoted: "The presence of the parties is suffocating," "As between ability and the party card, it's the latter that counts more, without doubt," and "The truth is that often they in the parties confuse public service with service of the public relations of the palace."[27]

RAI continued to be one of the most strongly contested arenas of the *sottogoverno* (subgovernment). In 1984, when the 16-member Administrative Council of RAI came up for reappointment, the bitter struggle was not resolved for nearly three years. In a political deal, the parties proposed to appoint not only the ten councilors selected by the

Parliamentary Commission but also the six IRI appointments, allotting two to the Christian Democrats and one each to the Socialists, the Social Democrats, the Communists, and the Republicans. Under an "avalanche of public criticism," the head of IRI refused to confirm the appointments.[28] However, the struggle was not only about the appointment to the six IRI seats but also over the election of the new president and vice-president of the council. Not until November 1986 did the parties reach agreement on the composition of the new council and the new president and vice-president.

THE GROWTH OF PRIVATE COMMERCIAL BROADCASTING

As RAI continued to be dominated by the parties, private commercial broadcasting grew to be a formidable competitor in the least regulated free market system in the world. In the mid-1970s, the Ministry of Post and Telecommunications had brought suit to shut down a private FM station operating in Milan. The matter was resolved by the Constitutional Court when it ruled in favor of the private station on June 25, 1976. Reasoning much as it had two years earlier, the Court confirmed RAI's monopoly of national programming, including the monopoly over national news and public affairs (but with the proviso that RAI had to provide impartial and comprehensive coverage along with the opportunity for expression of a variety of points of view). However, private commercial broadcasting was ruled legal as long as it was limited to regional and local broadcasting. Thus the Court legitimized the dozens of private commercial stations that had come into being in the two years since its 1974 decree.

In response, new stations sprang up like mushrooms. The early entrants into broadcasting included activists of the left and the right, the political parties, labor unions, publishers, and entrepreneurs like Silvio Berlusconi. Foreign broadcasters from Monaco and Switzerland and an Italian publisher hoping to broadcast from the island nation of Malta began to set up and expand their broadcast systems. By 1980, there were 972 private television stations, about half of them broadcasting daily programs.[29] There were more than twice as many FM stations.

These new stations, operating on any available frequency and often interfering with one another, constituted an unregulated free market broadcasting system. The major exception to the rule of government laissez-faire was the ability of RAI to have stations that substantially interfered with the RAI-allotted frequencies closed down (after extended court hearings).[30]

Everyone, including the Constitutional Court, expected that parliament would shortly enact regulations for private broadcasting. Indeed, in the subsequent years, numerous bills were introduced. However, none had been enacted by the end of 1990.

Beginning in 1980, television networks began to form.[31] Berlusconi, the young developer and cabler of new towns outside Milan, was the first to see that in order to compete and attract advertising, he would need to set up stations around the country. Through his firm, Fininvest, he built and operated a network of stations playing simultaneously duplicate cassettes of the various programs. Thus he was technically complying with the Constitutional Court requirement that private stations could not be interconnected beyond a very small region. Three publishers, Rizzoli, Mondadori, and Rusconi, put together networks based on the American model of affiliates, for whom they acted as brokers, assembling packages of television programs and advertising that they provided in cassette form to the independently owned stations. Berlusconi, however, through ownership of his stations, had greater control over the programming schedule and the fulfillment of advertising contracts and was therefore more attractive to advertisers. Moreover, he had an "American-style" organization of salespeople, much more aggressive at marketing than his well-established publisher rivals.

In 1981, Berlusconi challenged RAI's monopoly in two areas, live sports and RAI's exclusive access to the Telespazio earth station for uplinks and downlinks with television satellites. RAI had turned down broadcast rights to games of an ad hoc soccer league in Latin America involving teams from Brazil, Argentina, Uruguay, West Germany, the Netherlands, and Italy. Berlusconi then offered a large sum for the rights for all of Europe. This would require, of course, that Berlusconi be allowed to receive the games via satellite through Telespazio.

There was great demand on the part of Italian fans to see these games, which was intensified by the ensuing struggle involving Berlusconi, RAI, the Ministry of Post and Telecommunications, and parliament. The compromise was that Berlusconi was allowed to broadcast the games live over his Milan station but was required to broadcast them a day later by cassette throughout the rest of his network, Canale 5. RAI provided live broadcast of the major games for the rest of Italy.[32] Berlusconi then challenged RAI for the rights to broadcast the regular soccer games throughout Italy, offering more for the games than RAI was willing to pay. Again the politicians defended RAI's position as Italy's sports broadcaster, and RAI, with some concessions, continued broadcasting these games.[33]

By the fall of 1981, the ratings showed the three RAI television channels with a total audience of 7,808,000, versus 5,047,000 for the audience for the private networks and independent stations. RAI and the private networks were competing fiercely for audiences, and RAI's programming had, in response to the competition, become more commercial, with more purchases of foreign programming. In 1981, the Italian broadcasters bought about $70 million worth of programming from the United States, and Italy had become the largest market for U.S. programming.[34]

Because of the escalating costs, the Rizzoli network folded, leaving the field to RAI and the networks of Rusconi, Mondadori, and Berlusconi.[35] RAI indicated the lengths to which it would go in order to prevent competition, buying the Monaco-based network, Télé-Monte-Carlo Italia, which was also in financial difficulty and with which Berlusconi was negotiating. Berlusconi wanted the network because, as a foreign network, it had legal interconnection of the stations and, what is more, access to satellite broadcasting because of Télé-Monte-Carlo's membership in the European Broadcasting Union. RAI held on to Télé-Monte-Carlo until 1985, when a Brazilian firm, TV Globo, purchased the operation.[36]

By 1982, Rusconi had decided that his network, Italia-1, was too much of a financial gamble. Just as the sale of the network to Mondadori was being concluded, Berlusconi made a higher offer, later financing the purchase through the door-to-door sale of stock by his housing development sales force.[37] Berlusconi could now program two networks with the best possible counterprogramming against Mondadori's network, Rete-4. Finally, in the summer of 1984, Mondadori also sold out to Berlusconi. Berlusconi, with all three major commercial networks in Italy—Canale-5, Italia-1, and Rete-4—was the owner of the world's fourth largest private media operation (after the three U.S. networks).[38]

How had this happened? One of the Mondadori principals suggested that the publisher network owners were used to operating in a clearly structured, well-regulated business environment relatively free of major risks. Their efforts were to hold on to their networks until a law regulating commercial television was passed by the government, which would then stabilize their position. RAI also was awaiting regulations that would limit private broadcasters.[39]

However, Berlusconi did not want a law and was much more comfortable in the "Wild West shoot-out." Berlusconi was aided by the Socialist party in preventing passage of a regulatory bill and especially by his friend, the prime minister of Italy since 1983, Bettino Craxi.

Craxi had been the Socialist mayor of Milan and the person Berlusconi dealt with in building his new towns. They became good friends and also political allies. On several occasions, one or more of Berlusconi's stations were shut down by regional judges alleging that the networks were, by playing programs simultaneously, violating the Court decree on interconnection. Craxi's government would within hours put forward an emergency decree that allowed the networks to resume. This was, of course, popular with the public.

RAI, BERLUSCONI, AND THE COMPETITION
FOR BROADCAST ADVERTISING

The growth of private broadcasting led to a rapid increase in the size of the advertising market. During the years from 1970 to 1979, while the

Italian economy grew by 31 percent, the market for all advertising (newspapers, magazines, domestic and foreign broadcasting, movies, and billboards) grew by only 20 percent. However, in the years from 1979 through 1984, while the economy was growing by just 5.3 percent, the market for advertising showed a real increase of 66.4 percent. In 1979, some 62 percent of advertising revenue went to the press, newspapers, and periodicals, and only 28 percent went to broadcasting. By 1985, the press had only 42 percent of the market, and broadcasting had 53 percent. Television during this period grew from 20.8 percent of the advertising market to 49.7 percent. Thus in the course of five years, Italy became one of the few countries in the world to invest more in broadcast advertising than in the printed press.[40]

As this television advertising market was growing, Berlusconi's advertising firm, Publitalia, was growing also. In 1980, at the inception of the Berlusconi networks, Publitalia had only 1 percent of the whole advertising market in Italy. Sipra, the exclusive advertising agent for RAI, was the largest firm in the market, receiving 27.1 percent. During the next four years, Publitalia virtually exploded in size, growing to 26.9 percent of the market, the largest firm in Italy, followed by Sipra, which had declined to 19.5 percent of the market. In terms of the market for television advertising, in 1980 Sipra had 46.4 percent of the market while Publitalia had only 3.9 percent. By 1985, Sipra had declined to 31.4 percent of the market, and Publitalia was far and away the largest firm, with 59.3 percent of the market. In dollar terms, the market for television advertising had grown from a 1980 market of $383 million, of which Sipra had $178 million, and Publitalia had $15 million, to a 1985 market of $1.052 billion, of which Sipra had $330 million and Publitalia $626 million.[41]

In retrospect, it seems clear that there was a tremendous bottled-up demand for broadcast advertising in Italy when private television and radio came on the scene. Until that time, the only advertising outlet available was RAI (except for the foreign stations broadcasting in Italy). RAI, having only a limited time available for advertising because of its cap on ad revenue, was very difficult to deal with. RAI dealt only with major corporate advertisers, which meant that small and local businesses could not advertise on radio or television. RAI had very high standards for the quality of advertising it would accept, and placement of the advertising was decided by RAI. RAI's advertising agency, Sipra, operated on a policy that a sponsor had to invest 70 percent of its advertising budget in print media in order to be allowed to spend the remaining 30 percent on television, and Sipra would steer the advertisers to print media controlled by the Christian Democrats.[42]

When private broadcasters began offering advertising opportunities and even began sending sales people to knock on the doors of local businesses and corporations, and moreover were much less demanding about the quantity and quality of the advertising, they found willing and eager buyers. During this period, Berlusconi lost no opportunity to justify his networks on the basis of their offering of advertising opportunities to businesses other than multinational corporations. Berlusconi asserted that his networks were an important force for economic development in Italy and for the preservation of capitalism, offering the chance for heretofore competitively disadvantaged small businesses to grow and compete in the marketplace.

Berlusconi's evaluation of the importance of business advertising on television was, not unexpectedly, echoed by a principal of one of the large ad agencies in Rome: "When RAI was the only game in town, and only 300 firms had the privilege of airing spots, budgets earmarked for television were much less effective; Berlusconi and company have definitely been a shot in the arm to the industry."[43] As of early 1985, more than 2,000 firms advertised nationally or locally in Italy. Thus in a period of five years, Berlusconi had not only developed Publitalia into the dominate Italian advertising firm but had also built himself an ideological shield for his battles with RAI, the courts, and parliament.

RAI, of course, was handicapped, in part, by the parliamentary cap on its ad revenues. But "Mamma RAI," like that other mother, "Ma Bell," had to learn to market itself, to attend to the care and feeding of its customers in the new competitive environment.

COMPETITION IN THE 1980s: PROBLEMATIC RESULTS FOR RAI'S PROGRAMMING?

RAI has gone through three phases of reaction to private competition with profound effects on its programming. Its first reaction was astonishment, outrage, and attempts through various lawsuits to enforce its monopoly.[44] When this effort failed and its competitors began to build significant audiences with imported programming (mostly from the United States), RAI joined the battle in those terms. These years, through mid-1984, were especially difficult.

American distributors were happy to offer RAI first choice of their programming, and RAI purchased large amounts of it. In 1981, RAI played the first 14 installments of *Dallas*. When RAI dropped the series, Berlusconi picked it up without missing an episode. Demand for programming was so great that U.S. productions were being shown in Italy simultaneously with their airing in the United States. A RAI council member declared, "If we have to descend to the level of commercial broadcasting to retain our audience, we'll do it."[45]

In 1981, the Italian equivalent of *TV Guide, Sorrisi e Canzoni*, redesigned its format (at a cost of $8 million) to give the schedules of the private broadcasters equal space with those of RAI. By 1983, RAI was broadcasting $8^1/_2$ times as many hours of entertainment programming as it had in 1974. In percentage terms (RAI had increased the number of broadcast hours), RAI's entertainment programming on RAI-1 and RAI-2 had increased from 18 to 57 percent. News and public affairs programming remained constant at 18 percent. But cultural, educational, children's, and other programming had declined from 63 to 32 percent. RAI began to resemble more closely its private competitor networks, which were broadcasting 85 percent entertainment and only 3 percent news and public affairs.[46] By 1984, RAI was in trouble, with "revenues up a little, costs up like crazy. We've increased the hours of programming, the cost of programs, salaries, the cost of talent, the cost of sports—everything."[47]

The 1980 Olympics had cost the European Broadcasting Union (EBU) $5.8 million for the rights for all of Europe. In 1984, Berlusconi offered the Olympic Committee $10 million for the Italian rights alone, so the EBU was forced to pay $19.8 million. RAI was charged $6 million for the Italian rights because "its breast harbors the asp."[48]

Many of RAI's stars had been lured away by the private networks, which revamped their popular RAI programs and began to compete with RAI. The private networks had half of the audience, and, for the first time ever, RAI was having difficulty selling out its advertising slots.[49] RAI responded by developing new talent, greatly increasing the amount of its own production, entering into coproduction agreements with companies in the United States and in Europe, and being more selective about its foreign purchases. By the 1985–1986 season, RAI was producing 70 percent of its programming hours (85 percent if we include news programming).[50]

Some of this programming is of very high quality. Since the earlier productions such as *Marco Polo* and *Jesus of Nazareth*, RAI has added films and series such as *The Name of the Rose, Ortello, Garibaldi*, and *Christopher Columbus*. RAI has contracted for feature films from premier Italian filmmakers such as Fellini, Antonioni, Olmi, and Wertmuller. By the mid-1980s, RAI management, in contrast with the desperate days of the early 1980s, spoke proudly of "having roll[ed] up our sleeves" to "restore our public service image. . . . We raised the quality of our popular programs for home consumption and foreign marketing."[51]

During the last half of the 1980s, RAI and Berlusconi's three networks waged a costly struggle for audiences. During the 1987 season, the Berlusconi networks finally equaled RAI in share of the audience, each with about 43 percent.[52] The heavy (and very costly) weaponry for this struggle was largely imported programming. The rivalry drove up programming costs dramatically; the total value of imported programming increased from $127.7 million in 1986 to $324.7 million in 1987.[53]

In response to its audience losses to the Berlusconi networks, RAI also began to program its three channels in 1988 to maximize its total audience (rather than allowing head-to-head competition among the three). By the end of that year, RAI had regained its audience lead over the Berlusconi networks, 46.7 percent to 39.1 percent, with the remainder going to the mininetworks and independent stations.[54] Of course, another way of looking at these figures is to note that since about 1986, even with its virtual monopoly on live sports and news, RAI has captured slightly less than one-half of the Italian television audience.

One clear result of the competition of the 1980s is that RAI's programming has become much more appealing to mass audiences. Its highest-rated programs include such fare as game shows, a variety review linked to the national lottery, and numerous U.S. imports, and even such soap operas as *Capitol* and *Loving*.[55]

Commenting on RAI's recapturing the lead in the audience wars, RAI's deputy director general, Emmanuele Milano, noted that while RAI's prime responsibility remains informational and cultural programming,

> we still believe RAI must be at the center of the country's television panorama. When everyone has looked to invade our position, we have reacted. If our adversaries run at 100 kilometers per hour, we can run at 120 kilometers per hour. If they don't play the game at too high a level, we can again make television with more culture and information. In the end, it is up to them.[56]

But there is also strong criticism of RAI's programming; the mediocre quality of middle-brow, often imported entertainment programming and the relative paucity of educational, cultural, and strong news and public affairs programming are what RAI's critics find most disturbing.[57]

RAI'S REVENUE PROBLEM: SLOW GROWTH

RAI operates on an annual budget of just over $2 billion. The two major sources of revenue are television receiver license fees, which account for 58 percent of revenue, and advertising sales, which account for around 35 percent. (The remaining 7 percent derives from sales and services.) During the highly competitive 1980s, RAI often had annual deficits of $100 million or more. By 1990, these had accumulated into outstanding bank loans totaling $1.3 billion.[58]

These two revenue sources are largely out of the control of RAI and grow at substantially less than the rate of inflation. License fees are set by parliament and are currently among the lowest in Europe.[59] RAI receives only 75 percent of the fees, the other 25 percent going to various government agencies. The revenue raised from fees grows at about 3 percent per year because of the increased use of color receivers.[60]

Any increase in fees is a political issue. Increases of about 50 percent in 1980 brought forth worries that it would result in a lower level of compliance of payment and suggestions that the fees are regressive taxes and that funds for RAI should come from the treasury. After the 1980 increase, the fees remained constant for five years. In the last year of that period, before finally receiving a 30 percent increase in 1985, RAI ran an 8 percent deficit and required a government subvention of $107 million. This latest increase did not, however, match the increase in the cost of living during the five years, and, in fact, the license fees are effectively 35 percent lower than in 1980.

Advertising is the second major source of revenue for RAI. The advertising revenue cap is set annually by the Parliamentary Commission after the recommendation of a committee composed of representatives of RAI and the Italian Federation of Publishers (instituted as a part of the 1972 reform). It is based on a percentage of newspaper and magazine advertising revenue and in recent years has increased by about 6 percent annually. At present, RAI sells enough advertising to reach its allowed maximum. Advertisers like RAI because of its high audiences, of course, but also because RAI permits far fewer ads than Berlusconi does. But only a few years ago, in 1984, with RAI struggling in the ratings, RAI failed to sell out its advertising quota.

Taken together, and without an increase in the license fees, RAI's total revenue grows by about 5 percent per year. Although the inflation rate in Italy has declined to about 8 percent annually, clearly the annual increase in RAI revenues has not even kept pace with the rate of inflation. But RAI's programming costs have grown at a much faster pace than inflation. This inexorably increasing financial pressure provides a strong argument for a more efficient RAI.

LOTTIZZAZIONE AND A NEW REFORM OF RAI

Lottizzazione has hurt RAI in several ways in addition to encouraging the tendency of the political parties to attempt to control program content, especially in news and public affairs. Frequent political struggles over the appointment of a new RAI president, vice-president, and Administrative Council have not only made managing RAI's adaptation to its new environment more difficult but have also been demoralizing. At times, political uncertainty has become a preoccupation.[61] After an election or a government crisis, RAI may find itself with an entirely new board.

The RAI Administrative Council also involves itself, for political reasons, in what ought to be management decisions. For example, the scheduling of news programs on RAI-1 and RAI-2 (which channel would get which time slots) was decided by the council.[62]

In 1985, the tenth anniversary of the reform of RAI, Luigi Mattucci, the director of RAI's Milan production studios, described RAI in the following discouraging terms:

Today RAI is a large, old organization with enormous resources and professionalism, [but] not organized for new ends or new strategies. Its own inertia and its relationships with political power have reduced it to this. Each party prefers, rather than an autonomous RAI, a submissive agency without a head that doesn't function but at least obeys.[63]

One scholar, addressing the need to depoliticize RAI, has proposed weakening the ties between the Parliamentary Commission and the RAI council by creating an intermediate insulating entity.[64] However, it seems very unlikely that the parties would, in the foreseeable future, relinquish their control and patronage over RAI, even if only because of mutual distrust. This might only occur via referendum (which is how the divorce and abortion laws were changed). But a referendum is not part of any current agenda.

The press and public opinion strongly favor a noncolonized, efficient, and professional public broadcasting service. However, if there is to be a "reform of the reforms," it may come about because of the financial pressures on RAI.[65] For example, *lottizzazione* has placed a significant proportion of unqualified personnel in positions at all levels. But the financial pressures on RAI, coupled with the audience competition, have enhanced the value of professionalism and have made the deadwood more costly. RAI has a large cadre of first-class professionals, in its technicians, in journalism, and in general programming. The best young journalists, all agree, go to RAI.[66] These professionals must often ignore or bypass the numerous unqualified political appointees at the lower levels.[67]

The structure of RAI set up by the reforms was designed with the idea of RAI as a monopoly broadcaster. The three radio and three television networks each have separate heads with significant autonomy. Within each of these, the news and public affairs divisions also have their own heads and considerable autonomy. These channels were allotted to the parties and competed with each other. Most observers, including those within RAI, agree that RAI's internal structure is inappropriate and wasteful in the new competitive environment. RAI's top management has called the internal competition "absurd."[68] Rather, the three television channels should coordinate their program production, purchasing, and airing to control costs and maximize audiences. This would also provide better value to Italy's audiences.

There have been several attempts to increase cooperation between RAI-1 and RAI-2 in the past several years, with modest success. But a major obstacle to rationalization of the relationship between the two networks has been the Christian Democrat and Socialist parties' rivalry and suspicion and their unwillingness to forgo their proprietorship of the channels. Only when Berlusconi networks reached equal audience levels in 1986 was RAI able to curb this interchannel competition enough to program for maximum total audiences.[69]

RAI-3, the part-national, part-regional network born of the reform, with 21 regional broadcasting centers and five production centers, has only recently begun to develop real audience support. Yet its mandate for public service to the regions is of equal importance to the national mandate. RAI's deputy director general, Mario Motta, has described RAI-3 as like PBS in that it "can't find an identity, a character" and has "each station doing its own local news and regional programming, but also carrying national news and other programming from the network."[70] However, to integrate RAI-3 into RAI requires satisfying the Communists, to whom the RAI-3 was allotted.

At present, prospects for the depoliticization of RAI are slight. But the benefits from such a reform are recognized at the highest levels. Back in the gloomy days of 1984, RAI Council President Sergio Zavoli wrote that RAI's

> credibility can only be acquired in one way: by freedom of choice. The principle of political responsibility . . . does not mean a total dependence on the party system which penalizes and distorts every principle of the formation of government decisions and of company management.
>
> We are prepared to answer for our actions at any institutional session, as long as these are a result of our own autonomous and responsible work. We have a right to be able to work. It is for others to criticize and to correct it.[71]

The terms of the presently proposed regulations could, however, add to the pressures for a more autonomous RAI.

FUTURE REGULATION: NEW COMPETITION IN SPORTS AND JOURNALISM

For a decade and a half, Italian broadcasters have operated in an uncertain regulatory climate. Berlusconi has benefited from this and now presents parliament with the fait accompli of his multibillion-dollar, three-network empire. The publishers have returned to publishing. RAI has successfully defended its legal monopoly on news programming and has largely done so (but at great cost) with respect to live sports programming. With Berlusconi victorious over his private competitors but lacking interconnection for news and sports programming, the terms of the new regulations have been somewhat clarified, but the political problems remain thorny. The major points at issue concern antitrust measures, interconnection, live news and sports programming, advertising revenues, and the establishment of a "high authority" to regulate public and private television.

Berlusconi's three networks, with 40 percent of the audience and 60 to 70 percent of television advertising revenues, clearly raise antitrust problems. Under one proposed solution, Berlusconi would be forced to sell his three networks. In return, Berlusconi (and the minor networks) would be given the right to interconnect stations in a real network. Concomitantly, they would be allowed to provide national news and sports coverage and to receive satellite broadcasting for international sports and entertainment. However, Berlusconi is obviously strongly opposed to the sale of one network and has strong support among his friends in the Socialist party in parliament. Indeed, Berlusconi's support in parliament has turned the issue of antitrust in broadcasting into a larger issue of antitrust in the media. This more recent formulation would allow Berlusconi to keep all three of his networks but might force him to sell his newspaper, *Il Giornale*. However, it would also prevent the Agnelli/Fiat group, a potentially powerful competitor that owns the national newspaper *Corrière della Sera*, from becoming involved in broadcasting.[72]

Another part of the recent proposal would guarantee RAI's funding at 50 percent of the total broadcast advertising revenue. Since about two-thirds of RAI's funding comes from television fees, this proposal would also guarantee that the private broadcasters receive somewhat more than 80 percent of all broadcast advertising revenue. At present, Berlusconi receives approximately 90 percent of this private television advertising revenue.

On March 22, 1990, the Italian senate amended the broadcast regulation bill to prohibit commercial breaks (except at intermission points) in films shown on television. Since this policy is already enforced on RAI, RAI would not be affected by this amendment. However, Berlusconi programs multiple commercial breaks in films, which are a major source of revenue. The costs to Berlusconi of this prohibition have been estimated by his organization at $500 to $600 million and by others at $100 to $200 million.[73] In addition, a new broadcasting law will likely remove the present limitation of one channel per operator, which has prevented the growth of cable television in Italy. Finally, the law might replace the Parliamentary Commission with a single apolitical commissioner who could set the rules for both public and private broadcasting, though there is already opposition to this concept.

COMPETITION: GOOD FOR JOURNALISM?

Interconnection of the private networks and national news programming may further cut into RAI's audiences. However, with respect to the throttling of RAI news and public affairs broadcasting, competition with private broadcasters, which would be made possible by the agreement, might provide RAI journalists with a lever to pry themselves out of the grasp of the political parties.

RAI has strong public support and perhaps is gaining somewhat greater parliamentary acceptance of autonomous, professional news programming. For example, in 1985, RAI-1 began a late-night interview show, *Linea Diretta*, starring a popular and professional veteran news broadcaster, Enzo Biagi. Biagi, with great freedom to choose his topics, has interviewed the man who shot Pope John Paul II, the heads of the Christian Democratic and the Communist parties, feminist leaders, the editor of *Pravda*, and the head of the *New York Times*'s foreign news bureau, as well as the brother of an escaped convict, a police office in Palermo after a raid on a Mafia hideaway, and two regional Socialist leaders on trial for accepting bribes. The program was attacked bitterly by Socialist party leaders, and members of parliament have called on the minister of Post and Telecommunications to shut it down. However, Biagi received strong public support, including a majority in parliament, and the program continued.[74] Although *Linea Diretta* was not produced by RAI's news services, Biagi believed his programming and large audiences would help them: "It conditions everyone who sees it for a freer and fuller news approach. . . . It will be difficult to cancel this program."[75]

Perhaps an indication of another step toward journalistic independence was, ironically, the week-long broadcast suspension of a Biagi interview with Libyan Colonel Qaddafi, which had taken place only a few hours before the American aircraft attack in April 1986. The leaders of the five government parties, the minister of the interior, and the head of the Parliamentary Commission all wanted the program (now *Spot*, in prime time) cancelled. Biagi and the director of the news division TGL, Albino Longhi, threatened to resign. A huge public and press outcry ensued. The RAI council voted to broadcast the interview in the next week's program, and RAI Director General Agnes agreed.[76] However, in 1988, the program was cancelled by the new government; late in 1989, Biagi was reinstated by yet another new government.

Thus competition with private news could encourage this tentative and halting growth of the autonomy of RAI's broadcast journalism. But Biagi himself has observed that there is no guarantee of this. He notes that competition for audiences in RAI's entertainment programming has led to "more films, more serials, more magazine programs, and many more quiz programs."[77]

WHAT ROLE FOR RAI?

"Mamma RAI" has enormous professional and technical strengths and reserves of prestige and good will. Even its competitors from Berlusconi sometimes see it as a BBC rather than as a PBS.[78] But notwithstanding its recent success in the audience ratings, in the long run, RAI will have difficulty competing with its private competitors, given the present financing structure. Berlusconi's advertising revenues are already twice those of RAI and growing rapidly as the demand for television advertising grows. Soon, if not already, Berlusconi will be able to outspend RAI for programming by a substantial margin.

One obvious solution to this problem is to allow RAI to sell as much advertising as it can, subject to the limits on advertising time set by parliament. However, the Italian newspaper publishers, continually operating at a deficit (only one Italian in ten reads a newspaper) and receiving government financial subsidies, are not likely to relinquish willingly their power over the RAI advertising cap. And there is no reason for Berlusconi to want this. Indeed, he has stated at both the Christian Democrat and Socialist party conventions that he prefers an RAI with no advertising, since it is also supported by license fees.

Berlusconi also advocated that RAI not compete in the area of popular entertainment programming but limit itself to programming that is not commercially rewarding for the private broadcasters.[79] There have been, in the past, suggestions in the Italian press that RAI should become like PBS, the BBC, and ABC in Australia, which accept little advertising.[80] Under this scenario—only incremental changes in RAI's financial structure with attendant annual revenue growth of about 5 percent, coupled with the logic that RAI should not attempt to compete in entertainment programming—RAI would slowly become more like PBS, operating with an annually diminishing fraction of the budget of the private broadcasters and providing more demanding or more culturally oriented programming for smaller special audiences.

Alternatively, RAI's colonization by the parties could, ironically, produce sufficient political support to allow either a regular inflation-adjusted increase in license fees (more acceptable to RAI's media competitors) or a loosening of the cap on advertising revenues (more acceptable to the public).[81] Then RAI could compete with the private sector on roughly equal financial terms. As the publicly supported broadcaster, RAI would have added obligations, perhaps for political and parliamentary reporting, for its regional programming, and for cultural, scientific, educational, and children's programming and the like. But RAI would also have the advantage of greater technical resources and competence (at least initially) of its superior broadcast frequencies, of the possible synergy of both radio and television broadcasting, and of its great prestige as "Mamma RAI."

In this case, if the various pressures for a less political and more efficient RAI were to lead to greater political autonomy, RAI might become, over the next several years, an Italian BBC, while the BBC evolves into an English PBS.[82]

NOTES

1. The *sottogoverno* "include(s) most of Italy's large industrial firms; the major banks and credit institutions; social security and welfare agencies; state radio and television; hospitals; universities; research centers; opera houses; theatres; museums; and organizations for sport, culture, and recreation." More than 45,000 of these entities are funded, at least in part, by one of four state holding companies that themselves control over 1,000 subsidiaries. The Institute for Industrial Reconstruction (IRI) of which RAI is still a subsidiary, is the largest of these. See Frederic Spotts and Theodore Wieser, *Italy: A Difficult Democracy* (Cambridge: Cambridge University Press, 1986), p. 137.
2. In many agencies the application form has a place for the applicant to indicate his or her political sponsor.
3. Spotts and Wieser, *Italy: A Difficult Democracy*, p. 141.
4. The Socialists were described as "the party of vice-presidencies." See Spotts and Wieser, *Italy: A Difficult Democracy*, p. 147.
5. *"Lottizzazione"* is the now common Italian word used to mean the distribution of patronage jobs throughout an organization to the parties of the governing coalition, based approximately on their numerical contribution to the coalition. It is related to the English word "allotment."
6. Quoted in P. A. Allum, *Italy: Republic without Government* (New York, W. W. Norton, 1973), pp. 83–84.
7. Ibid., p. 84.
8. Quoted in William E. Porter, "The Mass Media in the Italian Elections of 1976," in Howard R. Penniman, ed., *Italy at the Polls: The Parliamentary Elections of 1976* (Washington, D.C.: American Enterprise Institute for Public Policy Research, 1977), p. 262.
9. Ibid.
10. Francesco Siliato, *L'antenna dei padroni* (Milan: Mazzotta, 1977), p. 49.
11. Ibid., pp. 34–35.
12. Ibid., pp. 52–53.
13. Eugenio Scalfari, "E ora, libertà de antenna, *"L'Espresso* (23 January 1972).
14. Norman Kogan, *A Political History of Italy: The Postwar Years* (New York: Praeger, 1983), p. 279.
15. Quoted in Siliato, *L'antenna dei padroni*, p. 109.
16. Hank Werba, "10 Years of Commercial Television in Italy," *Variety* (23 April 1986), p. 143.
17. Siliato, *L'antenna dei padroni*, p. 74.
18. Giuseppe Richeri, "Italy: Public Service and Private Interests," *Journal of Communication* 3 (Summer 1978), pp. 76–77.
19. *Tg* stands for *Telegiornale* and *Rg* for *Radiogiornale*.
20. Siliato, *L'antenna dei padroni*, pp. 98–101.
21. William E. Porter, "The Mass Media in the Italian Elections of 1979," in Howard R. Penniman, ed., *Italy at the Polls* (Washington, D.C.: American Enterprise Institute for Public Policy Research, 1981), p. 263.
22. Daniela Brancati and Laura Delli Colli, "Dieci anni di riforma e bisogna rifar tutto," *La Republican* (16 March 1986), p. 23.
23. Porter, "Mass Media in the Italian Elections," pp. 273–274.

24. Ennio Mastrostefano, "L'inchiesta televisiva: un genere sconodo," *Problemi dell' Informazione* 10 (July-September 1985), p. 415.
25. Siliato, *L'antenna dei padroni*, p. 116.
26. Porter, "Mass Media in the Italian Elections," pp. 273-274.
27. Bruno Tucci, "La Rai nel mortale abbraccio dei partiti," *Corrière della Sera* (4 January 1984), p. 7.
28. Spotts and Wieser, *Italy: A Difficult Democracy*, p. 137.
29. This total is from a census by the Ministry of Post and Telecommunications, cited in Paolo Murialdi, "Il giornalismo italiano dagli anni '60 a oggi," *Problemi dell' Informazione* 10 (July-September 1985), p. 321.
30. The Ministry of Post and Telecommunications would also occasionally shut down a politically extreme station.
31. Much of the following description of the rise of the Berlusconi broadcast empire depends heavily on Werba, "10 Years," p. 143.
32. Ibid., 144.
33. One of these concessions, worth millions to the owners, was the acceptance of sponsors' names on players' jerseys.
34. Werba, "10 Years," p. 144.
35. Berlusconi quickly bought Rizzoli's rich library of 400 feature films.
36. Werba, "10 Years," p. 144.
37. Ibid., p. 145.
38. Ibid., p. 168.
39. Personal interview.
40. *Media Key* (July 1985), pp. 19-41. The figures for 1985 are estimates.
41. Ibid.
42. *Television Radio Age International* (September 1980), p. 23.
43. "TV Advertisers Look at Government Decree as a Dream Come True," *Variety* (6 February 1985), p. 52.
44. For example, the Rizzoli network, defying the Court decree on interconnection, programmed a national news program that was deemed the best in Italy. RAI went to court and had it stopped.
45. Hank Werba, "Only One Way for Italo TV to Go—Up," *Variety* (22 April 1981), p. 106.
46. Anna Lucia Natale, "Culture di massa, giornalismo e servizio nei palinsesti televisivi della Rai e dei networks," *Problemi dell' Informazione* 10 (April-June 1985), pp. 205-243. The percentages are derived from a reworking of Tables 1 and 2, p. 206.
47. A "glum" RAI official quoted in Larry Michie, "Italy Squabbles while TV Law Dawdles," *Variety* (18 April 1984), p. 113.
48. Ibid.
49. "A Sip of Scotch and Thou: Blurbing Along in Italy," *Variety* (18 April 1984), p. 112.
50. Hank Werba, "RAI Up from the Pits to King of the Hill," *Variety* (17 April 1985), p. 123.
51. Ibid.
52. The remaining 14 percent of the audience was divided among several mininetworks and private independent stations.
53. *Variety* (27 April 1988), p. 207. Statistics are from the Ministry of Foreign Trade.

54. These are prime-time Auditel ratings reported in "RAI Holds Edge on Fininvest in Race for Italo TV Viewers," *Variety* (8 April 1989), p. 87

55. Claudio G. Fava, "Yank Soaps Are Cleaning Up," *Variety* (6 December 1989).

56. Quoted in "Milano Sez Hurt Pride Spurred RAI to Get Out There and Win," *Variety* (24 April 1988), p. 208.

57. See Giovanni Bechelloni, "Le tre televisioni," *Problemi dell' Informazione* 9 (April-June 1984), p. 151, and the comments of RAI's Enzo Biagi, p. 37.

58. RAI Annual Report, 1991.

59. In 1986, these fees were $65 for a color television set and $45 for a black-and-white set. The fees in France are about 8 percent higher, in Great Britain 12 percent higher, in Germany almost 30 percent higher, and in Switzerland more than twice as high.

60. Only one-third of Italian households had color sets as of December 1984.

61. Then Director General Agnes commented on the low morale at RAI: "That's less because of private TV competition than because of political uncertainty. It's a preoccupation." Quoted in Michie, "Italy Squabbles," p. 113.

62. Jay Stuart, "RAI Gets Live-Show Exclusive," *Variety* (26 November 1986), p. 109.

63. Brancati and Delli Colli, "Dieci anni," p. 23.

64. Paolo Murialdi, "Introduzione: il fare televisione e i fatti delle televisioni," *Problemi dell' Informazione* 9 (April-June 1984), p. 147.

65. An instructive case in the difficulty of establishing autonomy from the parties is that of the Constitutional Court. Although the judiciary is, in the words of the constitution, "an autonomous order, independent of every other power," the constitution's Court was only established in 1956, after a long struggle against the Christian Democrats, who then attempted to name not only the parliament appointees but also the Italian president's appointees. After this inauspicious beginning, the Court only slowly over the years established the prestige and autonomy that it enjoys at this time. See Spotts and Wieser, *Italy: A Difficult Democracy,* pp. 150-152.

66. Porter, "Mass Media in the Italian Elections," p. 262.

67. Tucci, "La Rai," p. 27.

68. "RAI-3's Missing Identity," *Variety* (18 April 1984), p. 112.

69. There is an argument from economics that a monopolist would provide more variety and thus better value in programming multiple channels. See Bruce M. Owen, Jack H. Beebe, and Willard G. Manning, Jr., *Television Economics* (Lexington, Mass.: Heath, 1974), pp. 49-78. Berlusconi's programmer, Robert Giovalli, describes his decision making in these terms, attempting to select from a library of programs a combination that will just exceed RAI's audiences (to satisfy Berlusconi's advertisers) but will not be greater than this size (which would be wasteful of expensive programming). See "Top Young Programmer's Young and Competitive," *Variety* (23 April 1986), p. 131.

70. "RAI-3's Missing Identity," p. 112.

71. "A Crisis of Credibility at RAI," *Variety* (18 April 1984), p. 124.

72. Agnelli/Fiat abandoned a proposed partnership in a minor network, Télé-Monte-Carlo, because of this proposal. See "Monte Carlo Television Network Must Reconsider Expansion," *Variety* (8 February 1989), p. 127.

73. Through his acquisitions, Berlusconi owns, in perpetuity, the broadcast rights for all of Fellini's films, among others. These films have been mercilessly cut for advertising breaks, provoking considerable popular outcry against the

practice. However, 70 percent of Italian films are supported, in part, by television coproduction funding; the president of the Italian Motion Picture Association has asked the Chamber of Deputies to kill the amendment.

74. "Biagi Puts Bite in News," *Variety* (17 April 1985), p. 122.
75. Ibid., p. 140.
76. Hank Werba, "Nix of Biagi Interview with Qaddafi Day of Air Strike Causes Flap," *Variety* (23 April 1986), p. 1.
77. Enzo Biagi, "Il network non basta far bella la RAI...," *La Repubblica* (8 May 1986), p. 6.
78. Vittorio Moccagatta, assistant to Silvio Berlusconi, in "Berlusconi's Private TV Webs Waiting for Parliament's Nod," *Variety* (18 April 1984), p. 114.
79. Werba, "10 Years," p. 145.
80. *Television Radio Age International* (September 1980), p. 13.
81. The cap might even be adjusted automatically to a fixed percentage of all national broadcast revenues, designed to provide a total revenue for RAI (with the inclusion of the revenue from license fees) roughly equal to that of its private competitors.
82. *The Economist* suggests that the next British government will attempt to turn the BBC into a "voluntary subscription service." See "Bending the Beeb," *The Economist* (7 February 1987), pp. 18-19.

CHAPTER **7**

The Public Service Basis of Canadian Broadcasting

Marc Raboy

ORIGINS OF THE CANADIAN PUBLIC SERVICE CONCEPT

Not surprisingly, given the historical circumstances of the country, broadcasting in Canada emerged as a hybrid of American and British models.[1]

Canadian broadcasting in the 1920s was largely a reflection of the market-based system then taking shape in the United States. With a few notable but marginal exceptions (an educational radio station run by the University of Alberta, two stations operated by the Manitoba telephone system, and a closed-circuit network serving the transcontinental passengers of the Canadian National Railways), Canadian radio developed in the private sector.

Not only were most early Canadian radio stations privately owned and commercially operated, but many of the most important ones were directly affiliated with U.S. networks. Thus by the late 1920s, the "Americanization" of the airwaves—through imported programming, imitative domestic program formats, and indirect network control—was an issue of concern for Canadian political and cultural elites.

Canada, between the wars, sought to assert itself as a nation, and broadcasting became one of the privileged arenas for this. The Royal Commission on Radio Broadcasting, chaired by the president of the Canadian Bank of Commerce, Sir John Aird, set the tone when it recommended in 1929 that all broadcasting in Canada be organized on the basis of public service and be placed under the authority of a national, publicly owned corporation.[2] "Canadians want Canadian broadcasting," the Aird commission reported, and the only way to guarantee delivery was by placing broadcasting in the public sector. Needless to say, this proposal was met with the strongest opposition from the radio station owners and by large segments of the private enterprise community.

Though the nationalist argument was the strongest factor, there was actually much more to the issue. A wide array of voluntary associations representing unions, farmers, women, educators, and other groups appeared before the Aird commission to argue that broadcasting should be seen as a vehicle of social and cultural development, not merely one of vulgar entertainment or commercial promotion. For these groups, broadcasting had to be more than simply "Canadian." Later, when the Aird commission's proposals appeared headed for oblivion, these groups coalesced into the Canadian Radio League, one of the most successful lobbying undertakings in Canadian history, generally credited with pressuring the government into creating the Canadian Broadcasting Corporation.[3]

Diverging views about the nature of Canadian nationhood also had to be taken into account. French-speaking Canadians, protected by the barrier of language, felt much less threatened by American radio programming so long as radio was available in their own language as well. Within the Canadian political context, the predominantly French-speaking province of Quebec sought jurisdiction over broadcasting within its borders, arguing that the new medium was a means of education (a sector placed under provincial authority by the British North America Act of 1867). The Aird commission had tried to take these considerations into account in its report, proposing that the national public broadcasting entity provide for autonomy over program content in each province.

The prehistory of Canadian public broadcasting was thus marked by three sets of tensions: between private capital and the state, over the economic basis of broadcasting; between the state and the public, over the sociocultural mission of broadcasting; and between dominant and alternative visions of the state, over the relationship of broadcasting to the politics of Canadian nationhood.

These tensions have continued to mark the evolution of broadcasting in Canada, and we shall see that they characterize the most significant problems facing Canadian public broadcasting to this day.

Structures

For a number of reasons, the government did not act on the recommendations of the Aird commission for nearly four years. Although sensitive to the nationalist argument, it was reluctant to attack the interests of its good friends in the private sector. (This was a general problem in Canada during this period, as political leaders came to realize that the demographic and geographic realities of their country meant a necessarily greater role for the state and state institutions if indeed there was to be a country.)[4]

The government was defeated in national elections in 1930, and its successor had to deal with the economic crisis of the Great Depression.

Also, it sought a court judgment on the constitutional question raised by Quebec. After the Supreme Court of Canada, and then the Judicial Committee of the Privy Council in London (still the highest legal authority over Canadian affairs at that time), ruled that radio broadcasting came exclusively under federal jurisdiction, Ottawa was ready to act.

The Canadian Radio Broadcasting Act was introduced in May 1932.[5] It created the Canadian Radio Broadcasting Commission (CRBC), a publicly owned authority with the mandate to own and operate stations, produce and acquire programs, expropriate private broadcasters, and regulate all broadcasting activity in Canada.

It was soon apparent that the new agency was hamstrung by the economic and political limitations built into the legislation. A small capital budget was provided to enable the CRBC to set up stations and begin broadcasting. Operations were to be financed by a user license fee and commercial advertising. No funds were provided for compensating private broadcasters who the CRBC might wish to take over. And no provision was made for provincial participation in running the system or input into programming. The CRBC opened stations and set up a national program service but never moved to acquire the private stations. It tried operating bilingually, in English and in French, but switched to separate services in each language in the face of opposition to bilingualism, especially in western Canada. Its attempts to regulate the private sector were met with scorn by broadcasters, who regarded the CRBC as a competitor.

After another change of government, the broadcasting legislation was rewritten in 1936 and the CRBC was replaced by the Canadian Broadcasting Corporation (CBC).[6] Although the CBC's mandate was similar to that of its predecessor, it marked a fresh corporate start for public broadcasting in Canada. The CBC was closely modeled along the lines of the BBC. (In fact, its first general manager was an expatriate Canadian who had until then spent his professional career as a senior executive with the BBC.)

By the late 1930s, then, the "mixed system" of Canadian broadcasting was well established. This system is based on the parallelism of public and private sectors with different financial bases and different mandates, under the regulatory authority of a single public agency. It is also based on a linguistic duality reflecting the historic origins of the Canadian nation-state: a range of parallel yet asymmetrical (that is, not always identical) services in English and in French, in both the public and private sectors.

World War II was a crucial period of consolidation for the CBC, which emerged as the undisputed central agency of Canadian broadcasting.[7] The lines between public and state broadcasting blurred in the context of the war, as the CBC (along with another new agency, the National Film Board of Canada) was used as an instrument to promote the national war effort. This was problematic, particularly with respect to French-

English relations, as the CBC was formally closed off to opponents of conscription in Quebec, for example. In later years, the CBC would often find itself under government pressure to promote national unity in the face of perceived threats of fragmentation coming from regional objections to national policy.

In the late 1940s, the CBC was given the mandate to develop and oversee the introduction of television to Canada. Despite pressure from the private radio broadcasters and other entrepreneurs, Canadian television began in 1952 under an effective CBC monopoly. During the first decade of Canadian television, privately owned station "affiliates" were allowed to coexist with CBC-owned and -operated stations, but the CBC was the only originator of programs, and there could be no more than one English-language and one French-language station in any single market.

Again, Americanization was an important early factor in programming. Many Canadian households in border areas (where the great majority of Canadians live) had already equipped themselves to receive U.S. television signals before Canadian television became available. A large proportion of these continued to remain tuned to the U.S. networks, which were, of course, beyond the scope of Canadian regulation. In order to compete, and because it was cheaper than producing its own, the CBC felt compelled to import many of the most popular American programs.

With the introduction of television, the financial basis of Canadian broadcasting went into crisis. Canadian radio had been lucrative for the private sector and more or less self-financed for the CBC. Canadian television could not pay for itself, given the high costs of production and distribution (relative to radio) and the small size of the potential market (the Canadian population is about one-tenth that of the United States). From the beginning, the CBC has had to go to Parliament annually, hat in hand, to seek an operating grant. (The license fee was abolished as ludicrously inadequate soon after the introduction of television.)

Repeated studies since the 1950s have recommended elaborating a statutory formula for financing public television, but the government has continued to operate on an ad hoc basis. As a result, there is a never-ending parliamentary debate about the proper extent of public treasury support for the CBC, and the politicians tend to expect a political dividend on the funds they grant each year.

The private sector continued to lobby on two fronts during the 1950s: for a greater role in television and for a separate agency to replace the CBC as regulator.[8] A conservative government elected in 1957 heard the industry's demands, and a major legislative reform in 1958 created the Board of Broadcast Governors (BBG),[9] an independent regulatory agency whose first major activity was to oversee the introduction of private-sector television. This was in place by 1961, when the national CTV network began operating. Most major centers in Canada acquired competing public and private television stations during the 1960s—in English from coast to coast and in French in Quebec.

Canadian political unity was seriously called into question by the emergence of radical nationalism in Quebec in the 1960s, and the federal government determined to use cultural policy, and the CBC in particular, as a strategic instrument.[10] Paradoxically, the discovery of a political purpose for public broadcasting was a financial boon for the CBC while sowing discord between the politicians and the professionals working in television. The CBC went through a series of melodramatic crises surrounding attempts to define and play out its proper role, with the net result of a serious loss of credibility, particularly in Quebec. When the broadcasting legislation was updated in 1968, the government wrote a specific mandate obliging the CBC to "contribute to the development of national unity and Canadian identity"—a measure widely seen as threatening to turn the corporation into a propaganda vehicle.

The 1968 Broadcasting Act enshrined the basic principles and structures of Canadian broadcasting as a single system comprising public and private elements, under the supervision of an independent public regulatory authority. It replaced the BBG with the Canadian Radio-Television and Telecommunications Commission in 1976, and reaffirmed that broadcasting frequencies are public property; broadcasting in Canada should be effectively owned and controlled by Canadians and should use predominantly Canadian creative and other resources; all Canadians are entitled to broadcasting service in English and French; Parliament should establish a national broadcasting service that is predominantly Canadian in content and character (the CBC); the national broadcasting service should be a balanced service of information, enlightenment, and entertainment; and where any conflict arises between the objectives of the national broadcasting service and the interests of the private broadcasting enterprises, it shall be resolved in the public interest, giving paramount consideration to the objectives of the national broadcasting service.[11]

This legislation remained basically unchanged until 1990. The system became increasingly complex as of the 1970s.[12] Technologically, the rapid and pervasive spread of cable distribution fragmented the audience and made more and more American signals available (especially after the introduction of pay TV services after 1982). Satellites made television potentially accessible to the most remote northern corners of Canada, creating a series of new financial, policy, and sociocultural considerations.

Socially, pressure from the opposition movements that grew up in the 1960s led to a range of community broadcasting initiatives that sometimes found their way into the system. Community radio operations that exist to this day were set up in such cities as Vancouver and Montreal; in Quebec, the provincial government decided to finance community radio and television as one way of occupying space in this sphere of federal jurisdiction; and native communities established their own media for the first time.

The political pressure to redefine the nature of the Canadian state finally led to the first provincial incursions into public broadcasting, in the guise of educational television networks set up first in Quebec and Ontario and later in Alberta and British Columbia. Quebec challenged Ottawa's jurisdiction over cable regulation, on the grounds that cable, unlike hertzian waves, could be confined within the territory of a province. As in 1932, however, the Supreme Court ruled for Ottawa.

Public dissatisfaction with the increasingly bureaucratic and centralized nature of the CBC poured out at CRTC hearings in 1974, at which the regulator rapped the knuckles of the public broadcaster and suggested that it seek a new relationship with its public as the best way to distinguish itself from the dominant North American commercial mold. One concrete upshot of the 1974 hearings was the abolition of advertising on CBC radio, which remains commercial-free to this day (and is generally considered far more successful than television vis-à-vis its public service mandate).

Following the election of a pro-independence provincial government in Quebec in 1976, the federal government called on the CRTC to conduct an inquiry into the CBC's news operations, alleging that the public broadcaster was failing to meet its national unity mandate. The CRTC exonerated the CBC of actually exhibiting unfair bias but found that comparing its French and English operations in fact demonstrated the extent of noncommunication between Canada's "two solitudes."

Meanwhile, more new private television stations were licensed in different parts of the country. By the end of the 1970s, many cities in English Canada had three stations—one CBC, one CTV, and one independent. A French-language private network, TVA, was created in Quebec, and in Ontario a regional private network, Global TV, was established. But in Canada as elsewhere, the real thrust toward privatization—and the accompanying decline in public broadcasting—became a phenomenon of the 1980s. One of the fundamental characteristics of public service broadcasting in Canada is that it means different things to different people. To cultural nationalists, public broadcasting represents the only effective means of competing with foreign (largely U.S.) programming. Their emphasis is thus placed on the need for a strong *national* public broadcaster like the CBC.

To public interest groups it represents the possibility of access to and fair representation on the air. They therefore tend to emphasize the need for more grassroots forms of communication, like community broadcasting, and qualitative rather than quantitative regulation of all broadcasting content.

To politicians and bureaucrats, it is a strategic instrument in the continuing struggle for pan-Canadian national unity. Here too, the emphasis is heavily on the CBC, but the degree of support for the national broadcasting service tends to fluctuate with the political context and the extent to which it is seen to be contributing to national policy goals.

Finally, private broadcasters came to see a role for public broadcasting. To them it is a safety valve, a state-financed service that should ensure the provision of commercially unviable but socially and culturally uplifting forms of programming. In this view, public broadcasting should fulfill virtually all national objectives of broadcasting and leave the marketplace to the private sector.

During the 1980s, these separate and often conflicting interests continued to clash over the evolution of the Canadian broadcasting system, particularly over the relative place of public broadcasting therein. The decade was especially febrile in the policy arena—in Canada as elsewhere in the Western world, the pressures of globalization, the fiscal crisis of public finances, and the prevailing ideological winds combined to hack away at the established position of public broadcasting. But the policy battle played itself out in a particularly Canadian way that provides some illuminating insights valuable for students of public broadcasting and policymakers in other countries as well.

POLITICS AND POLICIES OF THE 1980s

As stated earlier, one of the most important factors in the evolution of Canadian public broadcasting from the 1930s had been its perceived strategic role in the development and preservation of a strong sense of nationhood in the face of the external pressures of continentalization and the internal problem of weak national cohesiveness.[13]

The political entity of Canada is based on an uneasy pact linking two "founding peoples," the descendants of French and British colonists. During the 1960s and 1970s, the crystallization of francophone nationalist sentiment around the idea of political independence for Quebec prompted the federal government to mobilize a range of cultural institutions in support of its vision of Canada.

Perceptions of Canadian nationhood became even more complex with the manifestation of strong ethnic consciousness by representatives of the dozens of other immigrant groups that comprised more than one-third of the population by the 1980s and by the emergence of an articulate and militant movement for aboriginal political rights. These too had implications for broadcasting and were reflected in the policy debates.

The context shifted after the defeat of the Quebec nationalist position in a referendum in 1980 and the apparent (but ultimately temporary) resolution of the question in Canada's favor. This opened the way for an important policy shift from an emphasis on politics toward an accent on the economic aspects of culture and communication.

Less than two months after the Quebec referendum, in July 1980, an important reorganization within the bureaucracy moved responsibility for broadcasting from the arts and culture branch of the secretary of state's department to the Department of Communications, which, since its creation in 1969, had been essentially responsible for telecommunications and hardware.

This was more than of mere administrative consequence. It represented a major, perhaps irreversible policy shift. The minister of communications, Francis Fox, signaled the shift when he told a parliamentary committee that his department's activities would hitherto focus increasingly on industrial development and the growth of the cultural industries.[14]

This was the first time that the term *cultural industries* formally appeared in the policy discourse in Canada, and the new approach quickly upset the balance between culture and communications and offset the center of gravity for Canadian cultural policy.

A policy review committee reporting in 1982 endorsed the new economistic thrust and made concrete recommendations in the direction of privatization. Leaning on the Broadcasting Act's requirement that the system as a whole should provide a "balanced" program offering, this committee suggested that the role of the CBC should be to serve as "an alternative to private broadcasters."[15]

Skeptics recalled that the public broadcaster was supposed to be the central agency of the Canadian system and not a kind of "PBS North," but a possibly irreversible process had begun. The committee proposed that the CBC reduce its reliance on advertising revenue (an ambiguous proposal in the sense that it could only lead to improved quality if the government increased public funding) and eliminate in-house production in favor of contracting out to private producers in all areas but information programming.

The Minister of Communications integrated many of the committee's proposals into an important policy document published in March 1983.[16] The subtitle declares its orientation: "New Policies and Initiatives to Provide Canadians with Greater Program Choice and Make the Canadian Broadcasting Industry More Competitive: A Response to New Technologies and a Changing Environment."

The paper outlined a new strategy for broadcasting based on this general thrust. Its central point was to promote the private sector's capacity to produce quality television that Canadians would watch and that could be marketed worldwide. To aid this, it created a new broadcast program development fund (Telefilm Canada) to subsidize private-sector production projects. At the same time, recognizing the failure of regulatory attempts to prevent Canadians from consuming available foreign signals, it abolished licensing requirements for satellite dishes. Instead, it emphasized the importance of cable distribution as "the most cost-effective means of significantly expanding the viewing choice of most Canadians, while at the same time ensuring that the broadcasting system remains identifiably Canadian."[17]

The general orientation of the paper was unmistakable: The regulatory environment had to be made more flexible, especially with respect to the introduction of new services; the legislatory framework had to be revised, redefining and establishing new objectives for broadcasting in light of new technologies and new opportunities; and as for the CBC, the paper announced a fundamental review of its role "to ensure that it provides programming appropriate to the new broadcasting environment."[18]

Outside the government, especially in English-speaking Canada, the CBC was still seen as an instrument of resistance to American cultural domination. In 1979, fully 75 percent of English-language and 42 percent of French-language television viewing time was spent watching foreign programs; among young people, the figures rose to 83 and 56 percent respectively. CBC President A. W. Johnson told the parliamentary committee that year that the CBC should become "the unique and distinctive Canadian network" by increasing its Canadian content to 85 percent (as opposed to the 60 percent required by regulation). But, he said, this would require significantly more than the corporation's $600 million operating budget (of which roughly 80 percent came from Parliament and most of the balance from advertising revenue).[19]

Following the March 1983 policy statement of the Department of Communications (DOC), the CBC board of directors responded with its own proposals for the corporation's future,[20] and then the minister issued a second document, directed specifically at the CBC.[21] Here, the CBC was presented as "an essential instrument of Canadian cultural development" with "a massive task."

The Broadcasting Act mandated the CBC to provide "a balanced service of information, enlightenment and entertainment for people of different ages, interests and tastes," but given the expansion of components of the system, the document stated, "there is now less need for the CBC to provide such a comprehensive programming service."[22]

The new environment included not only traditional over-the-air private broadcasters (generally outnumbering the CBC 2 to 1 in every market), it also included, for the growing number of cable subscribers, the full gamut of U.S. networks and a range of pay TV services (available since 1982, these services, Canadian-owned and -licensed, were modeled on U.S. services like HBO and MTV and distributed largely American products). It also included important, if underdeveloped, alternative public services in the form of provincial educational and community broadcasters.

"In this new multi-channel environment," stated the DOC, "it has become ever more imperative that the CBC find a new and more relevant role—one which provides programming distinctive from the kind already so abundantly available from other domestic and foreign programming services."[23] The new role designated for the CBC was to be a provider of Canadian programming produced in the private sector through the assistance of the Telefilm fund. In other words, the government was continuing its support for Canadian television production and programming, but instead of doing so by financing a public corporation, it would henceforth put the funding into subsidies to private corporations. Thus program production was privatized, in the framework of a strategy aimed at the "Canadianization" of Canadian television.

Furthermore, contrary to the review committee's recommendations (and to repeated CRTC warnings about the difficulty of the CBC's meeting its objectives in a commercial environment), the CBC would be expected to continue to rely on television advertising revenue. There was an evident contradiction here. In spite of more stringent expectations that it distinguish itself from the commercial sector, the CBC would still have to compete for the mass audiences that deliver advertising dollars.

A new Conservative government in the Reagan-Thatcher mold was elected in September 1984, committed to a general policy of public-sector rollback. One of its first moves was to instruct the CBC to cut its budget by about 10 percent. In April 1985, the new minister of communications, Marcel Masse, set up the Task Force on Broadcasting Policy to propose "an industrial and cultural strategy to govern the future evolution of the Canadian broadcasting system through the remainder of this century":

> The strategy will take full account of the overall social and economic goals of the government, of government policies and priorities, including the need for fiscal restraint, increased reliance on private sector initiatives and federal-provincial cooperation, and of the policies of the government in other related economic and cultural sectors.[24]

This allusion to the broader context was critical to the evolution of broadcasting policy during the next five years. One of the government's main objectives was to conclude a bilateral free-trade agreement with the United States, to which it correctly anticipated widespread opposition among Canadian nationalists. Early on, Minister Masse endeared himself to the cultural nationalist milieu by warranting that cultural industries and Canada's right to promote them through special policy measures would be protected, notwithstanding the agreement. In this vein, one can appreciate his choice for cochairs of the broadcasting committee, Gerald Caplan, the former national secretary of the new Democratic party of Canada (opposed to free trade), and Florian Sauvageau, a professor of communications from Quebec and former journalist and CBC producer.

(Masse was still sure to hedge his bets: With one exception, the other five committee members were from the private broadcasting sector.)

The Caplan-Sauvageau task force took to its role in the fine tradition of Canadian broadcasting inquiries going back to the 1920s. Although the minister had asked for a quick and expeditious report, the task force held public meetings around the country and solicited public input from interested parties while conducting an ambitious research program. Finally, it produced an 800-page report, with more than 100 recommendations, in which the essential public service nature of Canadian broadcasting was reaffirmed and the key role of both new and old public broadcasting institutions (not only the CBC but also the provincial, community, and native broadcasters) was reasserted.

The task force proposals were referred to the parliamentary committee on communications and culture, which repeated the process with its own round of hearings and consultations, refining the proposals while maintaining the overall thrust favorable to support for public broadcasting. The government then introduced legislation to replace the outdated Broadcasting Act, and this was referred to yet another round of public hearings.

The result was a genuine public debate over the social purpose and possible structure of broadcasting in which hundreds of organizations and thousands of individuals got to speak out and present visions that corresponded to their own interests. The powerful broadcasting organizations, both public and private, were compelled to take part in the process as well in order to maintain their credibility (while obviously continuing their habitual behind-the-scenes lobbying activity).[25]

The broadcasting legislation was modified and remodified in several important areas before going to a vote, just as the government was preparing to call what would be known as Canada's "free-trade election" in November 1988. In this context, the legislation ended up full of small but meaningful concessions to women, aboriginal Canadians, disabled people, and educational and community broadcasters while reflecting the overwhelming national consensus in favor of maintaining a strong CBC. It also recognized the distinctive difference between French and English broadcasting, the legitimacy of separate development of the two services on the basis of perceived different needs and interests, and the principle of equivalency of publicly financed services in English and in French.

In a bizarre twist, the Broadcasting Act became a pawn in the grand national political drama when opposition senators in the nonelected upper house staged a filibuster just as the government was preparing to dissolve Parliament and call general elections.[26] Although it had been passed by the House of Commons, the bill thus died on the Senate agenda when the election was called. (It was finally reintroduced virtually intact and was eventually adopted in February 1991.)[27]

It is important to recognize, however, that while the public debate culminating in legislation was being carried on in the essentially symbolic sphere of policy discussion, the system was evolving according to the government's broad agenda. The CBC continued to suffer budget and service cuts between 1985 and 1988; the CRTC continued to license new private-sector services (notably, a range of 11 satellite-to-cable services introduced in 1987 along with a compulsory fee increment to all cable subscribers) and to reduce regulatory demands from private broadcasters; and more measures were taken to encourage and promote the industrial growth of broadcasting enterprise at home and abroad.

CURRENT ISSUES IN PUBLIC SERVICE BROADCASTING

As already intimated, the main issues in Canadian broadcasting have demonstrated remarkable consistency over a period of 60 years. The main questions today still concern the relationship of public and private enterprise in the overall system, the social (as opposed to "national") role attributable to broadcasting, and the role of broadcasting in defining and redefining Canadian nationhood and the political nature of the Canadian nation-state. An appropriate, as well as convenient, way of getting a handle on this is to look at the manifestation of each of these issues in the new Broadcasting Act, which provides, in many respects, a portrait of the situation at the beginning of the 1990s.

Public and Private

The new Broadcasting Act clearly affirms the public nature of *all* Canadian broadcasting by declaring that

> the Canadian broadcasting system, operating primarily in the English and French languages and comprising public, private and community elements, makes use of radio frequencies that are public property and provides, through its programming, *a public service* essential to the maintenance and enhancement of national identity and cultural sovereignty.[28]

But from this declaration to the actual realization of the public service objective is a long way indeed.

The fact is that public broadcasting is receiving less and less material support from public funds while the authorities are placing fewer public service obligations on private-sector broadcasters. The act, for example, mentions that private networks and programming undertakings should, *to an extent consistent with the financial and other resources available to them,* (1) contribute significantly to the creation and presentation of Canadian programming and (2) be responsive to the evolving demands of the public.[29]

In the past, private broadcasters have repeatedly returned to the CRTC to plead financial excuses for their incapacity to meet their promise of performance with respect to Canadian content. The primacy of financial considerations is now recognized in the law. At the same time, the law makes a policy objective out of the self-evident commercial sensitivity to consumer pressure. CBC programming, meanwhile, is specifically mandated to

> be predominantly and distinctively Canadian, . . . reflect Canada and its regions to national and regional audiences, . . . strive to be of equivalent quality in English and in French, . . . contribute to shared national consciousness and identity, . . . [and] reflect the multicultural and multiracial nature of Canada.[30]

One important aspect of this broad and detailed mandate that is deserving of attention is the need to serve the regions. The challenge of balancing national and regional program requirements has always been a strain on CBC management. National programming has a higher and more easily identifiable profile. It is prestigious and, to a certain extent, internationally marketable. It is based in two major production centers, Toronto (English) and Montreal (French), and can be more easily attuned to the expectations of national politicians in Ottawa.

Regional programming, by contrast, is difficult to contain, and its effect is difficult to measure. Closer to the populations it serves, it often reflects the potentially divisive undercurrents of regional politics and is frequently out of tune with national policy objectives, in a broad sense. Good, popular public broadcasting in a region is also threatening to the financial security of local private broadcasting outlets.

In the most draconian round of budget cuts since the ax began to fall in the early 1980s, the CBC virtually eliminated its regional television services in December 1990, closing 11 stations in different parts of the country and reducing nonnational programming to two daily newscasts in each province. These cuts provoked massive public outcry, not only in regions with a long tradition of contesting Ottawa's centralism, such as the Prairies and the city of Windsor, across the river from Detroit. City councils sought injunctions to require the CBC to fulfill its legal mandate, mayors petitioned members of Parliament, laid-off CBC employees and their unions prepared proposals to purchase their stations and run them as cooperatives, and users took to the streets.[31]

Further CBC cuts were expected. At the same time, the recent balance sheets of private television companies were showing the effects of the recession, and the private broadcasting lobby was stepping up pressure on the government to oblige the CBC to be less aggressive in competing for advertising revenue. Another task force has been looking into the finances of Canadian television and virtually endorsed this view when it reported in May 1991.[32] The gap between the rhetoric of public policy and the antipublic bias of existing broadcasting in Canada has never been so great.

Social Issues

The new Broadcasting Act has raised public expectations enormously by providing that the system should

> through its programming and the employment opportunities arising out of its operations, serve the needs and interests, and reflect the circumstances and aspirations of Canadian men, women and children, including equal rights, the linguistic duality and multicultural and multiracial nature of Canadian society and the special place of aboriginal people within the society.[33]

This was one of the most hotly contested and repeatedly modified sections of the legislation. Broadcasters argued (mostly in private deliberations) that employment equity would impose too onerous a burden on them, but reference to employment was added to the legislation at the amendment stage following a campaign by women's groups and with the support of Flora MacDonald, the minister of communications who succeeded Marcel Masse.

On the whole, this section reflects changing attitudes toward the nature of Canadian society during the 23 years that the previous broadcasting legislation was in effect: It actually specifies broadcasting measures that are contained in other legislation; in areas such as official languages, employment equity, and multiculturalism; and in the charter of rights that is part of the Canadian constitution of 1982.

The CRTC has been sensitive to social issues in a general way, for example, requiring the broadcasting industry to adopt codes on sexual stereotypes in programming and imposing adherence to these codes as a condition for broadcasters' license. The government, through various programs, has supported a range of aboriginal broadcasting activities that have greatly contributed to the social and cultural development of Canadian native communities.

Broadcasting has always been an object of pressure on the part of social groups struggling for empowerment. The new Broadcasting Act recognizes the legitimacy of many of these struggles and will undoubtedly be used as a legal peg on which to hang their future demands.[34]

The National Question

The question of Quebec remains the Achilles heel of the Canadian political system, and here too broadcasting (and culture and communications generally) continues to play a central role.

As shown earlier, Quebec opted for the status quo in its referendum of 1980. But that option was tempered by federal promises of a new constitutional arrangement that would take into account Quebec's historic demands. Instead, the federal government, with the support of the nine other provinces but over the objections of Quebec, repatriated the Canadian constitution from London in 1982. One of the objectives of the new government elected in 1984 was "national reconciliation" in the wake of further deteriorating Ottawa-Quebec relations as a result of the constitution.

Communications, and specifically broadcasting, was one area in which the Mulroney government made significant overtures to Quebec, giving the province a de facto say in the development of new services (which remained under formal federal jurisdiction), providing special support for francophone cultural industries, and opening the way for Quebec to participate directly in international projects like the French-language satellite service, TV5.

The government's general policy toward Quebec resulted in the 1987 Meech Lake Accord, in which Ottawa and all the provinces agreed on a formula to bring Quebec into the constitution. One of the most controversial clauses of the accord referred to Quebec as a "distinct society" within Canada—a reference with vague but possible far-reaching implications that raised the hackles of conservative elements in English-speaking Canada, as well as social groups, including groups representing women and natives, who felt that their own distinctive needs were consequently undermined.

The Meech Lake Accord died on June 23, 1990, after two provinces reneged on their initial support, and Canada entered a new phase of constitutional crisis as Quebec francophones were shocked into reawakened nationalism. At significant political cost to its popularity in English-speaking Canada, the government maintained special provisions on the distinctiveness of Quebec broadcasting in the final version of the Broadcasting Act. The main section in this respect reads: "English and French language broadcasting, while sharing common aspects, operate under different conditions and may have different requirements."[35] The act also toned down the section of the CBC's mandate referring to an obligation to contribute to the promotion of national unity. These were precisely the types of prescriptions that had rankled opponents of the Meech Lake Accord while mollifying the important segment of Quebec opinion that held that the only way Quebec would remain within Canada was on the basis of equality—with the irrevocable right to question its continued participation in the federation.

In 1991, Canada's political and constitutional future was as unclear as it had ever been. The options under consideration by Quebec ranged from outright separation from Canada to some form of binational federation to a radically renewed federalism. But with respect to communications, all projects on the drawing board spoke of full-scale repatriation of all jurisdiction over culture and communications—meaning that, as an opening bargaining position at least, Quebec will be demanding the legal authority to organize and regulate all broadcasting activity on its territory according to its own agenda.

CONCLUSIONS

The evolution of broadcasting worldwide was marked in the 1980s by the convergence of two parallel sets of changes, one technological and the other ideological. On the one hand, we became equipped with unprecedented capacity for the production and distribution of audiovisual material. On the other, we (or our leaders, to be more precise) came to believe that this new capacity should be used for market-based broadcasting business.

This evolution manifested itself in different ways in different contexts, resulting in a general questioning of the historic function of national broadcasting in a public service framework. Canada provides a particularly interesting vantage point for observing these changes because the types of questions they raise have been with us for such a long time—since the beginning of Canadian broadcasting.

What is the appropriate mix of public and commercial broadcasting activity within a single system? What is the appropriate relationship of foreign to domestic program origin, of national to regional program content? What is the appropriate social role for broadcasting?

Whereas the basic nature of broadcasting has usually been posed as a dichotomy in western Europe (broadcasting: public service or business?), in Canada, since 1932, broadcasting has been a hybrid entity (public service and business). Business has most of the time held the upper hand. Yet all broadcasting, regardless of ownership, vocation, or relationship to the marketplace, is deemed to be responsible to a principle of public service and can be challenged, at least formally, to meet that obligation.

There is no question that if this is so, it is only because of public pressure to keep it so. The Canadian example shows that not only have the most active and vociferous elements of Canadian society struggled to establish, promote, and sustain public broadcasting, but they have also struggled for the notion that public broadcasting should contribute to the democratization of public life—implying a range of institutions and practices beyond the classical model of a state-run or, as we call it, crown corporation.

In the intense debates on the future of Canadian broadcasting in the 1980s, there was a palpable shift from the traditional idea that public broadcasting could and should refer exclusively to a national broadcasting service. The Canadian Broadcasting Corporation remains the centerpiece, the most important single institution of the Canadian broadcasting system, but the space it occupies continues to diminish. At the same time, however, the total space occupied by public service broadcasting in Canada has been enhanced by the addition of provincial services in the four most populous provinces, by the formal recognition of community broadcasting as a distinct and legitimate part of the system, and by the active involvement in the policymaking process of representative organizations from dozens of less-than-national publics.

The public service commitment of Canadian broadcasting faces grave challenges, in spite of the rhetorical reassurances enshrined in the legislation governing it. These can be grouped in three categories that correspond to the geopolitical context.

The first set of problems is national and concerns the relationship between public service and capital within individual nation-states. Policymakers are currently encouraging, through regulatory favoritism and public funding, the emergence of broadcasting industries that they hope will be capable of competing on the world scale. The consequent contribution to public service is dubious to say the least.

The second set of problems is international and concerns the relationship between politically sovereign states. Although the cultural industries were formally excluded from the Canadian-American Free-Trade Agreement that came into effect in 1989, a "notwithstanding" clause enables either party to take reprisals if it can show preferential treatment of cultural industries by the other. Canadian cultural policy is on thin ice in this regard—as other countries are discovering as they attempt to protect and promote their cultural industries as well.

The third set of problems is less than national and concerns the relationship between groups that make up individual nation-states. The historic experience of broadcasting in the saga of Canada's constitutional development illustrates the problem of fragmentation brought about by the need to accommodate divergent national interests within the broadcasting systems of states where the question of nationhood is not resolved. At the same time, it illustrates the extent to which the politics of broadcasting constitute a microcosm of political life itself.

These three problem areas are symptomatic of the changing economic and political context of broadcasting in all Western nations. Clearly, they can be addressed only by looking at the overall ecology of broadcasting, locally, regionally, and globally, as well as nationally.

As in any attempt to take an ecological approach to problem solving, initial assumptions will be crucial. That is why we must look at the over-all context in which broadcasting takes place as a public service environment.

NOTES

1. The historical material in this chapter is drawn largely from Marc Raboy, *Missed Opportunities: The Story of Canada's Broadcasting Policy* (Montreal and Kingston: McGill-Queen's University Press, 1990).
2. Canada, Royal Commission on Radio Broadcasting, *Report* (Ottawa: King's Printer, 1929).
3. The role of this unique organization is discussed at some length in Raboy, *Missed Opportunities*, chap. 1. See also Margaret Prang, "The Origins of Public Broadcasting in Canada," *Canadian Historical Review* 46 (1, 1965), pp. 1-31.
4. On this question, see Herschel Hardin, *A Nation Unaware: The Canadian Economic Culture* (North Vancouver, B.C.: Douglas, 1974).
5. Canadian Radio Broadcasting Act, *Statutes of Canada* (1936), p. 51.
6. Ibid., p. 24.
7. See Raboy, *Missed Opportunities*, chap. 2.
8. Ibid., chap. 3.
9. Broadcasting Act, *Statutes of Canada* (1958), p. 22.
10. Raboy, *Missed Opportunities*, chap. 4. A particularly candid and revealing statement of government policy on this point is to be found in Canada, House of Commons, *Debates* (Hansard, 1964-1965), 10080-10086 (summarized in Raboy, *Missed Opportunities*, pp. 158-160).
11. Broadcasting Act, *Statutes of Canada* (1967-1968), p. 28; also in *Revised Statutes of Canada* (1970), p. B11.
12. Raboy, *Missed Opportunities*, chaps. 5 and 6.
13. Ibid., chap. 7.
14. Canada, House of Commons, Standing Committee on Communications and Culture, *Minutes* (1980-1983), pp. 2, 9.
15. Canada, Federal Cultural Policy Review Committee, *Report* (Ottawa: Minister of Supply and Services Canada, 1982), p. 273.
16. Canada, Department of Communications, *Towards a New National Broadcasting Policy* (Ottawa: Minister of Supply and Services Canada, 1983).
17. Ibid., p. 6.
18. Ibid., p. 20.
19. Canadian Broadcasting Corporation, "The Canadian Broadcasting System," in Canada, House of Commons, Standing Committee on Communications and Culture, ed., *Minutes* (Appendix 2, 1979), 4A, pp. 1-27.
20. Canadian Broadcasting Corporation, *The Strategy of the CBC* (Ottawa: Canadian Broadcasting Corporation, 1983).
21. Canada, Department of Communications, *Building for the Future: Towards a Distinctive CBC* (Ottawa: Minister of Supply and Services Canada, 1983).
22. Ibid., p. 7.
23. Ibid., p. 8.

24. Canada, Department of Communications, "Review of the Canadian Broadcasting System: Terms of Reference for the Task Force" (Ottawa: DOC Information Services, 9 April 1985).

25. This process is the object of a research project currently being conducted by the author. For a preliminary report, see Marc Raboy, "Policymaking in the Public Sphere: Pleading for Power in Canadian Broadcasting," paper presented at a meeting of the International Association for Mass Communication Research Congress (Bled, Yugoslavia, August 1990).

26. See Marc Raboy, "Two Steps Forward, Three Steps Back: Canadian Broadcasting Policy from Caplan-Sauvageau to Bill C-136," *Canadian Journal of Communication* 14 (1, 1989), pp. 70–75.

27. Broadcasting Act, Bill C-40, passed by the House of Commons (5 December 1990) and the Senate (1 February 1991).

28. Ibid., art. 3.1.b, emphasis added.

29. Ibid., art. 3.1.s, emphasis added.

30. Ibid., art. 3.1.m.

31. See Marc Raboy, "Lack of Bucks Riles Canucks: Public Broadcasting Taking the Heat in Canada," *Screen* 32 (4, 1990).

32. Canada, Department of Communications, *The Economic Status of Canadian Television: Report of the Task Force* (Ottawa: Minister of Supply and Services, 1991).

33. Ibid., art. 3.1.d.iii.

34. For further development of this question, see Marc Raboy, "From Cultural Diversity to Social Equality: The Democratic Trials of Canadian Broadcasting," *Studies of Broadcasting* 26 (1990), pp. 7–41.

35. Broadcasting Act, Bill C-40, art. 3.1.c.

CHAPTER 8

Public Service Broadcasting in the United States: Its Mandate, Institutions, and Conflicts

Willard D. Rowland, Jr.

HISTORICAL CONSTRAINTS

The concept of public service broadcasting developed slowly and late in the history of U.S. radio and television. Indeed, the public service notion has been institutionalized only marginally in the United States and, by comparison with most other advanced industrial, capitalist countries, at a rather low level of social and political commitment and material support. As Raymond Williams once argued, American public broadcasting has been added only "as a palliative" to the weaknesses and contradictions of the heavily dominant private, commercial system.[1] It has never had the centrality to American culture and politics that it has had in Britain, in virtually all western European and Scandinavian nations, and in several other countries (including Canada, Australia, New Zealand, and Japan). Though public service broadcasting in most of those countries is currently being challenged on various ideological, economic, and technological grounds,[2] it remains at the center of their cultural consciousness and communications policy debates; its predominant status and authority may be under concerted attack, but it is still the sine qua non of the national, electronic media experiences abroad. In the United States, for all the increases in financial support, station numbers, program sources, distribution means, and personnel during the past quarter century, public broadcasting remains a relatively remote and minor feature of American mass media and telecommunications and hence of sociopolitical discourse.

U.S. public service broadcasting was disenfranchised from the very outset.[3] During the emergence of popular mass audience radio broadcasting in the 1920s, there were few doubts about the public interest

157

adequacy of private, commercial forms of control and use. The ideology of a progressive, socially responsible private-enterprise economy had been so successfully resuscitated during the antitrust reform era and became so closely associated with equally optimistic expectations about the positive values of commercial forms of modern, popular communication that throughout the decade before the Great Depression there was little support for fashioning radio under any other template. The assumption remained that there was such considerable identity between private and public interests in broadcasting that, as in the simple models of eighteenth-century libertarianism, the best public services would emerge in a largely unfettered private enterprise. Occasionally, doubts were expressed about such prospects, and there were even explicit attempts to develop alternative, noncommercial radio services, typically under the auspices of educational, religious, labor, or municipal government institutions. But those concerns and institutional alternatives were at such odds with the predominant world view that they remained relatively weak and ineffectual during the crucial "ballyhoo" years of the 1920s, when the basic structure of American broadcasting was being erected. As a result, the Radio Act of 1927 made no provision for supporting or developing noncommercial broadcasting, and much of the work of the new Federal Radio Commission (FRC) also militated against the few existing public service efforts.

During the early 1930s, as the Depression deepened and a broader debate raged about appropriate economic and social reforms, there emerged a certain degree of dissatisfaction with the extent of public service in commercial radio.[4] Many educational institutions, particularly land-grant colleges and universities, tried to develop a separate system of educational stations, and to support that effort they sought legislation attempting to reserve AM frequency space for noncommercial or nonprofit licensees.

But by the mid-1930s, such statutory efforts, most notably the Wagner-Hatfield amendment to the 1934 Communications Act, had failed. As a result of the Depression and the discriminatory spectrum reallocation and other licensing policies of the FRC, many public agencies and private nonprofit institutions had withdrawn from radio operations (frequently selling out to commercial interests). With the number of active stations drastically reduced, the opportunity for much noncommercial production and for audiences to experience it were concomitantly lessened. In the absence of any major alternatives, the public was increasingly cultivated with the light-entertainment forms of commercial radio. Meanwhile, the industry was making considerable claims about its intentions of working with noncommercial interests to offer alternative educational and high cultural programming, and indeed for a period it seemed actually to be doing so. The educational leaders were themselves divided over how thoroughly separate a system of broadcasting was necessary. Simultaneously, whatever else the Roosevelt administration was accomplishing through its New Deal programs, it was not contemplating any significant restructuring of the U.S. broadcasting system.

Throughout this period, a small group of noncommercial stations, largely at state colleges and universities, did survive, and eventually, by the late 1930s, the Federal Communications Commission (FCC) had set aside reserved frequencies for their exclusive use. But those reservations had come late; they were only in the new, as yet unavailable FM band; and they were never extended back into the then predominant AM band. Further, they were preserved for a limited class of stations— "noncommercial educational." The name evoked something far less popular and less universal than the concept of public service broadcasting being developed abroad. This form of radio, in the United States, was seen to be necessary only in a relatively restricted domain of instructional, formally pedagogic service. Its models were principally those of the classroom—the lecture, the textbook, and the training film. Only fitfully did it dwell in the realms of drama, public affairs, or the popular. It was merely an alternative, at best a minor, secondary service with tiny resources and few public expectations that it should be anything more. During the heyday of American AM radio (1927-1955), noncommercial licensees had almost no presence in the medium, particularly in large population centers. There was no national, interconnected network, and funding remained minuscule by any standard abroad. With this poor heritage, the noncommercial radio service was so narrowly defined, so locally based, and so technologically limited that well into the 1970s it was barely audible in U.S. media culture.

By the time of World War II, as the economy was beginning to recover and international political crises stimulated wider debate about the meaning and health of American democracy, certain contradictions in U.S. mass media structures and practices had become somewhat more apparent. The inconsistencies between the promises of libertarian expectations for the several mass media and their actual performances were discussed in the report of the Commission on Freedom of the Press (the Hutchins Commission, 1943-1946).[5] More specific critiques of the radio industry were rendered in a special Hutchins Commission study, the White report,[6] and in a parallel FCC staff report, the Blue Book (1945-1946).[7] All three documents were couched in terms of what was becoming known as the social responsibility theory of the press and media behavior,[8] in which the failures of private, commercially sponsored, profit-driven media institutions were decried and recommendations for improved public service were issued. The Blue Book seemed to be laying the groundwork for stricter FCC regulation of public service performance by commercial licensees, and the Hutchins recommendations, supported by the critical White analysis, actually included provisions for a stronger noncommercial broadcasting effort and the introduction of federal government support.

However, neither the Blue Book nor the Hutchins report was ever adopted as official policy. They were too controversial, too explicitly threatening to the existing private enterprise interests and free-expression mythologies. They therefore had no immediate effect on basic terms of communication ownership, purpose, and control. The social responsibility theory was capable of sharp criticism, but as an essentially neolibertarian construct, it had little capacity for significantly affecting public and political attitudes about major, necessary structural changes. It was too much a creature of the progressive liberal reform ideology that had been fostering precisely the failures and contradictions that it was criticizing, and it never could transcend that dilemma. Despite mounting evidence to the contrary, the public interest was still thought to reside in an overwhelmingly private, commercial system tempered by the existing form of federal regulation. Public service communication values and institutions were never widely understood in the broader British, European, and Canadian terms. Indeed, the public service organizations abroad tended to be seen, and dismissed, as "state" broadcasting. It remained an article of faith that whatever weaknesses there were in the United States could be overcome in time through the workings of enlightened, public-spirited, private broadcasting leadership; moderate FCC oversight; and the introduction of yet another, newer electronic technology.

In this light, it is clearer why U.S. television also proceeded on a line of development that, patterned after radio, provided only a small space for formal public service institutionalization in anything approaching the models abroad. It is true that the FCC provided noncommercial frequency reservations earlier in the history of television (1952), preserving a somewhat broader initial niche. But again, the concept of television in this realm was strictly limited, and the practical resources to realize anything more were not there. To its academic, philanthropic, state educational, and private, high-cultural constituencies, noncommercial television was more exciting than educational radio and therefore, from the outset, it did attract somewhat more substantial support locally and nationally. Yet that support still tended to view this form of television in restricted terms. Its very name, ETV, evoked the old problem of "noncommercial educational" broadcasting. It was to be a service that was only a secondary alternative to the dominant private commercial enterprise, with little or none of the expectations of popularity, universal service, and wide-ranging subject matter associated with public television elsewhere. There remained a strong belief that private-enterprise, commercially supported television would provide enough to satisfy the public so that no other option need be addressed. As before, the belief was that any failures that might emerge in the commercial realm could be corrected by appeals to private broadcasters' consciences, gentle regulatory coercion, and an ETV service supported at minimal levels, largely by local interests, universities, and state authorities.

Furthermore, any tendency to question such assumptions or to invoke other public service models from abroad could be little advanced during the early Cold War/McCarthy era. That environment fostered jingoistic appeals to the most simplistic images of what was right and just in American values and institutions, and it trafficked in fear of anything alien or foreign, especially in such sensitive areas as communication, with all its trappings of concern about propaganda and freedom.

The weaknesses of the commercial-adequacy assumption were sufficiently apparent by the late 1960s that federal policy for broadcasting began to institutionalize certain adjustments. Federal support had moved beyond providing reserved frequencies to funding a few forms of instructional programming (1958) and the construction of noncommercial facilities (1962).[9] Now, particularly in the wake of the Carnegie Commission report of 1967 (Carnegie-I),[10] the government was bringing itself to the point of beginning to provide funds for more general programming, national systems of public radio and television interconnection, and other grants for local licensees to use at their discretion. That apparently changing federal policy reflected the interest among various national centers of private and public power and among many state governments and associated local private interests in increasing the number of local public television and radio facilities. Simultaneously, the more substantial federal initiative stimulated the state and local tendencies, with the result that the Public Broadcasting Act of 1967[11] helped lead to the creation of a larger, more powerful national-level superstructure, including the Corporation for Public Broadcasting (CPB), the Public Broadcasting Service (PBS), and National Public Radio (NPR); a proliferation of public stations; stronger regional activities; more hours of national programming; and a generally more widely available and attended range of services.

The change in name and status signaled a certain broadening of purpose and potential service; it seemed to be stating the case for a substantially refurbished and upgraded public service enterprise. There were wider expectations that public broadcasting should reach more people, address more interests, and generally elevate the quality of electronic media discourse. This was a trend that had begun in the mid-1950s, with the widening institutional basis of ETV licensee organizations in response to the expanding range of interests in noncommercial television's use. Various philanthropies, industrial interests, and other cultural organizations at the local level, most typified nationally by the Ford Foundation, had organized "community licensees" and had influenced other more traditional educational interests to encourage all forms of ETV stations to produce and carry a range of programming that was less formally instructional in nature. Efforts in drama, music, children's programming, and even public affairs began to be introduced with a broader, more general audience in mind. Such trends were particularly encouraged through the Ford-supported national production and distribution center, National

Education Television (NET), from the mid-1950s to the late 1960s.[12]

Meanwhile, during the 1960s and 1970s, licensee governance broadened to include a wider range of citizenry—leaders and representatives of an expanding realm of professional and social interests. Community group and state telecommunications authority licensees became increasingly prominent in local and national public broadcasting affairs, while local school district licensees actually declined. Although the number of university and state educational authority licensees increased, their boards, advisory committees, and managements tended to reflect a broader, less strictly educational orientation. These changes accelerated after the 1967 Public Broadcasting Act, which introduced additional federal funding and attracted attention to and support for noncommercial radio and television as a national enterprise, a public broadcasting "system." But as important as all these developments were, they were slow in coming, and they either papered over old tensions and problems or introduced new ones.

CONTEMPORARY ISSUES AND PROBLEMS

Identity and the Problem of the Public

When Carnegie-I invoked the term *public*, it was clearly trying to create a new image for the enterprise. It could not dismiss entirely the educational label, for too much policy support at the local, state, and federal levels had been built on the assumption of the inherent worth of the association with education. However, Carnegie did try to transcend the issue by incorporating broad notions of general audience service and high production quality that would earn much wider funding support from private and public sources, while yet retaining enough of the traditional educational values to qualify legitimately as something other than conventional commercial television.

Widely though not universally supported within public broadcasting, this approach did much to improve the attractiveness of the service to the broad moderate center of U.S. political and cultural tastes. But that very condition led to an increasing dilemma: the contradictions of popularity and publicness. For as noncommercial broadcasting had begun to call itself "public" and to use that title to justify calls for increased federal and state funds, it had also begun to be asked whether it ought not to be able to demonstrate a considerably wider audience reach on a more frequent basis. Yet at the same time, it was vulnerable to charges of trying to be too popular ("commercial") and also being too unaccountable to the public now providing it more support.

The popularity matter was, and remains, awkward. If more tax-based resources were to be dedicated to public broadcasting, should not it be both more universally available and more attractive to larger, even majority audiences, as with public broadcasting elsewhere? The technical problem of inadequate and unavailable signals could be overcome with more federal and state construction money. But what then? Should public broadcasting be expected to attract more of that newly available audience, and if so, how? Could public attention be increased through programming or services targeted to various special social, ethnic, and economic groups or through material of more general audience appeal? But then, by whatever means it might be becoming more popular, how would it avoid charges of engaging in ratings competition? If successful in building popular new program services, how would it adjust to charges of depressing the revenues of private broadcasters? How would it respond to losing some of its programs to the commercial marketplace, and would it generally manage to maintain a separate, supportable identity? On the one hand, there was concern about whether public broadcasting was not going to be popular enough, whether it would remain the province of educational and cultural elites and therefore unworthy of public funds whatsoever, let alone substantial increases. On the other hand, there was concern that it would become too popular, becoming indistinct from the conventional commercial services and in the process drawing so much audience and profitability from them that it would threaten the as yet fragile national policy consensus supporting its relatively recent elevation to a somewhat higher order of activity, presence, and status.

Simultaneously, the notion of publicness had also introduced difficult questions about governance, access, and accountability. These questions rose amid the 1960s and 1970s debates about the redistribution of power throughout U.S. society and institutions—the basic concerns about democratization in the struggles over civil rights, Vietnam, consumerism, and the environment. In that context, noncommercial broadcasting found that it could not claim to be public and yet avoid scrutiny about its responsibilities to that public. To accept more tax-generated funding, especially at the federal level, was to invite inquiry into its criteria and mechanisms for choosing governing boards and managements, for determining necessary services, and, generally, providing participation for diverse interests, particularly for those that had historically been underrepresented in U.S. broadcasting. Educational broadcasting had long been exempt from concerns about accountability—it had, after all, been fostered primarily in the halls of higher education, where considerations of academic freedom and protection from intense direct public scrutiny usually prevailed. As an educationally "liberal" activity, noncommercial broadcasting had also been accustomed to the benefit of the doubt about its social responsibilities—a presumption of inherent goodwill, progressivism, and general improvement over what existed in the commercial realm. Consequently, public broadcasting was not initially well prepared for charges of discrimination, elitism, and fiscal irresponsibility.

Few public broadcasters or their principal policy supporters seemed to be able to put these concerns into any historical perspective. In all the commentary and research on public broadcasting published in the period between Carnegie-I and the second Carnegie Commission report in 1979 (Carnegie-II),[13] there was virtually no recognition of the depth of the problem of publicness, no apparent awareness of the rich arguments about it stretching back through American history, with particularly acute expressions in the early-twentieth-century debates about pragmatism and progressivism.[14] Broadcasters and public policymakers seemed to have little or no knowledge of these arguments and about how they might bear on contemporary struggles over the new media. Demonstrating a relatively shallow social and political consciousness about this institution they were building, public broadcasters had few tools for understanding how serious, and not merely partisan and special-interest-based, were many of the questions being raised about its publicness.

As a result, when such questions became a more regular part of the policy debates in the mid- and late 1970s, many public broadcasting responses, as expressed in board meetings, national conferences, and political lobbying, were fearful and defensive, appearing to be insensitive and even reactionary. There was such resistance to inquiries about governance, accountability and access that many of the generally friendly forces in the policymaking arena were discomfited. Public interest groups, minority and feminist spokespersons, independent producers, and others began to suggest that public broadcasting was too inbred, too reflective of a white, male, upper-middle-class outlook that was much more closely associated with established, unprogressive forces in the social and economic order than it realized and hence that substantial alterations in policy for funding and oversight were necessary.

That criticism became institutionalized in the form of increasingly organized efforts by local citizen activist groups and, particularly, independent producers. The national program development policies worked out by CPB, PBS, and the stations during the 1970s heavily favored submissions from the existing stations, particularly larger "community" licensees in the major cities that had built substantial production plants. Writers and producers unaffiliated with such stations, and therefore independent of their managements, boards, and funding structures, had almost no access to the federally provided production funds channeled through CPB or to the national schedule controlled by PBS and its member stations.

In response to this situation, many of the independent producers and associated nonstation interests began to call for changes in the structure of national program funding. By at least the time of the 1978 Public Telecommunications Financing Act,[15] the influence of these groups was being felt and reflected in Congress. Some accommodations were made during the early and mid-1980s, but the independent producer community continued to feel that the program funding process was still stacked too systematically against it. Accordingly, through a steady process of representations before CPB and PBS, as well as a few major stations, the independents continued to organize themselves and achieve even more sympathetic hearings in Congress. Their efforts were parallel to, if not strictly modeled on, a similar set of activities abroad. Most other public broadcasting establishments had also come under fire for allegedly restricting production and programming practices, and those disputes had led to significant changes in national broadcast policies. Perhaps the most notable of these cases was the debate in Britain over the concept of the proposed Open Broadcast Authority and the eventual creation instead of Channel 4.[16]

In the United States, the independent efforts achieved a somewhat less dramatic but nonetheless unprecedented success when in 1988, as part of a new federal reauthorization bill, CPB was forced to set aside portions of its funds for the support of independent program efforts.[17] The new law also directed CPB to create and fund a new independent production service. The result was the formation in 1989 of a formal organization, the Independent Television Service (ITVS), that would coordinate program grants to nonstation producers to expand program diversity and innovativeness and thereby, presumably, to foster a wider range of program voices within the public television community.[18]

Meanwhile, from quite opposite, more conservative directions, public broadcasting was continuing to be accused of being, in fact, too immoderate, too "liberal," if not leftish, and too much a part of that coalition of old New Deal and recent Great Society forces that had been characterized as undermining traditional U.S. economic and spiritual values. It was also seen to be contributing to an overly large, stifling, and inflationary public sector and, like the National Endowments for the Arts and Humanities, to be serving the interests of too few in American society—in effect representing a public subsidy of private tastes and interests that should be forced to sustain themselves in the commercial marketplace.[19] From these various neoconservative perspectives, the post-Carnegie-I support for expanded federal aid had been a mistake, and a retrenchment to more traditional instructional purposes, if not outright elimination, was in order.

Finding public broadcasting under concerted attack from the left and the right, the liberal center, which during the late 1970s and early 1980s was otherwise under assault on a wide range of more general social and economic issues, felt much of its ground shifting, and the recent consensus over the unquestioned value of steadily and substantially increasing federal support for public broadcasting began to unravel. Meanwhile, public broadcasting itself continued to be unable to articulate a clear vision of what is meant by its claim to being a public enterprise and how that unexpressed philosophy should translate into a larger and more effective role in American social experience. As late as the early 1990s, there remained little evidence of public broadcasting leaders (including board members, chief executives, senior managers, and producers in the various national, regional, and local station organizations) being able to write or speak at length and in depth about the philosophy, history, and social expectations of their institution, let alone the broader realm of related questions about its role in American culture, politics, and social order.

Weak Public Discourse About Culture

The problem of articulating public broadcasting's identity and pursuing a sophisticated internal and external discussion about its role, goals, and needs has been fostered by a long-standing weakness in U.S. civic debate about culture and the role therein of broadcasting. Reflecting the ambivalences of the New World in its attitudes toward matters European and foreign, American popular commentary has always been confused about how to treat the fine arts and cultural institutions. What role should they play in education, daily life, and the very fabric of the Republic? Are they inherently elitist and antidemocratic? Can one be both a populist and a promoter of excellence in painting, sculpture, music, drama, and literature? Who is responsible for their support—governments, powerful quasi-public institutions, wealthy individual patrons, or the commercial marketplace? To what extent is it necessary to ensure balance among such sources? These questions became all the more confused with the rise of industrial mass communication and popular culture and the growing role of commercial mechanisms rooted in indirect indicators of taste, interest, and need as measured by circulation, box office, and ratings statistics.

Since the mass media have themselves been products of such forces, they have not been able to promote a systematic debate about their contradictions. A regular, daily argument about cultural policy and the arts has long been beyond the ken of most of the American press and media. As a result, the matter of broadcasting and especially of television has been all the more elusive. "Culture" tends to be treated as something apart from real life, and therefore it is relegated to the Sunday feature sections of the largest or most status-conscious newspapers or to the "lifestyle" sections of the rest. The daily coverage of television has consisted largely of program schedules, synopses, and Hollywood gossip generated by media promotion offices. In the traditional newshole, coverage of cultural and media policy matters has been shallow and, at least until quite recently, remarkably uninformed and naive. Reporters and commentators, even for the better papers and magazines, tend to come to the subject with little background in the broader, more difficult currents of contradictory American experiences with culture and industrialized media. Only rarely do the media columnists manage to transcend these constraints and build a record of sophisticated criticism into which the more subtle cultural policy considerations of public broadcasting can fit.

Occasionally, public broadcasting becomes embroiled in a debate about a particular public affairs program or documentary, and that episode may draw a certain amount of sustained newspaper and even television journalistic attention. But that is usually the extent of public broadcasting coverage, and that is precisely the problem. As with coverage of federal or state arts and humanities programs, public broadcasting is likely to be considered newsworthy only if it reflects some evidence of overt government interference or if there is some financial scandal. Once the immediate crisis is over, the reporter and periodical move on to other subjects. They seldom revisit the topic, and those who will pick it up later typically do so unaware of what has been written before.

Given this background, it is not surprising that public knowledge of and ability to discuss public broadcasting has been rather limited. To be sure, public broadcasting is typically seen as a "good thing" by the few reviewers who pay it any regular attention, and it has therefore probably been more praised than condemned in the popular press. Even in the cases of complaints about its public affairs coverage, the origins of the critiques are usually so clearly partisan that little damage is done by them. In such instances, public broadcasting may even earn sympathetic support. More important, perhaps, public broadcasting tends to benefit from the periodic, almost ritualistic outbursts of argument and handwringing by politicians and editorialists over commercial television—its amounts of gratuitous violence, its lack of serious service for children, its appeal to lowest-common-denominator values, and its overall "poor quality." But as has long been the case, the tendency in such rhetoric is to see public broadcasting only as a relatively minor corrective. There remains in the United States almost no literature or ongoing critical commentary that can state the case for public broadcasting in broad, universal terms, envisioning it as a major cultural and political institution that might command sustained majority attention. Even people within public broadcasting itself seldom make this case.

Without overstating the quality and range of cultural debate abroad, it is fair to say that one will tend to find in other industrialized countries a more regular, informed discussion of public broadcasting. At the very least, one encounters quite frequent, often daily, reviews of programs, as well as weekly treatments of institutional and policy issues in readily accessible publications. Throughout such coverage there runs an ability to take all forms of media and public broadcasting seriously, to tie them to broader themes of social and political debate, but to do so without being either pedantic or sensationalistic.

The absence of comparable U.S. coverage of the media has been a serious weakness in internal American discourse about popular culture, and it has been especially harmful to an understanding and general promotion of public broadcasting. As a set of media and program services that ideally stand in opposition to conventional American ways of organizing broadcasting, public broadcasting is hampered by a public commentary that remains relatively unschooled and purposeless. Meanwhile, the institution itself has done little to lead or foster the debate in ways other than individual program promotions or periodic fund-raising appeals.

On the surface, the problem of weak public discourse about culture might seem to be less substantial than other issues, such as funding difficulties and structural tensions. Yet in the end, precisely because it suggests the way in which so much in American culture and communications is taken for granted, little discussed, and poorly understood, it might be one of the serious, lasting problems facing the institution.

Technology and the New Commercial Marketplace

Throughout the post-Carnegie-I period, most private and public centers of policymaking activity had been developing an increasing interest in, if not fascination with, the emergence of the new electronic technologies and related reassessments of federal economic and regulatory policy. Many communication policy positions, emerging during the late 1970s and early 1980s, including the continuing efforts to revise the basic communications legislation, were based on attacks on traditional statutory and regulatory assumptions about spectrum and information technology realities. They centered on proposals for encouraging a wider range of technological application through broader uses of marketplace mechanisms. Those propositions were developed and made ever more central to the policy debate through a vast amount of private, official, and academic literature.[20]

The history, terms, and ultimate contradictions of the new policy premises wrapped up in that literature have finally begun to come under closer critical review.[21] The counterpremises in the current critical communication literature raise questions about the universal adequacy of marketplace models in communication, the truly revolutionary potential for new technology, the actual applied meanings of diversity and service in the deregulated environment, and the nature of the primary interests being served by the new orthodoxy. These findings clearly have significance for public broadcasting policy options and may in time have some corrective impact on the policy climate. But such perspectives were so thoroughly ignored in the initial embrace of marketplace rhetoric that there was not much capacity for having a sophisticated debate about their implications for the relative needs and problems of public broadcasting.

Public broadcasters were hardly unaware of the significance of the technological changes enveloping them. A series of studies, conferences, and planning documents from 1977 to 1980 give evidence of the degree to which many public broadcasting professionals were engaged in debate about the extent of change in telecommunications technology and their role in it.[22] But discussion and planning are one thing; action and implementation are another. For all their insight into the changing environment of delivery systems and content categories associated with the developments in cable, satellites, ITFS, MDS, videotex, ISDN, and other aspects of informatics, and for all the attempts in many corners of public broadcasting to provide new, diverse services that would take advantage of such opportunities and demonstrate to policymakers the indispensable nature of those activities, public broadcasters found it difficult to make major, dramatic changes. Having only just hit their stride in the post-Carnegie-I phase of establishing a certain pattern of programming services and having made apparently successful accommodations with major segments of their audiences around those program forms, public radio and television reflected a degree of inertia and caution that worked against suggestions for rapid new redefinitions of themselves as "public telecommunications." Accordingly, all the extensive proposals for revised and broadened multiple programming and delivery services, new funding commitments, and a wholesale expansion of public broadcasting capacity in the 1978–1981 period were reduced to minor corporate restructurings that largely begged the long-term questions about purpose, identity, and impact.[23]

By the late 1980s, public television had once again begun to rediscover the changing technological and program market conditions. But its responses remained sluggish, piecemeal, and severely restricted. Most of what had been predicted in the planning efforts—and then ignored—a decade earlier had come to pass. Via cable and satellite, a majority of U.S. households were now able to receive two to three dozen television signals, with the result that the old single public television station was increasingly lost in a much bigger sea of television offerings. That situation had been exacerbated by the rapidly growing videocassette recorder and video rental industries, which were making inroads in both general and vocational viewing patterns. Simultaneously, as noted earlier, the independent producer community had continued to grow and, as a result of the persistently reluctant responses to its challenges, had managed to secure special legislation diverting federal funds to it and otherwise empowering the independents against the stations and older national agencies.

The trajectory of the public television responses to the rise of competing program services and delivery mechanisms was particularly telling. The initial planning efforts in the 1978–1980 period had pointed directly at the rise of the sorts of services that came to be institutionalized in such channels as Arts & Entertainment, Discovery, and Nickelodeon. Here were precisely the elements of high culture, science, and children's programming that defined much of the core of public television. Yet at the outset, when some of these services had experienced initial growing pains and fiscal difficulties, the response by the public television community had been to see those problems as signs of long-term weaknesses and as evidence that they would fail. Hard analysis gave way to wishful thinking. Much to its surprise and dismay, however, public television found that the new commercial services would not, in fact, disappear and that it had to begin to deal directly with them. By 1990, having failed to establish its own claims in these areas, public television was actually seeking joint production and distribution agreements with the commercial cable television arts and special-interest ventures.[24]

Meanwhile, there were other programming elements that might be considered legitimate public service forms that the public television community seemed largely to ignore. These included such things as live legislative proceedings and even minority sports with which public television had at various times experimented. However, throughout the 1980s, it had increasingly left such efforts to others in cable, most notably C-SPAN, the local government channels, and ESPN.

Then, in the late 1980s, Whittle's Channel One, a commercially sponsored schools broadcasting service, and Jones Intercable's Mind Extension University, providing accredited degree programs via cable, struck directly at one of the principal legs of noncommercial public broadcasting—its longtime and heretofore exclusive instructional and educational mandate. Beginning in 1989 the cable industry even went so far as to create formal, new capacities for coordinating and promoting its educational efforts.[25] Though in large part this was an effort to impress Congress, which by the late 1980s was hearing enough public complaints about the effects of its Cable Communications Act of 1984 to be considering new regulatory legislation, the cable industry was nonetheless actually beginning to provide formal instructional television services. The public television response to these initiatives was largely bemused and in some quarters even hostile. As with the cable arts, science, and children's program experience earlier, many in public television responded by denying the quality of the upstart services and their capacity to survive and hoping they would just go away.[26]

Finally, although the number of public television stations had grown to the point that two or three were frequently available in each community, most of the overlapping stations remained largely competitive with one another. In spite of all the evidence of the changed technological and program market environment, the public television system was still unable to reorganize its local delivery capacity to take advantage of precisely the opportunities that others were using to challenge it.

A model of multiple, complementary program services, to be delivered variously by broadcasting, cable, satellite, cassette, and video disk, providing a range of distinct forms for children's, public affairs, drama, independent production, instruction, and possibly many other areas, had been laid out for it at least a decade earlier.[27] This model would have permitted public television to take advantage of all the broadcast television frequencies available to it while also folding in the many other delivery opportunities that were appearing, thereby permitting it to make much more efficient use of its available facilities and adapting new ones to its purposes. Yet in 1989–1990, as in 1979–1980, it was spending the bulk of its energy and internal political resources on merely another corporate restructuring, this time to consolidate the power of program decision making in one office at PBS.[28] Not necessarily an inappropriate change, and clearly mandated in some form or another by section 7(h) of the 1988 Public Telecommunications Act, that adjustment was nonetheless only a small piece of what was necessary. The almost exclusive focus on it by Congress, public television, and the popular press ignored the much bigger nature of the problem. It reflected a restricted, single-service image of public television, a pattern of thinking that had remained relatively unchanged since Carnegie-I. Public television was still reacting to, not anticipating and getting ahead of, the commercial high-technology ventures in its own backyard.[29]

Public radio had faced a number of similar challenges. But initially, most of its readjustment efforts had gone into the search for venture business and other enterprises to help NPR deal with budget reductions. NPR fiscal management had gone seriously awry during the early 1980s, and far from being able to think through all the appropriate new programming directions for NPR and the radio system generally, the stations and CPB were faced with the substantial task of staving off NPR bankruptcy.[30] During the mid-1980s, there was a series of debates within public radio about its organizational structure, programming, and fiscal distribution mechanisms. At the outset, those discussions tended to focus largely on matters of corporate structure and plans for increasing audience ratings, and although they led in part to a reorganization known as "unbundling," they did not attend to the larger, more enduring questions about public radio's role in American society.[31] Beginning in 1988, however, the public radio community undertook a far more sophisticated strategic planning debate about its purposes, necessary services, and appropriate position in a rapidly changing social and technological environment. That process included a wide-ranging set of position papers, hearings, conferences, and planning reports and discussion of such notions as a shift from public radio to "public audio" and more diversified audience communities. This debate closely resembled the initial and most promising phases of the public television planning efforts a decade earlier, demonstrating a similar sensitivity to the more important social issues.[32] The question remained, however, whether the far-reaching recommendations about public radio expansion emanating from that review could begin to be implemented or whether, as with the prior public television experience, they would eventually be reduced to the minor aspects of internal, organizational restructuring.

FUNDING

Several difficulties have always been associated with the funding of public broadcasting, most of them involving particular structural weaknesses among the various sources of revenue. However, far and away the most serious problem about funding has been its utter inadequacy. Whatever other problems it might reflect, U.S. public broadcasting simply has not had anywhere near the amount of resources necessary for it to provide the extensive range of services that are consistent with its central cultural role abroad and even the most modest U.S. models of public telecommunications.

Because the poverty lament was so old and persistent, many supporters of public broadcasting, and indeed many within the enterprise itself, had grown weary of the argument. They pointed out all the positive signs. By 1990, annual revenues—over $1.5 billion (see Table 8.1)—were sufficient to support roughly 1,000 radio and television stations, a sophisticated satellite distribution system, two full-time national networks, and various other national and regional services; thousands of hours of original programming every year, much of it of exceptionally high quality; and a professional cadre of over 10,000 employees.

But by almost any other measure, U.S. public broadcasting was grossly undersupported. Its total revenues were only about 4 percent of those of American commercial broadcasting, its numbers of stations were only 10 percent of those in the commercial industry, and its national program production funds were only one-fifth or less of what the commercial cable television industry was already spending on programs.[33] Its per capita rate of support—the annual amount of public broadcasting revenue per citizen of the country—remained well below that of all other advanced industrial first-world nations, and its program production rate, particularly in television, was far smaller than all other public service broadcasting institutions around the world.[34]

Clearly, public broadcasting's financial situation had improved considerably over the previous quarter century. The infusion of federal funds helped strengthen the other public and private sources of support (see Table 8.2). However, although its capital and program service base was some 16 times that of what it was in the late 1960s, it must be kept in mind that such growth was measured against a tiny, almost invisible baseline and was therefore deceptively large.

The specific funding problems were all serious and can perhaps best be understood by analyzing each of the key categories of support in turn.

Tax-Based Funding

Federal Funds.   Other than the relatively small amounts of ETV facilities and ITV production support prior to the late 1960s, federal

TABLE 8.1 Total Funding of U.S. Public Broadcasting (millions of dollars)

Fiscal Year	Federal		Nonfederal						Total	
	Total	Percent	State and Local Tax-based	Percent	Private	Percent	Total	All Percent	Sources	Percent
1972[a]	59.8	(25.5)	107.7	(46.0)	66.8	(28.5)	174.5	(74.5)	234.3	(100.0)
1973	55.6	(21.8)	127.3	(50.0)	71.9	(28.2)	199.2	(78.2)	254.8	(100.0)
1974	67.1	(23.1)	139.1	(47.9)	84.3	(29.0)	223.4	(76.9)	290.4	(100.0)
1975	92.3	(25.3)	156.6	(42.9)	115.9	(31.8)	272.4	(74.7)	364.8	(100.0)
1976	130.1	(30.0)	175.9	(40.6)	127.3	(29.4)	303.2	(70.0)	433.3	(100.0)
1977	135.3	(28.1)	191.3	(39.7)	155.6	(32.3)	346.8	(71.9)	482.1	(100.0)
1978	160.8	(29.1)	218.2	(39.5)	173.4	(31.4)	391.6	(70.9)	552.3	(100.0)
1979	163.2	(27.0)	245.5	(40.7)	194.7	(32.3)	440.2	(73.0)	603.5	(100.0)
1980	192.5	(27.3)	271.6	(38.5)	240.7	(34.2)	512.3	(72.7)	704.9	(100.0)
1981	193.7	(25.2)	277.5	(36.1)	297.7	(38.7)	575.2	(74.8)	768.9	(100.0)
1982	197.6	(23.4)	301.0	(35.6)	346.6	(41.0)	647.6	(76.6)	845.2	(100.0)
1983	163.7	(18.2)	318.3	(35.4)	417.1	(46.4)	735.5	(81.8)	899.2	(100.0)
1984	167.0	(17.1)	334.5	(34.3)	472.8	(48.5)	807.3	(82.9)	974.2	(100.0)
1985	179.2	(16.3)	358.4	(32.7)	558.7	(51.0)	917.1	(83.7)	1,096.3	(100.0)
1986	185.7	(16.4)	378.8	(33.4)	569.5	(50.2)	948.3	(83.6)	1,134.0	(100.0)
1987	243.0	(18.8)	389.2	(30.1)	662.3	(51.2)	1,051.5	(81.2)	1,294.5	(100.0)
1988	247.5	(18.1)	415.8	(30.4)	704.1	(51.5)	1,119.9	(81.9)	1,367.4	(100.0)
1989	263.9	(17.3)	451.3	(29.5)	812.3	(53.2)	1,263.6	(82.7)	1,527.6	(100.0)

[a]First year for which detailed nonfederal data are available. All percentages are of total federal and nonfederal income.

SOURCE: Association for Public Broadcasting; Corporation for Public Broadcasting.

173

TABLE 8.2 Federal Funding of U.S. Public Broadcasting (millions of dollars)

Authorizing Legislation	Federal: Fiscal Year	Corporation for Public Broadcasting		Facilities		Other Grants and Contracts	Total Federal Funds
		Authorization	Appropriation	Authorization	Appropriation		
Public Broadcasting Act of 1967 (PL 90-129)	1963-67			—	32.0		32.0
	1968	9.0		—	—		
Public Broadcasting Financing Act of 1970 (PL 91-411)	1969	9.0	5.0	12.5	3.2		8.2
	1970	20.0	15.0	15.0	5.4		20.4
	1971	35.0	23.0	15.0	11.0		34.0
	1972	35.0	35.0	15.0	13.0	11.8	59.8
CPB Appropriation Authorization (PL 92-411)	1973	45.0	35.0	15.0	13.0	7.6	55.6
CPB Appropriation Authorization (PL 93-84)	1974	55.0	47.8[a]	25.0	15.7	3.6	67.1
	1975	65.0	62.0	30.0	12.0	18.3	92.3
Public Broadcasting Financing Act of 1975 (PL 94-192)	1976[b]	110.0	96.0	30.0	12.9	21.2	130.1
	1977	103.0	103.0	30.0	14.0	18.3	135.3
	1978	121.0	119.2	30.0	18.0	23.6	160.8
	1979	140.0	120.2	40.0	18.0	25.0	163.2
	1980	160.0	152.0	40.0	23.7	16.8	192.5

Public Telecommunications Financing Act of 1978 (PL 98-214)	1981	180.0	162.0	40.0	19.7[a]	10.0	193.7
	1982	200.0	172.0	20.0	18.0	7.6	197.6
	1983	220.0	137.0[a]	15.0	15.0	11.7	163.7
Omnibus Reconciliation Act of 1981 (PL 97-35) and FCC Authorization Act of 1983 (PL 99-272)	1984	145.0	137.5	12.0	11.9	17.6	167.0
	1985	153.0	150.5	—	24.0	4.7	179.2
	1986	162.0	159.5	24.0	22.9[a]	3.3	185.7
Consolidated Omnibus Budget Reconciliation Act of 1985 (PL 99-272)	1987	200.9	200.0	28.0	20.5	22.5	243.0
	1988	214.9	214.9	32.9	19.6	13.9	247.5
	1989	238.0	228.0	36.9	19.8	16.1	263.9
	1990	254.0	229.4[a]	39.0	20.0		
Public Telecommunications Act of 1988 (PL 100-626)	1991	245.0 +200.0[c]	242.1[d] +56.8[c]	42.0	20.8		
	1992	265.0	251.0 +76.3		22.5		
	1993	285.0	253.3 +65.3				

[a]Less than final appropriation due to impounding, recission, or sequestration.
[b]CPB data for 1976 includes transition quarter (appropriations, $17.5 million).
[c]Added figures are for the Satellite Replacement Fund.
[d]Appropriations for 1991–1993 are not final; they remain subject to further reductions.

SOURCE: America's Public Television Stations; Corporation for Public Broadcasting.

revenues were unavailable for noncommercial broadcasting. After the 1967 legislation and the creation of CPB, the total amount of federal support (for CPB, facilities, and ITV) grew from some $7 million in 1966 to over $250 million in 1990. But by any expectation that public broadcasting should become a major influence in American life, such figures remained tiny.

Furthermore, efforts to generate the federal funds have proved to be controversial and difficult. They have required the expenditure of considerable amounts of political capital and energy by public broadcasting leaders, and they have regularly been subject to serious reconsideration and even cuts. Those realities have had substantial costs that many people would consider to be too high. For such a relative pittance, public broadcasters have had to engage in constant, intensive lobbying and begging, thereby exposing themselves to regular political oversight and its vicissitudes and requiring them to divert considerable energy and resources from other presumably more essential tasks, such as program service development and production.

When Carnegie-I first proposed a system of federal funding, it envisioned a taxing mechanism that would generate substantial and increasing revenues placed in a trust fund so that regular government influence over their disbursement and use would be prevented. It was felt that nothing like the receiving-set licensee fee so common in most other countries would be feasible. Nor was it thought appropriate that advertising revenue should be permitted. Instead, funding proposals focused on various tax options, particularly on the sales of receiving sets, on commercial broadcasting revenues or profits, and on commercial uses of the spectrum. Yet none of these had sufficient political support, and when the 1967 act was passed, it left the matter of federal funding up to Congress and the president as part of the annual authorizations and appropriations process typical for the vast majority of government programs. Furthermore, the amounts generated by that process were initially quite low, well below even the modest levels that Carnegie had contemplated as necessary for a minimally effective public service enterprise.

Within a few years, the weaknesses of the annual authorization and appropriation process became widely apparent, particularly in the wake of the Nixon administration's veto of the 1973 authorization measure and associated charges of political interference with the CPB board and public affairs programming.[35] Many professionals still held out hope for a dedicated, more permanent source of federal funds, but because the political will for establishing such a mechanism did not seem to be strong enough and because it was unclear that even a trust fund would be free of regular appropriations review by Congress, a compromise arrangement was reached. The new scheme had three essential principles: Funds for CPB would come from general treasury revenues with authorizations guaranteed five years in advance and appropriations for three of those, the amount of federal funds would be generated by a "system match" formula that constituted a fixed ratio between federal funds and the total amount of nonfederal financial support (NFFS) raised by all the licensees up to the ceiling provided by the authorizations, and the amounts to be distributed to the different media (radio and television) and to the licensees would be stipulated statutorily. These provisions went into effect in 1975 and were extended and adjusted in 1978.

For a period, the new provisions seemed to be having positive effects (see Tables 8.1 and 8.2). The guaranteed authorizations were progressively high enough (from $65 million in 1975 to $220 million in 1983) to encourage significant NFFS growth under the system match formula, and the terms of that ratio, initially 2.5 (federal to nonfederal), were improved to 1:2. Total nonfederal income more than doubled between 1975 and 1981 ($272.4 million to $575.2 million).

However, at the very moment of its initial success, the new federal funding mechanism began to break down in significant ways. The main difficulties were that the 1975 law's multiyear authorizations, which had been in effect barely two years, were reduced from five to three years in the 1978 act; the three-year advanced appropriations were actually only being made in the first of the three years, thereby making them, in effect, only two-year advances; and the authorization and appropriation steps remained separate, as with all government programs. The result was that the federal funding process was not at all long-range, nor was it particularly well insulated, in that it was requiring public broadcasting to return to the administration and Congress at least every two years to seek renewed appropriations. Then, during the Reagan administration's major federal budget reassessments of 1981–1983, the actual appropriations for public broadcasting, which had reached a peak of $172 million in 1982, were rescinded and cut. Federal support for CPB fell back to $137 million in 1983, and the facilities funds, which had peaked at $23.7 million in 1980, dipped to $11.9 million in 1984.

During the mid- and late 1980s, the situation improved somewhat, as the CPB appropriation rose to $229.4 million and the facilities program to $20 million by 1990. But in spite of these improvements, the situation remained tenuous, the stable federal funding recommended by Carnegie-I still out of reach. The carefully crafted compromise principles for federal revenue generation in the 1975 and 1978 financing acts were in shambles. For two years (1984–1986), public broadcasting had actually been without federal authorizations, and for all intents and purposes, the system match mechanism had been abandoned, as the actual federal appropriations fell well short of the amounts that would have been generated by the existing NFFS ratio. Public broadcasters struggled long and hard during the 1983–1986 period to secure renewed multiyear authorization measures. However, in 1984, two such bills, seemingly well supported by Congress, were vetoed by the president, and those vetoes were sustained. It was not until

1986 that an authorization measure was finally signed. Yet even then the advance authorizations were only for three years, until 1990, and the appropriations only for two, until 1989. In 1988, a new authorization bill was passed, but again for only another three years, and the eventual appropriations through 1992 continued to fall well short of the authorized amounts.[36]

Similar conditions dogged the facilities program. Although the Reagan administration had failed to eliminate facilities support, it succeeded in greatly reducing the authorizations for several years and forcing the appropriations to level out at about $20 million a year.

Much of the overt Reagan era hostility to public broadcasting funding began to ebb during the first two years of the Bush administration. Public broadcasters were also blessed during that period with the passage of an important three-year satellite replacement program (1991–1993). However, those improvements should not be overinterpreted. The authorizations were well below the levels the old system match formula would generate, and the actual appropriations continued to be less than even those authorizations.[37] The facilities funds were also far below what was necessary to build a truly substantial multichannel system of public radio and television. Meanwhile, under the new Gramm-Rudman-Hollings deficit reduction program, those already reduced CPB and facilities appropriations came to be subject to "sequestration" (further fixed-percentage reductions). Likewise, although the satellite program has been treated as an additional benefit, it almost certainly had the effect of helping to restrict the growth in both CPB and facilities funds.[38] Furthermore, the three- and two-year authorization-appropriation process, particularly with the annual sequestration battles, kept public broadcasting on a short tether. Its leadership and supporters appeared to have given up hope of any major funding increases and of anything like the long-promised middle- or long-range guarantees of even the modest amounts it was receiving.

During the 1980s, public broadcasting continued to enjoy sufficient bipartisan congressional support to prevent a hostile administration from realizing its goal of eliminating federal funding. That support even permitted certain recoveries by the late 1980s. But that help proved to be too weak to prevent such assaults from regularly reappearing, particularly under the guise of the seemingly more objective criteria of budget deficit reduction targets.

Even with the renewed upward trend of federal authorizations and appropriations, public broadcasting was forced back into the defensive posture of having to appeal annually for every funding measure while also struggling against recission and sequestration cuts in the appropriations up through the end of every year for which they were granted. The effects of this process were to continue to focus public broadcasting leadership energies on short-term problems and to bind them tightly to the political agenda of the moment. As revealed during the 1990–1991 efforts to prepare for the next reauthorization bill (to extend to 1996 the legislation that would expire in 1993), public broadcasting had neither the time nor the energy to stand back from these essentially annual funding struggles to look ahead and plan for any significant rearticulations of its purpose and needs. The very mechanisms of the federal funding process, as much as the inadequate amount, almost guaranteed that public broadcasting would be capable of only the most modest reassessment of its goals and capacities. It could reorganize a particular national program service office or align itself with a renewed interest in education, but it could not plan for, let alone implement, significant, far-reaching changes in the entire range of services and national and local delivery means.[39]

State and Local Funding.   State and local government support for educational or public broadcasting has always been a larger source of capital and recurring revenue than federal income (see Figure 8.1). That support for university licensees and state educational board and telecommunications authority stations, as well as for various state and local instructional programs, sustained a considerable portion of the system growth in the 1960s and 1970s. Its steady increase during the late 1970s and early 1980s, when state government budgets were otherwise widely leveling off or dropping, did much to offset the reductions in federal support. That growth remained remarkably solid even through the breakdown of the system match principle in the federal funding process.

However, while state and local support was significant and even increasing, the fact remained that its growth was slow and modest enough to guarantee only minor continued increases in public broadcasting facilities and program services. Proportionately, it also declined from about 50 percent of overall public broadcasting revenues in the early 1970s to about 30 percent in the late 1980s.

State government funding also varied widely in type and amount across the country; many states did not make public broadcasting a high priority. Even where such support was substantial, it was typically annual and at the most biennial in character, its overall levels showed no dramatic increases, and its actual proportion of overall public broadcasting funding was still shrinking. Thus while state support remained a substantial pillar of U.S. public broadcasting, it was unclear whether it could become the basis for anything more significant (that is, for a major increase in the numbers of noncommercial public service channels and program efforts).

State funding had always been predicated on the educational and instructional potential of public broadcasting. The strength of its persistence and even growth over the years suggested the possibility of a continuing willingness of states to invest in the enterprise. It was also clear throughout the late 1980s that many state governments were intrigued by the possibilities of more sophisticated educational telecommunications, particularly under the rubric of "distance learning." As improved quality of education became a popular political response to questions about economic

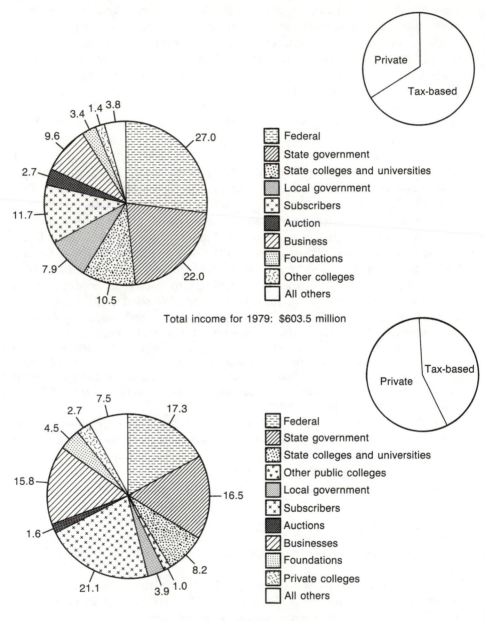

FIGURE 8.1   Sources of funding for U.S. public broadcasting, 1979 and 1989

SOURCE: Corporation for Public Broadcasting.

recovery, state governments were widely offering incentives to all levels of education (elementary and secondary schools, junior colleges, and universities) to become much more involved in the use of advanced technologies to deliver instructional programs. As always before in debates about the uses of new technologies in education, the premises of such initiatives were hotly argued, but the renewed state interest in the matter suggested possibilities for continuing to develop the state commitment to the educational public broadcasting enterprise. A few people within public broadcasting had always seen the potential of expanding the linkages in this realm, particularly through the "public telecommunications center" or "public teleplex" concepts,[40] but there remained sufficient uncertainties about it that there were never the sorts of fully developed, nationally led programs that would explore the full service and funding potential of such models. As a result, few public broadcasters were directly and forcefully testing the states' willingness to work with them in this area and thereby leverage more state funding.

Private Funding

Altogether, the various forms of private funding grew at substantial rates after the early 1970s. Sources included membership subscriptions, commercial underwriting, and foundation grants. Accounting for only about one-fifth of all public broadcasting funds in 1970, they amounted to more than one-third by 1980, and then, during the 1980s, they more than trebled, accounting for well over one-half by 1990. The success of private funding was such that it almost perfectly replaced state and local tax-based funds as the dominant form of public broadcasting support. Among its elements were two principal forms that merit brief discussion.

Memberships and Subscriptions.   Up through the late 1950s, memberships and subscriptions were little used outside of a few listener-supported radio stations and the new community corporation ETV licensees. In time, particularly with the emergence of the Carnegie notion of public broadcasting, stations of all sorts began soliciting membership subscriptions, even eventually school and university licensees. Such patronage practices were already common in the arts and other cultural and social activities, as in the support of symphony orchestras, opera companies, museums, and hospitals. Their adoption in noncommercial broadcasting reflected a certain expectation that public radio and television might play comparable roles in communities around the country. By the late 1980s, membership solicitation came to provide over 20 percent of public broadcasting's total income.

The initial rapid growth and sustained availability of such support had been highly encouraging for public broadcasting throughout the 1970s. It signaled a sort of audience loyalty and commitment that offset the discouraging news of regularly low ratings. It also provided a significant margin of increased income for public stations, permitting the necessary extra element in various important program service and capital projects. But there had always been certain reservations about the role and costs of such support. For instance, it raised a fairness issue about whether viewers and listeners should have additional responsibilities for public broadcasting above and beyond the funds they provided through taxes. Simultaneously, it raised the publicness question—that is, for whom does public broadcasting exist and by whom should it be controlled? Since only about 10 percent of the regular public broadcasting audience subscribed, there emerged the possibility of a special set of rights for those members to determine program service content. Such rights often seemed to be acknowledged by fund-raising campaigns that impressed on the audience the extent to which their contributions were necessary to confirm station decisions about purchasing or producing particular programs. Those appeals raised questions about how much disenfranchisement of the rest of the taxpaying audience might be occurring.

Meanwhile, the considerable efforts necessary to secure subscriptions had other substantial costs. Station managements had to invest considerable amounts of time and energy in their fund-raising efforts. They had to build up large development staffs, and in many cases, particularly in public television, they had to make trade-offs for such activities against local program planning and production efforts. In many of the television stations, the local program production staffs were eliminated or folded into the development office, so that the sole or major local production activities became the annual auctions or fund-raising appeals. As a result, much of the community program service effort was absorbed by the local cable access groups, who quite often had little or no relationship with the public broadcasting licensee. This drift exacerbated the estrangement between public broadcasters and the independent production communities; most significant, it took public broadcasting out of the realm of local political and social affairs. Particularly in television, public broadcasting's identity was increasingly that of an outlet for a national service, not as a forum for local voices and issues.

Finally, there was the continuing question about the long-term prospects for membership revenue. With federal deregulation permitting increases in cable subscription fees, with the persistence of various special pay services on cable, and with the changes in the federal income tax law governing deductions of charitable contributions, it was unclear that individual membership could be expected to grow much more. Indeed, by 1989-1990, there was a marked leveling off in this area for public television.[41]

The FCC's reluctance to maintain firm cable must-carry provisions for public television stations also seemed to undermine the subscription base. As a result, public television had to expend considerable energy, and political capital, just to restore the minimum terms of traditional local reception guarantees.[42] These efforts diverted attention from the broader questions about the desirability and costs of this entire system of revenue generation; perhaps more important, they also diverted public broadcasters and interested political parties from working on the even larger task of framing a wider vision for the service.

Underwriting and Advertising. Industrial and corporate support for programming and even transmission operations became perhaps the most sensitive area of public broadcast funding. Never explicitly defined and authorized in legislation, the practice of soliciting underwriting developed early in the history of community ETV licensees, where appeals to foundations and various other private interests had become, like individual membership subscriptions, a symbol of its legitimacy as a particular kind of cultural institution and as a material necessity. In time, as public broadcasting's popularity grew and its evening audiences took on a particular demographic character—somewhat disproportionately upscale, professional, and politically significant—many national and local corporate interests began to perceive important public relations and political value in reaching such audiences with news of their support for certain kinds of programs. At first, such identification was possible only in brief, strictly regulated underwriting credits. But as program costs rose, federal funding proved more problematic, corporate interests in reaching public broadcasting audiences grew, and federal policy actually began to encourage expansion of private, commercial support and even outright advertising, these practices became increasingly liberalized.

All of these tendencies were reflected in the experience of the Temporary Commission on Alternative Financing (TCAF), which, as part of its 1982-1983 study of the nonfederal income potential for public broadcasting, actually conducted experiments in public broadcasting advertising.[43] Though not willing to recommend advertising's permanent emplacement, the TCAF actually helped legitimize the serious discussion of advertising's merits and at the very least fostered an environment more congenial to liberalized sponsorship. The TCAF report recommended practices that the FCC soon authorized as "enhanced underwriting," thereby taking public broadcasting a significant step further into the realm of direct commercial advertising. During the 1980s, such support grew by 65 percent, from less than 10 percent to about 16 percent of all public broadcasting revenues (see Figure 8.1).

Public broadcasters and their critics have remained sharply divided over this issue. There were strong concerns that any increasing commercialization of public broadcasting was unhealthy, that it drove the institution ever closer to the programming and audience considerations that guide commercial broadcasting and against which public broadcasting must stand. At the very least, questions were asked about what programming efforts and voices went unheard when underwriting resources were unavailable. Another practical concern was that increased commercialization would seem to threaten all the other significant forms of revenue generation without any guarantee that it would offer sufficient replacement funds. Other observers, however, felt that none of the other forms of financial support would ever provide the extent of revenue necessary for public broadcasting to survive, let alone to grow and substantially increase its range of services and appeal. From this perspective, the argument was that there were no realistic alternatives to increased commercial revenues and that although there were dangers associated with them, they could be managed well enough to ensure that the better, unique characteristics of public service programming would persist and even prosper.

Whatever the relative merits of these arguments, they tended to occur outside of any sustained debate about the purposes and needs of public broadcasting. There was little recognition in the 1980s that the measure of increased commercialization's merits or demerits could be taken only in light of a clearer sense of public broadcasting's objectives.

INSTITUTIONAL STRUCTURES AND RESPONSIBILITIES

The crazy-quilt structure of U.S. public broadcasting has always been a mystery to foreign observers and never easily explained even domestically. Just to describe it, let alone analyze and critique it with any sophistication, is a tremendous task that is seldom undertaken. A considerable amount of confusion persists about the various roles and lines of power among the myriad entities of public broadcasting, including CPB, other federal agencies, the national interconnection and program services, the regional networks, the state authorities, the producing entities, and the stations.[44]

The complexity in public broadcasting derives from the fact that much of its structure, as weak and poorly supported as it was, had been built before the 1967 Public Broadcasting Act and that that structure, both before and since, has been determinedly antifederalist, reflecting the traditional Jeffersonian constitutional concerns with checks and balances. Educational radio and television had grown up as considerably decentralized institutions with relatively broad local autonomy. The new institutions, particularly CPB, PBS, and NPR, were superimposed on that structure, and, while their very establishment and access to larger sources of federal funds fostered tendencies toward more centralized control at the national level, their various powers have always remained circumscribed.

At the time of the creation of CPB and in the immediate aftermath, there were powerful tensions over the locus of authority for program production and distribution. In 1967 alone, there were significant swings between what Carnegie-I envisioned for its Corporation for Public Television and what Congress actually provided in CPB. The tendency toward decentralization and widespread power sharing introduced a long-term pattern of ambiguity such that by as late as 1990 there remained important uncertainties about the respective roles of CPB and all the various other institutions. At one level, CPB seemed to have a great deal of responsibility. Yet due largely to concerns about its potential for becoming a government broadcasting service, as a body with a presidentially appointed board of directors and a recipient of congressionally appropriated funds, there were important restrictions in the scope of its operations. Unlike virtually all other national public broadcasting corporations abroad, CPB could not own or operate networks or stations, it could not produce programs, and the vast majority of its funds had to pass through to the stations. It could underwrite program production, and it was authorized to carry out a variety of tasks that imply leadership—research, planning, training, and publicity. Yet its direct program support capacity was restricted by law, and the residue it could retain for its discretionary use for activities other than programs and station support was remarkably small.

Neither the licensees nor the other national and regional public broadcasting agencies, which were all themselves variously creatures of the licensees, were particularly interested in seeing CPB authority increased. Indeed, many of the restrictions that the laws imposed on CPB were there at the behest of the stations. Meanwhile, the actual experience of the constitution of its board and expectations to perform held by various administrations had given credence to the fears that without such restrictions, CPB would act more to focus partisan political pressure than to deflect it.[45]

On practical grounds alone, it had also been argued that to have national television program commissioning authority split between CPB and PBS has been highly inefficient—hence the efforts in 1989–1990 to centralize program decision making in PBS and to eliminate the Station Program Cooperative (SPC), a long-standing station program fund pooling mechanism that had been created precisely as a counterweight to CPB influence.[46] The new power in PBS was thought to be a reasonable gamble because it could be checked by the fact that PBS was owned and operated by its own member stations and by the ultimate right of CPB to reexamine the arrangements at any time. But by comparison with most other broadcast programming organizations in the world, public or private, the structure and dynamics of U.S. public television national programming remained awkward and of uncertain merit.

Meanwhile, similar confusions of authority abounded among the other organizations.[47] PBS and NPR were both membership organizations that programmed national services for television and radio, respectively. But because of differential relative capacities for national program development between the radio and television stations when the national services were formed, NPR could produce programs, but PBS could not. Likewise, while the licensees, many of whom were members of both NPR and PBS, invested NPR with a certain amount (but by no means all) of their institutional lobbying authority, they have taken away most of that power from PBS, placing it in a separate organization, America's Public Television Stations (APTS). Yet because of its central role in national program scheduling and distribution, PBS had always enjoyed a certain leading and often independent voice in the policy debates. In both public radio and television, there have been many other important institutions, some actually also owned by the stations, that compete as national program producers, distributors, and lobbyists.

Even at the local level, there were questions about the relative relationships and necessity of the given numbers and locations of the various independent public stations. In some cities, there were two or three public television stations and as many as three or four in radio, yet frequently there was considerable service overlap among them, and because of their separate institutional affiliations, there was often little capacity for working out distinctly different service patterns. Viewing the situation from another dimension, even in those cases, particularly in television, where there was only one station, there was frequently such similarity of program schedules from one station to the next that it was unclear why many local stations had to be staffed and operated as fully separate entities. Without more local programming, and with a common carriage of the majority of the national core service, the redundancy of management, programming, and development staffs in many such stations was becoming difficult to justify.

The matter of redundancy aside, there have been considerably different agendas among the stations. Licensed to different institutions—community groups, universities, state telecommunications authorities, and others—many have had different purposes and needs. Some were closer to formal educational goals, while others were far removed from such considerations. Some also had remarkably differential power within the system. For instance, several statewide licensees, particularly in the South and the Midwest, had long been successful at bringing educational and public television services to the most remote areas of their rural communities. They were so successful at this, particularly in the long years before cable brought in more than three or four television signals, that they built exceedingly strong local political support that has been regularly reflected in congressional action on public broadcasting.

The large-city community television licensees presented a particularly difficult problem. Several of these, particularly in New York, Boston, Washington, Pittsburgh, Chicago, and Los Angeles, had traditionally been major sources of national program production. As such, they commanded resources that far exceeded those of the vast majority of the other licensees. They reflected a commonality of interest that could put them at odds with other stations. Because of their large, expensive production facilities, they also had particularly strong vested interests in the national program commissioning and scheduling structures and therefore could stand in opposition to either CPB or PBS, or both. Those tensions were once again revealed during the debates over the new national program planning process at PBS.[48]

Yet even that debate, essentially over commissioning and scheduling authority, did not address another continuing problem: the extent to which production capacity would ebb and flow within each station and among them collectively with each new grant. Even with the persistence of several stations as major national program producers, most new efforts would require the amassing of new production teams and resources, which would then be disbanded after completion of the program, to be reassembled again only after a new grant was secured. With the important exceptions of a few long-standing production efforts such as those for *Sesame Street* at the Children's Television Workshop, the *MacNeil-Lehrer NewsHour* at WETA and WNET, or the domestic and foreign dramatic performance series at WNET and WGBH, there was relatively little stability in the ongoing national program production capacity, and as a result, a considerable amount of production energy and talent has been lost over the years.

By the late 1980s, the situation was becoming even more complex, unstable, and potentially wasteful. For some time, a number of stations and licensees that had not been explicitly created as national program producers had nonetheless come to play significant roles in national and even international program production efforts.[49] Important contributions to the national service and reflective of diverse, regional creative capacity, such efforts nonetheless also contributed to the dispersion of energy and resources throughout public television. Then, as internal competition for program dollars increased, it became clear that some stations were actually willing to compete with one another and to try to lure producers and underwriters away from others.[50]

In the end, the public broadcasting "system" has never been particularly systematic in organization or behavior. By 1990, it was not nearly as well integrated—its component parts simply not as well rationalized—as the term *system* suggests. The diversity of its institutions and their varied agendas militated against coordinated thought and action. Its patterns of internecine warfare were remarkably Byzantine and intense, sorely trying the patience and goodwill of friendly critics and political supporters, lending a general air of confusion to its image, and diverting too much of its leadership energies.

Altogether, then, there existed widespread uncertainty about the appropriate levels and dimensions of responsibility in public broadcasting. Under these conditions there was considerable institutional drift. Many activities considered basic to other industries and certainly to other public broadcasting institutions abroad were being allowed to fall through the structural cracks. There were only limited means for considering questions about goals and needs. Sophisticated research about directly relevant technological and social matters was virtually nonexistent. Planning for new program services and for improved uses of existing station and distribution facilities, including new technologies, was haphazard, and even something as simple and crucial as professional recruitment and development was being ignored. Put another way, one of the principal problems of U.S. public broadcasting was that it had little capacity for determining just what its more serious problems were, let alone knowing how to address them.

SUMMARY AND PROSPECTS

By the early 1990s, and by comparison with the size and resources of American commercial broadcasting and of public broadcasting abroad, the U.S. public service institution remained small and underfunded. It was plagued by divergent, often mutually incompatible goals, limited services, small audiences, and minimal significance in the nation's cultural and political debates. It was hardly a failure, as aspects of its programming could regularly demonstrate. It had made substantial contributions to American life and continued to offer much promise. But the institution was still not widely understood; it was marginal in the lives of most Americans; and with the exception of a small, intensely loyal core of viewers, listeners, and corporate and political sponsors, its needs were largely ignored.

As the history of pre-Carnegie-I educational broadcasting reveals, the institution always had difficulty reaching consensus on general objectives and appropriate strategies for development. The irony of its growth during the quarter century after 1967 was that many of its diverse elements had expanded and strengthened to the point that consensus and coordination had probably become more difficult than before, particularly on any truly fundamental changes. As a result, it was now even less easy to identify the most important problems and take appropriate remedial steps.

There is a certain mystique about the salutary possibilities of national commissions and outside intervention. The rosy glow of the Carnegie-I experience permeates much thinking in this regard, particularly as its twenty-fifth anniversary approaches. But far too much of that remembrance is fuzzy, ignoring how much of Carnegie-I was never implemented and failing to understand the serious traps and contradictions implicit in much of what was adopted.[51]

While many of the expectations in Carnegie-I may remain generally valid, the more recent experience of Carnegie-II may be more useful in debates about what to do during the 1990s. The Carnegie-II report was an unusually ambitious document. It tried to deal comprehensively with many of the identity, service, funding, and structural problems discussed here. But in contrast to the reception of Carnegie-I, the more recent report was virtually ignored. There had been a great assumption that the mere existence of Carnegie-II would so well crystallize the debate about public broadcasting that it would automatically lead to significant changes in public broadcasting's structure and levels of support. Yet for all of its passionate interest in promoting a significant advancement of what it called a "public trust," Carnegie-II was too aloof from both the general U.S. telecommunications policy environment and the realities of the structural changes and power relationships within public broadcasting that had emerged since Carnegie-I to be effective in the applied political realm where its recommendations would have to be enacted. There were none of the prior understandings with Congress and the White House that had guaranteed those aspects of success achieved by Carnegie-I.

With that experience in mind, recent calls for a third Carnegie-like study will bear careful scrutiny. It is clear that public broadcasting itself is currently organized in such a way that it is having considerable difficulty recognizing and dealing with its principal problems. But that very structure will do much to confound and dissipate the impact of any single external review effort. It actually works against any sort of review, single or otherwise. People concerned about public broadcasting who are interested in addressing its more important problems and thereby trying to promote significant increases in its resources and services are going to have to find better ways of working within that structure while simultaneously working with the external policy forces. Such means probably imply a considerably more patient, ongoing process of review and analysis, one that is close enough to the operational realities and diverse elements of public broadcasting to speak authoritatively about it while still being sufficiently autonomous and taking a broad enough view of U.S. cultural and telecommunications policy needs to be able when necessary to take the critical perspective.

However, if such a process of review is to be established and implemented, it must not permit the continuing drift of the status quo. U.S. public broadcasting is nowhere near as significant a force as it ought to be; yet it is remarkably quiescent on that score. It is almost as if it is too content with its restricted status. It is loved, perhaps too easily, by the few who attend to it, and in varying ways it offers a certain status and reasonable remuneration to its boards, staff members, and production teams. But it may have become too comfortable with the commercial language of the marketplace and modern communications technocracy, bringing it ever closer to the very realm of enterprise and thought that would smother it. Hardly overfunded, against a standard of major, far-ranging public service, U.S. public broadcasting is nonetheless too complaisant. It is not as if its people do not work hard; they do. It is more a question of what they are working for.

Public broadcasting can do much more by way of vital programming, information, and educational services that simply will not exist in American life without it. It can thereby stand for much more of what is best and necessary in American culture and social experience. But it cannot do these things if the institution itself has no internal gyroscope, no vision of what is possible, no burning fire in the belly, no willingness to challenge the stultifying forces that surround and seduce it.[52] The question now is whether it will grapple with these problems or hew to the complacency of recent years and thereby slide back into the relative invisibility out of which it only recently emerged.

No major commission report, no matter how prestigious, is going to overcome the existing inertia. Nor will any particular structural change address the complex, limiting constraints. What is necessary is a more permanent process of introspection and self-criticism, one that is willing to question the givens of old and new conditions and will engage the talents and interests of the thousands of professionals and citizens working in support of the institution. This process can be helped by outside resources and perspectives, but it is unlikely that it will succeed through any single cataclysmic intervention, as in 1967. The process now will have to be one that combines a more continuing and comprehensive pattern of self-examination with a tougher, less satisfied attitude about what has been accomplished and what may yet be.[53]

NOTES

1. Raymond Williams, *Television: Technology and Cultural Form* (London: Fontana/Collins, 1974), p. 37.
2. Willard D. Rowland, Jr., and Michael Tracey, "Worldwide Challenges to Public Service Broadcasting," *Journal of Communication* 40 (2, 1990), pp. 8–27; and Willard D. Rowland, Jr., *The Challenges to Public Service Broadcasting*, Aspen/Berlin Conference Report No. 5/86 (Berlin: Aspen Institute, 1986).
3. Willard D. Rowland, Jr., "Continuing Crises in Public Broadcasting: A History of Disenfranchisement," *Journal of Broadcasting and Electronic Media* 30 (3, 1986), pp. 251–274.
4. Robert J. Blakely, *To Serve the Public Interest: Educational Broadcasting in the United States* (Syracuse, N.Y.: Syracuse University Press, 1979), pp. 55–64.
5. Commission on Freedom of the Press, *A Free and Responsible Press* (Chicago: University of Chicago Press, 1947).
6. Llewellyn White, *The American Radio* (Chicago: University of Chicago Press, 1947).
7. Federal Communications Commission, "Public Service Responsibility of Broadcast Licensees" (4 March 1946), in Frank J. Kahn, ed., *Documents of American Broadcasting*, 3d ed. (Englewood Cliffs, N.J.: Prentice Hall, 1978), pp. 132–216.

8. Theodore Peterson, "The Social Responsibility Theory," in Fred Siebert, Theodore Peterson, and Wilbur Schramm, eds., *Four Theories of the Press* (Urbana: University of Illinois Press, 1956), pp. 73–103.

9. The initial reservations (12 percent of all television allocations) were included in Sixth Report and Order, 941 FCC 148, 158 (14 April 1952), in Kahn, ed., *Documents of American Broadcasting*, pp. 236–245; the instructional television support, for $3 million to $5 million a year for research and experimentation in broadcasting and film, was in Title VII of the National Defense Education Act; and the construction funds, for up to 50 percent of the total cost of projects—initially only in television, not radio—were authorized by the Educational Television Facilities Act of 1962. See Blakely, *To Serve the Public Interest*, pp. 89–93, 135, 142–144.

10. Carnegie Commission on Educational Television, *Public Television: A Program for Action* (New York: Bantam, 1967).

11. Public Broadcasting Act of 1967, PL 90-129, 81 Stat. 365 (7 November 1967).

12. Stephen B. Jones and Willard D. Rowland, Jr., *NET Programming: A History and Appreciation of the Programming Service of National Educational Television, 1952-1970* (Contract No. A86-31, Library of Congress, February 1990).

13. Carnegie Commission on the Future of Public Broadcasting, *A Public Trust* (New York: Bantam, 1979).

14. See, for example, Walter Lippmann, *Public Opinion* (Orlando, Fla.: Harcourt Brace Jovanovich, 1922); and John Dewey, *The Public and Its Problems* (Fort Worth, Texas: Holt, 1927).

15. Public Telecommunications Financing Act, PL 95-567, 92 Stat. 2405 (2 November 1978).

16. Simon Blanchard and David Morely, eds., *What's This Channel Fo(u)r? An Alternative Report* (London: Comedia Publishing Group, 1982).

17. Public Telecommunications Act of 1988, PL 100-626, 102 Stat. 3207 (7 November 1988).

18. "New Public TV Service Names Board," *Broadcasting* (18 September 1989), p. 65; Janice Drickey, "Larry to the Third Power," *Current* (11 December 1989), p. 23.

19. Robert J. Samuelson, "Highbrow Pork Barrel," *Newsweek* (21 August 1989), p. 44.

20. Primary examples include Sloan Commission on Cable Communications, *On the Cable: The Television of Abundance* (New York: McGraw-Hill, 1971); Cabinet Committee on Cable Communications, *Cable: Report to the President* (Washington, D.C.: U.S. Government Printing Office, 1974); U.S. House of Representatives, Subcommittee on Communications, *Options Papers* (Staff Report), 95th Cong., 2d Sess. (Washington, D.C.: U.S. Government Printing Office, 1977); and Mark S. Fowler and Daniel L. Brenner, "A Marketplace Approach to Broadcast Regulation," *Texas Law Review* 60 (2, 1982), pp. 207–257.

21. A fine recent example is Robert Britt Horwitz, *The Irony of Regulatory Reform: The Deregulation of American Telecommunications* (New York: Oxford University press, 1989).

22. See Hartford N. Gunn, Jr., "Window on the Future: Planning for Public Television in the Telecommunications Era," *Public Telecommunications Review* 6 (4, 1978), pp. 4–54; Carnegie Commission, *A Public Trust*; Hartford N. Gunn,

Jr., et al., "In Search of the Formula; The System Planning Project Papers," *Public Telecommunications Review* 8 (3, 1980), pp. 1–103; "Public Radio: Where It's Been, Where It's Going," *Public Telecommunications Review* 7 (2, 1979), pp. 1–95; and Sheila Mahony, Nick De Martino, and Robert Stengel, *Keeping Pace with the New Television* (Washington, D.C.: Public Telecommunications Press, 1980).

23. See Willard D. Rowland, Jr., "The System Planning Project in Retrospect," *Public Telecommunications Review* 8 (3, 1980), pp. 1–3.

24. Kim Mitchell, "PBS, TDC Study Merits of Educational Network," *Multichannel News* (25 June 1990), p. 10; Richard Barbieri, "Competition Tops Agenda in Dallas," *Current* (23 July 1990), p. 4.

25. "Cable Goes to School," *Broadcasting* (2 October 1989), p. 39; what began as a consortium effort known initially as the Cable Alliance for Education (CAFE) was renamed Cable in the Classroom (CIC) with membership made up of 20 cable programmers and 43 cable operators.

26. Jack Robertiello, "Public TV Maps Whittle Strategy," *Current* (21 June 1989), p. 1; "How to Make Enemies and Influence Educators," *Current* (11 December 1989), p. 16; "Mind Extension, TI-IN Join in Cable Venture," *Current* (7 May 1990), p. 3; Jeannie Aversa, "Mind Extension in University Agreements," *Multichannel News* (31 July 1989), p. 12; Lynn Hirschberg, "Is Chris Whittle the Devil?" *Vanity Fair* 53 (3, 1990), p. 196.

27. Gunn et al., "In Search of the Formula."

28. Richard Barbieri, "It's a Deal: PBS to Manage Half of CPB Fund," *Current* (27 November 1989), p. 1; "CPB Sends Report to Congress," *Current* (12 February 1990), p. 4; Peter D. Lambert, "PBS Poised to Take Charge of National Schedule," *Broadcasting* (2 April 1990), pp. 99–102.

29. During 1991 plans for the new public broadcasting satellite (Telestar 401, to become operational in 1993) began to be more widely discussed. The new satellite's larger carrying capacity helped focus renewed attention on the multichannel question, especially with regard to education. But the extent to which the new opportunity would be used to address the full range of multiple service issues facing public television remained to be seen. See "PBS to Dicker with Educators on Sharing New Satellite," *Current* (21 October 1991), p. 10; "PBS Trumpets 'Education Satellite,' Will Test VSAI," *Current* (18 November 1991), p. 4.

30. "What Happened to Mankiewicz?" *Broadcasting* (25 April 1983), p. 28; "Mankiewicz Steps Down at NPR," *Broadcasting* (25 April 1983), p. 76.

31. See, for example, Audience Building Task Force, *Task Force Report* (Washington, D.C.: National Public Radio, 1986), and a continuous series of audience research reports in *Current* throughout the 1980s. See also Bruce Ingram, "Public Radio Confab Will Chew 'Unbundling' Bone of Contention Even Though NPR Voted for It," *Variety* (18 May 1988), p. 136; and "NPR Carriage Not Hurt by 'Unbundling,' " (31 October 1988), p. 52.

32. Arlie Schardt, *Public Radio: Opportunities for Leadership—A Discussion Paper from the Working Group on Public Radio in the 1990s* (Washington, D.C.: National Public Radio, May 1989); Public Radio Expansion Task Force, *Public Radio in the 1990s: Fulfilling the Promise* (Washington, D.C.: National Public Radio, January 1990); National Public Radio, *Strategic Plan for the 1990s* (Washington, D.C.: National Public Radio, February 1990).

33. Total commercial broadcasting revenues for the years 1986–1988 grew from $29.0 to $32.7 billion (Source: Morgan Stanley & Co., Inc., *Communications Industry Datebook*, August 1988). In 1990, operating commercial radio and television stations in the United States numbered nearly 10,300 (*Broadcasting*, 24 September 1990, p. 88); total operating noncommercial stations numbered nearly 1,900, but of those, roughly 800 were religious or student-run stations not supported by CPB.

34. As just one simple example, the federal government of Canada provided the Canadian Broadcasting Corporation with $981.4 million (U.S. $858.7 million) in 1990. The Canadian population of 25 million was about one-tenth that in the United States, meaning that the Canadian federal government commitment to public broadcasting was about $34 per capita versus about $1 in the United States. See Canadian Broadcasting Corporation, *Annual Report* (1989–1990), p. 39, item 7, "Parliamentary Appropriations." Note, too, that these figures do not include the additional millions of federal dollars in other national and provincial public service telecommunications programs.

35. Carnegie Commission, *A Public Trust*, p. 205; Willard D. Rowland, Jr., "Public Involvement: The Anatomy of a Myth," in Douglass Cater and Michael J. Nyhan, eds., *The Future of Public Broadcasting* (New York: Praeger, 1976), pp. 120–126.

36. Late in 1991 Congress seemed to be closing in on the new authorization bill with terms that would provide CPB with a ceiling of $310 million in 1994, $375 million in 1995, and $425 million in 1996, and PTFP with $42 million each for the years 1992–1994. But by year's end it had not passed the bill, though it had settled on a 1994 CPB appropriation of $275 million.

37. Had the match system been working in the late 1980s, it would have generated $630 million to $650 million in federal funds for 1991 or 1992, or more than twice what had been appropriated in the 1988 law.

38. Jack Robertiello, "CPB Spending Set for 1993," *Current* (6 November 1990), p. 1.

39. During 1990–1991, with the quality of U.S. education becoming a salient political issue, CPB and others began to reemphasize the educational nature of public broadcasting both to justify the new authorization bill and to seek special smaller allocations in various education funding bills. Although possibly useful in the short term, this tactic struck many as being a political expedient that was at odds with much of the general audience programming trends in public broadcasting since Carnegie-I and that in any event did not constitute a major reassessment of overall goals and services.

40. Central Educational Network, *The Public Telecommunications Complex* (March 1989); George Hall and James Fellows, "Teleplex: A Brave New World, a Bold New Concept," *Current* (4 June 1990), p. 39; see also the regular columns in *Current* by George Hall on behalf of the PBS Office of New Technology Initiatives (ONTI).

41. Richard Barbieri and Jack Robertiello, "TV, Radio Face Different Revenue Picture," *Current* (23 July 1990), p. 1.

42. "CPB Backs NAPTS Cable Must-Carry Position," *Broadcasting* (26 March 1990), p. 98; "NCTA and Public Television Agree on Must Carry," *Broadcasting* (2 April 1990), p. 117.

43. Temporary Commission on Alternative Financing for Public Telecommunica-

tions, *Final Report* (Washington, D.C.: Federal Communications Commission, 1983).

44. For a summary of the national-level structural changes and tensions in the 1967–1980 period, see Robert K. Avery and Robert Pepper, "An Institutional History of Public Broadcasting, " *Journal of Communication* 30 (3, 1980), pp. 126–138.

45. The most outstanding examples of this concern were expressed in the funding vetoes and CPB board appointment experiences during the Nixon and Reagan periods, the latter best reflected by the 1986–1987 controversy over CPB's proposal for a content analysis of the objectivity and balance of CPB-sponsored programs. See Rowland, "Public Involvement," and Michael Tracey, "Less than Meets the Eye," *Current* (13 January 1987), p. 3. For an authoritative treatment of the problem of CPB governance, see Joseph D. Hughes, "Heat Shield or Crucible?" *Public Telecommunications Review* 5 (6, 1977), pp. 14–36.

46. Fred Esplin, "It's Time to Get Rid of the SPC," *Current* (29 January 1990), p. 19; Richard Barbieri, "SPC Halted," *Current* (6 August 1990), p. 1.

47. This confusion was often manifested in press stories about public broadcasting where "public broadcasting system," "public broadcasting service," and "PBS" were often used interchangeably without any awareness of the distinctions among them—that is, between the Public Broadcasting Service (the public television network company) and the public broadcasting system (including everything from CPB, PBS, and NPR to the smallest noncommercial radio and television stations).

48. Jeremy Gerard, "Stations Oppose a Streamlined PBS," *New York Times* (20 September 1990), p. B2.

49. For instance, Maryland Public Broadcasting (*Wall Street Week*); WPBT, Miami (*Nightly Business Report*); KTCA, St. Paul (*Alive from Off Center*); and KCTS, Seattle (*Miracle Planet*).

50. Intriguing examples involve the shifts among such major programs as the *National Geographic Specials* and *In Performance at the White House*, involving stations WETA (Washington, D.C.), WQED (Pittsburgh), and WXXI (Rochester, N.Y.). See Jack Robertiello, "WXXI-TV Gets 'In Performance,' " *Current* (24 September 1990), p. 3; and Stephen Singer, "The 12-Minute Year," *Current* (11 December 1989), p. 1.

51. James Fellows, "Carnegie-I: The Legacy," *Current* (27 January 1987), p. 2.

52. Occasionally, though not often, similar concerns are voiced from within public broadcasting. See, for instance, Richard W. Smith, "For Public Broadcasting, Survival Is Not Enough," *Current* (22 September 1987), p. 2.

53. Two significant developments in the late 1980s offered some promise of renewed efforts in this regard: the incorporation in 1989 of the Hartford N. Gunn Institute and the effort in public radio to engage a new systematic, comprehensive strategic planning process.

Epilogue

Taken together, the eight chapters in this volume provide a representative profile of the origins, evolution, and current status of public service broadcasting in western Europe and North America. Although each reveals highly idiosyncratic circumstances in which the public service concept was given roots and permitted to develop, all emphasize the dramatic changes in the evolving media environment. Increasing political pressures, the proliferation of new technologies, declining public funds in the face of increased operating expenses, and growing competition from the private sector are characteristic of the problems confronting public service broadcast institutions in each of the countries examined. These challenges, coupled with broadening public skepticism about the very ideals and conceptual foundations on which the systems were built, reveal a complex and interrelated set of issues that must be addressed in the 1990s if public service broadcasting as we know it is to survive well into the twenty-first century.

The specific nature and extent of these interrelated elements vary considerably from country to country, though none was left unaffected by the ideological, technological, and economic upheaval of the 1980s. Clearly, the United States has had the longest history of trying to sustain an alternative public broadcasting system within a media framework totally dominated by private enterprise. Britain has also witnessed the coexistence of public service and commercially supported systems for nearly 40 years. And while the recommendations of the Peacock Committee sent shock waves throughout the United Kingdom, both the United States and Great Britain continue to provide, at least for the present, public broadcast programming that is not markedly different from that offered before the assault of marketplace forces.

Systems that were less firmly grounded and ill prepared for the arrival of new political pressure and competitive broadcast outlets show signs of reduced institutional stability and deteriorating program standards and schedules. Though some critics of American and British public affairs programs have been fond of characterizing offerings as bland, sterile, or unduly cautious, Sepstrup's analysis of public service broadcasting in Denmark, for example, illustrates the highly visible impact of commercial competition. If his case study is representative of trends in Scandinavian broadcasting, it is reasonable to conclude that the introduction of advertising has already altered programming in both form and content. The packaging of news is becoming more a function of attracting viewers than maintaining journalistic standards. There is less attention to domestic children's programs and a corresponding increase in imported entertainment series. Similarly, the amount of time devoted to advertising messages has been expanded and undoubtedly will continue to increase under the less restrictive guidelines adopted by the European Community in 1989.

In Denmark, as elsewhere in western Europe, the costs associated with both innovative program development and the ability to capitalize on technological initiatives deprive public service broadcasters from keeping pace with the large private telecommunications manufacturers, producers, and distributors. And as more of the economic resources accrue within the private sector, European public service institutions can expect the political climate to become increasingly bleak. The revitalization of national economics is far more central to the political agendas of policymakers than the preservation of public service idealism.

As audiences discover a new array of commercial channels, declining ratings will make it increasingly difficult for public service advocates to mount convincing arguments for the financial resources necessary to sustain the enterprise. Viewers are already calling for a reprieve from taxes and license fees, which have been the principal source of public broadcast funding. With new commercial broadcast channels and the introduction of cable networks, and the availability of so-called premium channels offered in addition to the basic subscription fees, viewers will be confronted with new electronic media expenses that will seem more directly related to their own personal viewing patterns. And the likelihood that European viewers will find the new cable channels appealing is very high, given the experience of cable entrepreneurs who have examined audience preferences in the United States. For example, a study conducted by the Cable Television Administration and Marketing Society in May 1991 reported that attitudes toward cable television services were highly positive, with 87 percent of existing subscribers indicating a desire to continue or increase current service levels. The study also revealed a high positive correlation between cable television subscription and videocassette recorder ownership, thus suggesting a viewing preference for yet an other alternative to public service broadcasting.

One of the limitations inherent in a case-by-case analysis of the kind provided in this volume is that it necessarily emphasizes the emergence of problems and the generation of possible solutions that are often peculiar to a particular country or region. That is, each individual study suggests that potential answers are rooted in the regulatory, cultural, and economic exigencies surrounding the existing broadcast institutions that operate within national boundaries. As several chapters suggest, finding individual solutions in the European countries will be made increasingly difficult with the implementation of European unity in 1992 and corresponding pressures that are market-driven. But even without the EC Council Directive adopted in 1989, which will dramatically alter the media menus for some 325 million European consumers, the gradual shift toward a global marketplace makes individual nation-bound solutions less practical. The kinds of mechanisms that might once have been involved to protect noncommercial entities are no longer effective. In a multinational media environment where the forces of commercialization dictate player performance, no existing government, regulatory, or policy formation mechanism can hold the forces in check. Recognizing that the complex and interrelated industrial infrastructures of a multinational, information-based economy cannot be regulated by any existing set of laws, directives, or policy constraints, government officials have been increasingly prone to relinquish the reins of control to the private sector.

In a competitive free-enterprise system where economic initiatives are born in service to the private investor, the calls for regulatory reform will surely come from the people who stand to profit most. Policy directives and regulatory practices that promote the private commercial concerns of media investors will clearly take precedence and will be only incidentally related to the educational and cultural needs of society. The new breed of business entrepreneurs emerging in western Europe already suggest that the challenge to traditional broadcast ideals and support structures will not subside. Relaxed concerns about protecting social institutions from commercial attack has permitted moguls with the vision of Silvio Berlusconi to undermine the well-intentioned motives of government officials.

Realistically, then, the future of public service broadcasting as a proactive force in the multichannel environment of the twenty-first century will not be based on fruitless attempts to stem the tide of commercialization or to preserve institutional boundaries and traditions for the sake of maintaining the status quo. Public service broadcasters must recognize and accept the inherent failings of the institutions they themselves inhabit—rightly criticized for inefficiencies, cost overruns, and bureaucratic excessiveness—and move quickly to build alliances that will preserve the spirit, if not the form, of public service idealism.

Public service broadcasters must recognize that consumers welcome the multiplicity of delivery modes and must therefore stop thinking of themselves as programmers for one or two broadcast services. Alliances with cable companies and videocassette distributors, for example, permit public broadcasters to become partners in receiving commercial revenues to be derived from educational and cultural programs, along with the income from the sale of study guides, books, and other instructional materials. As early as the mid-1960s, Marshall McLuhan was proclaiming that the educational environment of the electronic media had become richer than the traditional institutions of learning and that by turning off television and going to school, children were interrupting their education. He knew then that education had become big business, but it would take the creative zeal of entrepreneurs to demonstrate it in the marketplace. In the United States, cable interests are moving rapidly to tap into this market, bolstered by the early success of Whittle's Channel One, an in-school broadcast service supported by advertising to a captive audience. As Willard Rowland explained, the U.S. cable industry has even gone so far as to create a new organization to coordinate and promote educational efforts—the Cable Alliance for Education in Washington, D.C. And by 1991, the Discovery Channel had taken over the Learning Channel and established a programming alliance with the National Education Association to develop in-service teacher training programs as well as children's programs for use in the classroom.

For some time now, PBS President Bruce Christensen has argued that the future success of public television in the United States would require a return to the instructional roots of noncommercial educational broadcasting. His predictions were given increased credence in March 1991 when the Corporation for Public Broadcasting released a study conducted by the Boston Consulting Group.[1] The study recommended three strategic directions as guiding principles for the future development of public television:

1. Significantly increase investment in national programming for home audiences, regardless of distribution source.
2. Renew an investment in services to schools and the education community generally.
3. Expedite the use of diversified distribution channels, particularly in providing services to schools.

Exactly how these recommendations might best be implemented was yet to be determined, but the prospect of increased alliances with commercial producers, distributors, and instructional packagers seemed imminent.

With the building of these new commercial alliances and increased diversification of entrepreneural ventures, there is the very real risk that public service broadcasters will lose their original sense of identity and mission; that the individual audience member will increasingly be seen as a consumer rather than as a citizen in an informed democracy.

In the early days of American noncommercial educational television, there was something special about working within the ranks of underpaid professionals and dedicated volunteers who felt a calling to a higher purpose of public good. There was a spirit, a genuine belief that we were part of an enterprise that would have a profound positive influence on American society. Indeed, Donald Taverner, president of Pittsburgh's WQED, was fond of reminding us that we were not working for a television station but an *educational institution* that deserved to be ranked alongside Carnegie-Mellon and the University of Pittsburgh. Though those days seem more grand in memory than they did in real life, it is worth recalling that the commitment to a public service ideal, regardless of how misdirected or ill informed some critics might claim that commitment had been, provided the motivation to build an alternative service that just might, every once in a while, make a difference in the lives of our viewers. As terminology such as *audience flow, market share, profit margin*, and *cost per thousand* begins to pervade the public broadcasting institutions, there is a danger that the dedicated professionals working on behalf of various newly created services could lose sight of their heritage, identity, and public service mission.

In 1991, the thirtieth anniversary of Newton Minow's famous "vast wasteland" speech to the National Association of Broadcasters was celebrated at the Gannett Foundation Media Center in New York City. Invited to reflect on his historic remarks with the benefit of three decades of technological achievements and numerous shifts in the communication media landscape, Minow identified America's four principal failures: to use television for education, to use television for children, to fund adequately a public broadcast alternative to commercial television, and to use television properly in political campaigns. To correct these failings, he called for a return to the creative energy and idealism of the 1960s:

As we return, I commend some extraordinary words to the new generation. E. B. White sat in a darkened room in 1938 to see the beginning of television—an experimental electronic box that projected images into the room. Once he saw it, Mr. White wrote: "We shall stand or fall by television—of that I am sure. . . . I believe television is going to be the test of the modern world, and that in this new opportunity to see beyond the range of our vision, we shall discover either a new and unbearable disturbance to the general peace, or a saving radiance in the sky. That radiance falls unevenly today. It is still a dim light in education. It has not fulfilled its potential for children. It has neglected the needs of public television. And in the electoral process it has cast a dark shadow."[2]

He concluded his address with a challenge to the new generation to make television a saving radiance by putting the vision back into television.

Minow's challenge serves as a fitting conclusion to this volume as well. As our electronic media continue to account for more and more of what constitutes our collective reality, the need for a firm and unwavering commitment to a public service ideal is more important now than at any previous moment in broadcasting history. The mounting forces of a new competitive marketplace have diffused and sidetracked the energies of those who have been entrusted with making public service broadcasting an essential part of the educational and cultural mosaic of Western democracies, permitting the original vision to grow pale and undernourished. Just as the passion and idealism of a young American generation in the 1960s gave birth to a new sense of social consciousness, a rededication to the intellectual, cultural, and moral fabric of a thriving democracy could infuse a renewed sense of vision and restore a belief in the principles that have been allowed to drift. How political leaders, policymakers, broadcast administrators, and the citizens they all have been empowered to serve respond to the call for a rededication to the betterment of our society will determine whether public service broadcasting will flourish or wither and die in the evolving multichannel environment.

NOTES

1. Boston Consulting Group, *Strategies for Public Television in a Multichannel Environment* (Washington, D.C.: Corporation for Public Broadcasting, 1991).
2. Newton N. Minow, *How Vast the Wasteland Now?* (New York: Gannett Foundation Media Center, 1991), p. 19.

About the Authors

ROBERT K. AVERY

Mr. Avery is Professor of Communication at the University of Utah. His research interests are in the areas of telecommunication policy, visual communication, and interactive media. A former public television administrator, Mr. Avery served as Chair of the National Association of Educational Broadcasters. He is the author of numerous articles on the subject of public broadcasting and coauthor of *The Politics of Interconnection: A History of Public Television at the National Level* (1979) with Robert Pepper and *Research Index for NAEB Journals* (1980) with Paul E. Burrows and Clara J. Pincus. He is the Founding Editor of *Critical Studies in Mass Communication* and Coeditor of *Critical Perspectives on Media and Society* (1991).

JAY G. BLUMLER

Mr. Blumler is a professor in the College of Journalism at the University of Maryland, and Professor Emeritus of the University of Leeds, where he directed its Centre for Television Research. Past President of the International Communication Association, Mr. Blumler is among the leading scholars in mass communication with an interest in policy studies, political communication, and media audiences. Among his books are *Television in Politics: Its Uses and Influence* (1968) with Denis McQuail, *The Uses of Mass Communications: Current Perspectives on Gratification Research* (1974), *Broadcasting Finance in Transition: A Comparative Handbook* (1991) with T. J. Nossiter, and *Television and the Public Interest: Vulnerable Values in West European Broadcasting* (1992). He is a Joint

Founding Editor of the *European Journal of Communication* and International Editor for *Journal of Communication*.

JÉROME BOURDON

Mr. Bourdon has been a Research Fellow with the Institut National de l'Audiovisuel (French National Institute of Broadcasting) since 1983. A graduate of the Institut d'Études Politiques de Paris, he holds a Ph.D. in Contemporary History. Mr. Bourdon is the author of *Histoire de la télévision sous de Gaulle* (1989) and has published numerous articles on the history and sociology of French broadcasting.

KAI HILDEBRANDT

Mr. Hildebrandt is Associate Professor of Communication Studies at the University of Windsor, Ontario, Canada. His research interests are in political communication, community cable channels, public broadcasting politics in Europe, and research methods. Mr. Hildebrandt's publications include *Germany Transformed* (1981) with K. Baker and R. Dalton, and various articles on German and comparative voting behavior, value change, and access to justice

JOHN F. KRAMER

Mr. Kramer is Professor and Chair of Political Science at Sonoma State University, Rohnert Park, California. His research interests are in the areas of political communication, public opinion, and communication regulatory policy. Research for this essay was supported in part by a Fulbright Grant (1986) and by a funded sabbatical from Sonoma State University.

DENIS MCQUAIL

Mr. McQuail is Chair of Mass Communication at the University of Amsterdam. Prior to that, he was a member of the Sociology faculty at the University of Southampton, England. His main research interests have been in the study of media audiences, political communication campaigns, media policy, and the evaluation of media performance in relation to public policy. His books include *Television and the Political Image* (1961) with J. Trenaman, *Television and the Political Image* (1968) with Jay G. Blumler, *Towards a Sociology of Mass Communication* (1969), *Communication as a Social Process* (1975), *Analysis of Newspaper*

Content (1977), *Mass Communication Theory* (1983, 1987), *New Media Politics* (1986) with Karin Sinue, and *Media Performance* (1992). He is Joint Founding Editor of the *European Journal of Communication.*

MARC RABOY

Mr. Raboy is Associate Professor in the Department of Information and Communication at Laval University, Quebec, Canada. His interests include media policy from a political economy perspective, the relationship between media and social movements, and the role of media with respect to democracy. His major publications include *Movements and Messages: Media and Radical Politics in Quebec* (1984) and *Missed Opportunities: The Story of Canada's Broadcasting Policy* (1990), and he is the Coeditor of *Communication for and against Democracy* (1989) and *Media, Crisis and Democracy* (1992).

GERTRUDE J. ROBINSON

Ms. Robinson is Professor and Past Director of the Graduate Program of Communications at McGill University, Montreal, Canada. She publishes widely on comparative media policy in Europe, the history of the North American communication discipline, and women's issues and is the Editor of the *Canadian Journal of Communication.* Her major publications include *Tito's Maverick Media: The Politics of Mass Communication in Yugoslavia* (1977); *Women, Communication, and Careers* (1980); *News Agencies and the News in Canada, the United States, and Yugoslavia* (1981); and *Women and Power: Canadian and German Experiences* (1990).

WILLARD D. ROWLAND, JR.

Mr. Rowland is Professor and Dean of the School of Journalism and Mass Communication at the University of Colorado in Boulder. A former director of research for the Public Broadcasting Service, he has published extensively on all aspects of public service broadcasting and is a frequent consultant to professional organizations. His research interests focus on issues of communication history and policy, and, in addition to many book chapters and journal articles, he is the author of *The Politics of TV Violence: Policy Uses of Communication Research* (1983) and Coeditor of *Interpreting Television: Current Research Perspectives* (1984).

PREBEN SEPSTRUP

Mr. Sepstrup is a professor at the Aarhus School of Business Administration and Economics in Denmark. His interests include research on electronic media and the consequences of sponsoring and advertising for television, the transnationalization and commercialization of western European television, and the United States' influence on western European television. He was a member of the Royal Commission on the Media and serves as a member of the Board for Denmark's Radio. He has accomplished media-related work for UNESCO, the European Community Commission, and the Nordic Council and currently serves as a member of the Network of Media Economy Research Group, Europe.

THIERRY VEDEL

Mr. Vedel is a Research Fellow with the Centre National de la Recherche Scientific (National Center for Scientific Research) in Paris. His research work deals with public policies in the area of communications and he has published articles in such journals as *Media, Culture and Society*, *MediasPouvoirs*, and *Technologies de l'Information et Société*. He has also contributed to several books, including *Wired Cities* (1987), *Les déréglementations* (1988), and *Communication and Culture across Space and Time* (1991).

Index